Christmas 2000

Oysters

Oysters

A   Culinary

Celebration

Joan Reardon

 THE LYONS PRESS · New York

Printed in the United States of America

DESIGN BY BARBARA M. BACHMAN
COLOR PHOTOGRAPHS BY WILLIE NASH

Color photographs made possible by the gracious
cooperation of The Oyster Bar at Grand Central Terminal
in New York City. Special thanks to Michael Garvey,
General Manager, and Sandy Ingber, Executive
Chef, of The Oyster Bar

10 9 8 7 6 5 4 3 2 1

Library of Congress Cataloging-in-Publication Data
Reardon, Joan, 1930–
Oysters : a culinary celebration / Joan Reardon.
p.   cm.
ISBN 1-55821-944-7
1. Cookery (Oysters). 2. Oysters. I. Title.
TX754.098R43   1999
641.6 '94—dc21   99-35886
CIP

To

Doe Coover

for her

continued patience,

humor, and

savoir-faire

The purpose of a
cookery book is one and
unmistakable.
Its object can conceivably
be no other than to
increase the happiness
of mankind.

—JOSEPH CONRAD,
"Introduction" to *Home Cookery*

Contents

CAESAR:
I have been in Britain,
that western land of
romance . . . I went there
in search for its
famous pearls.
The British pearl was a
fable; but in searching
for it I found the
British oyster.

APOLLODORUS:
All posterity will
bless you for it.

—GEORGE BERNARD SHAW,
Caesar and Cleopatra

To Begin Again

To borrow from M. F. K. Fisher, wordsmith of memorable phrases and author of the quintessential book on oyster lore and recipes, "One of the fine feelings in this world is to have a long-held theory confirmed." That oysters have always been and will always be utterly seductive is mine. My first introduction to this fabled bivalve occurred in a well-frequented restaurant across the road from the Barnstable Courthouse on Cape Cod, but my taste for oysters was confirmed and enhanced during the ten years I lived in the nearby village of Cotuit, an idyllic place partially surrounded by the shelter of the bay that proudly bears its name. For years, the village has shared its oysters with connoisseurs, given a serendipitous way of life to its villagers, and, unusual for a seashore community, Cotuit has always given a place and "space" to both year-round residents and summer people to pursue serious intellectual and creative work.

Oysters: A Culinary Celebration could not have been written in any other place, and for this reason it is imperative to acknowledge a deep debt of gratitude to Cotuit, to the resources and staff of the local library, to the Cotuit Oyster Company (since 1837, the oldest brand name of oysters in the United States), to all the friends and neighbors who contributed to the first edition of this book, and especially to Ruth Ebling who labored over the manuscript with so much dedication.

Since the cookbook was published in its original form in 1984, however, the Cotuit Oyster Company has weathered low yields of oysters, fortunately a temporary condition, but a sobering one. The village of Cotuit reluctantly has expanded, and many of its houses have been renovated, with a slight loss to the eccentricity of former owners, and the neighbors who tasted and tested many of the recipes in the original edition of this book by necessity or choice have left Cotuit. Parnassus Press has also moved from Orleans to

Hyannis with new owners replacing Trumbull Huntington and Ben Muse. Time has been kind but not too kind.

And in the years between 1984 and the present, I have savored *portugaise verts* on a boat in Arcachon Bay; dined on that delicious combination of hot spicy sausages and ice cold oysters, *huitres a la charentaise*, in Bordeaux; dipped into bowls of *huitres chaudes au cidre et aux poireaux*, a blend of briny oysters, cider, and leeks, along Brittany's northern coast; and sampled the rich variety of Belons, Marennes, and *papillons* in the huge and accessible Les Halles de Lyon. Closer to home, New Orleans offered the plump Louisiana Gulf oysters in everything from Antoine's Rockefellers to French Quarter "po" boys, while a visit to Tomales Bay yielded enough bivalves for an oyster stew at M. F. K. Fisher's Last House. Although the first stop in New York City has been and will always be the Grand Central Oyster Bar with its selection of more than thirty oysters, from Washington State Bakers to Cape Cod Wellfleets, closer to home there is always the yearly opportunity to "roister with the oyster" at Shaw's Crab House in Chicago. But the taste of Cotuits lingers.

So, many more oysters later, many more opportunities to learn about the history of the oyster, the oyster industry, the "Great Oyster Craze" of the late nineteenth century, and the enduring oyster bars from the Union Oyster House in Boston to the Swan Oyster Depot in San Francisco, the time has come to revise *Oysters*.

Now a member of the culinary community myself, I have had the great good fortune to share ideas with others in that community, and I especially would like to thank Christopher Koetke, a professional chef and instructor at the School of Culinary Arts, Kendall College, for his thoughtful reading of the text and helpful wine, beverage, and recipe suggestions. Chef-instructor Elaine Sikorski-Tritsch offered valuable recipe suggestions for fish and shellfish entrées. My gratitude also extends to Elaine Gonzalez for sharing her family's recipes for Salsa Fresca and Salsa Verde. Time has only enhanced my indebtedness to David Nosiglia, former owner of the Smokehouse in Hyannis, Massachusetts, who gave generously of his time and advice in perfecting the recipe for Oyster Sausages and supplied his own recipe for the Oysters and Sausages appetizer. Richard Black's culinary expertise and advice, which were indispensable in editing the 1984 edition, continue to inspire my efforts, as does the Culinary Collection at the Schlesinger Library, Radcliffe, and the curator of published books, Barbara Haber.

I also wish to thank Houghton Mifflin for permission to quote lines from Anne Sexton's *Book of Folly*.

Without Cotuit and the justly fabled oyster that bears the village's name, this book could not have been written; without the commendation of Craig Claiborne, Pierre Franey, M. F. K. Fisher, Marian Morash, and Jasper White, the first edition would not have been as successful as it was; and without the confidence of my agent Doe Coover, editor Lilly Golden, and Barbara Bachman's design, the Lyons Press edition would not have become a reality.

JOAN REARDON
Seaward II
Lake Forest, Illinois, 1999

Introduction

R is for Oyster

—M. F. K. Fisher

Rumors

The history of the oyster has been told many times, in many ways, and, like a come-hither buffet table, there's a little something for everyone in the story.

Folklore enthusiasts who delight in the human dimensions of simple tales will find their share of Neolithic humor in the account of the unsuspecting man who picked up a yawning oyster, thought it a stone, and then got his index finger caught in the snapped-shut shell. The conclusion was predictable. When the man freed his finger and put it into his mouth to relieve the pain, he tasted the oyster liquor and discovered that the incredible oyster was also edible.

Oyster buffs will, no doubt, be interested in the remnants of four thousand miles of barrier reef that since ancient times extended from Scandinavia down the Atlantic coast into the Mediterranean and along the coastline of France and Italy to Greece. The flat and smooth European oyster, *Ostrea edulis*, and a score of other shellfish bedded in the reef, were a seemingly inexhaustible supply of food. The desire to learn more about these gifts from the sea motivated the Greeks to make modest forays into the practice of farming oysters, although it seems there was a treatise on fish cultivation written by a Chinese author Fan-li circulating in 850 B.C. It's intriguing, moreover, to learn that as early as the fourth century, B.C., it was a known fact that oysters did not necessarily reproduce in the waters where they grew well, and that aquaculture probably began at that time.

Fascinating reading, also, are the lengths and depths *Homo faber* plumbed in order to preserve and transport this indolent mollusk. Because the Romans discovered the Breton oyster at a fairly early date, they set up icehouses between Brittany and Rome to replenish the snow and ice in the oyster carts traveling over land. During the summer months, cistern carts filled with salt water were used. And there is an amazing tale of a Roman refrigerator devised more than two thousand years ago to keep oysters and other perishable comestibles fresh during the warm weather. Basically a deep-freeze set in a windowless rock wall secured by a tight door, it was a construct of vertical caves reached by a narrow wooden staircase. On the floor of the lowest cave, a wooden box was set in two or more feet of trampled, hardened snow. Cold springwater flowed underneath it and kept the oysters cold until needed.

Later on, the Romans discovered the magnificent flavor of Colchester oysters growing in the estuaries of the Thames River and introduced oyster cultivation into Britain by A.D. 407. With the surfeit of delicious bivalves, there were even more dramatic measures taken to transport oysters by boat. Seamen commandeered double-hulled galleys for the voyage, which occasionally was so long that fear of spoilage necessitated pickling the oysters in vinegar, salt, and laurel berries and storing them in barrels fumigated with pitch.

Then there are the many accounts of outrageous banquets, a facet of the oyster's history that has had more than its share of notoriety. Pliny called oysters "the palm and pleasure of the table," and he savored many a bivalve. In fact, Romans consumed bushels of oysters, relishes, mushrooms, peacock's eggs, and sardines as appetizers. But oysters were so popular that they were also used as accompaniments to roasted boar and other entrées and were served throughout an entire orgy. Documented or simply rumored, there are stories that virtually every influential Roman statesman, military hero, and emperor had more than a passing interest in oysters. Perhaps Gibbons's account of the Emperor Vitellius feasting on a thousand, or some such fabulous number, sums up the situation. Freud would have had something interesting to say about that, and, no doubt, the guests at the banquet did too. But, alas, the glory that was Rome faded away.

Although seafaring people like the Vikings ate oysters as a matter of course, the Visigoths, who had little fear of anything else, were apprehensive about oysters and acquired no taste for them. Happily in those "dark ages," however, there were a few recorded closet oyster lovers who were adamant about including oysters in their diet. Chronicles of the eighth century show that a certain St. Evremond ate several dozen for breakfast and lived to be at least ninety. During the years of his exile in England, the French king Louis IV developed a taste for British oysters, and later, when he was imprisoned in Normandy, he requested a ration of them regularly. And little more than a century later, when the Normans under the leadership of William the Conqueror invaded England, they seized the oyster beds in Kent and Essex. The British oyster was definitely one of the jewels of the crown, and fittingly, by 1319, Edward II established the custom of opening the oyster season with a feast held on the day of St. Deny's Fair.

Unfortunately, in spite of these modest medieval examples of oyster savoring, the halcyon days of wine and peacock feathers were over, and the interest in oysters rekindled in the Renaissance had a slightly different orientation. Even though Queen Elizabeth often feasted on raw Colchesters as a first course, and oysters on the half shell were still considered important banquet fare, an era of serious oyster cookery had begun in England. Elizabethan cookbooks got down to the brisk business of pickling, stewing, roasting, and saucing the oyster.

In France, extravagance, oysters, and royalty

remained inseparable. The trendsetting court of Louis XIV consumed oysters with abandon, and the king kept a private "park" at Versailles to guarantee an adequate supply for royal banquets. A hundred years later, one of the "Sun King's" less-than-fortunate successors, Louis XVI, stocked private beds of oysters at Etretat, which supplied him and Marie Antoinette with more than one royal repast before royalty was no more.

From the mid–seventeenth century until the early nineteenth century, oysters, like power, ceased to be the private domain of the aristocracy and passed to the man in the street. The oyster became the darling of the bourgeoise, the fashionable food. Casanova, adventurer manqué that he was, consumed fifty a day with his evening punch. And early gastronomic authors, like Brillat-Savarin, were of the opinion that "oysters furnish[ed] very little nourishment" and did not spoil one's appetite for dining. Little wonder that by the mid–nineteenth century, Charles Monselet, another French gastronomer, admitted with some chagrin, "Oysters seem to be losing ground this year. It can't be more than a breathing spell, a bad joke of fortune."

While France lamented the difficulty of obtaining oysters, the "Rhymesmith" of the "Preston Oyster and Parched Pea Club" in Lancashire, England, expressed the satisfaction of the British middle class with the surfeit of oysters and political good fortune that they enjoyed: "Nelson has made the seas our own,/ Then gulp your well-fed oysters down,/ And give the French the shell."

During the eighteenth and nineteenth centuries, oysters were plentiful, nourishing, and available to the poor and not-so-poor in England. Gentleman's clubs and university clubs, pubs, fairs, and oyster tubs in rows, oyster girls and oyster wenches, and a certain amount of high jinks down in the oyster cellars flourished.

The oyster was the subject of paintings, the object of amatory speculation, and a frequent topic for journalists and writers. In *All the Year Round* (1859), Dickens wrote a wonderful account of a free company of oyster dredgers who prospered in Whitstable in the mid–nineteenth century and turned oystering into a very profitable business, indeed. "Without stint or limit," they shipped the famous Whitstables to London's markets, where they were always in demand. Seemingly, there was no limit to the oyster craze in England.

Recollections

Across the Atlantic, there was another oyster, *Crassostrea virginica*, another dining scene, and another story. Mounds of shells along the eastern seaboard give more than enough evidence of the huge storage pools that the Indians used for oysters and other shellfish. Seven million bushels of shells were found off the coast of Maine. Remnants of a significant number of weirs were located in the marsh area that was reclaimed and now known as Boston's Back Bay. And such a heavy concentration of oyster beds and shells was found on Cape Cod that many of its bays and harbors were simply named "oyster" by the early explorers.

The changing role that oysters played in American cuisine from the wigwams of the Wampanoags to the private dining rooms of Delmonico's was definitely a saga that progressed from sheer necessity to serendipity. And even the culinary footnotes are different from the history of oyster savoring in Europe.

On both the Atlantic and Pacific coasts pre-Columbian Indians ate oysters only after they boiled them for five or six hours to make them tender. And it is fair to assume that the Indians taught the settlers to make oyster stew with different combinations of roots, vegetables, and grains in order to compensate for the absence of milk-giving animals. But necessity did little to dispel the Pilgrims' prejudice that oysters were fit only for farm animals.

Some colonists, however, adapted their taste for British oysters to the rough-shelled, different-tasting American oyster. In 1607, during the Christmas season, Captain John Smith wrote that in Virginia, "we were never more merry nor fed on more plenty of good oysters . . . in England." But from Massachusetts to Maryland, their appreciation of oysters waned every spring because supplies of food dwindled and a diet of oysters was the only way to keep from starving.

In the New World, wars were even started because of oysters. When Charles I gave Lord Baltimore the area up to the high-water mark on Virginia's side of the Potomac River and the projection of that line into Chesapeake Bay, he gave Maryland the lion's share of the oyster beds. And if the colonists failed to appreciate the gift, the potential of one of the greatest oyster-producing areas was soon discovered. Gunshots were—and are still—heard across those waters. But that's another story.

At some point in time between the years when the early settlers reluctantly dined on oysters and the years of community "oyster roasts," American attitudes changed. By 1857, Charles Mackay, an English visitor in the States, concluded that "the rich consume oysters and champaigne; the poorer classes consume oysters and *lager bier*, and that is one of the principal social differences between the two sections of the community." During the mid- and late 1800s, one of the major markets in the States was New York City, where oyster boats, known as arks, brought over six million oysters a day to wholesale dealers.

Up and down the eastern seaboard, oysters became synonymous with conviviality, profit, and regular tavern fare. Express "oyster wagons" crossed the Alleghenies to Pittsburgh where, by either boat or wagon, oysters were rushed to "parlors" in Cincinnati and Chicago. Every large town had an oyster cellar, saloon, bar, or parlor, usually down a short flight of steps, and identified by an oyster balloon displayed above the establishment. Open for business any time of the day, these parlors were often regarded as places of resort for politicians and public office holders. As far away as downstate Illinois, Abraham Lincoln included oyster roasts in his campaign strategy.

Menus in important restaurants like New York's Astor House featured "boiled cod fish and oysters" and "oyster pie." Almost every testimonial banquet ranging from $100 to $5,000 a plate began with Lynnhavens on the half shell, and a London gentleman wrote that New York City consumed £3,500 worth daily. The Revere House in Boston used one hundred gallons of oysters a week. In Philadelphia almost no oysters were served in 1810, but by 1840, four thousand tons were sent annually from Chesapeake Bay. And in the West, two of the costliest ingredients, eggs and oysters, were used in tandem to make what must have been the most expensive omelet in the world, presumably paid for in gold. By 1850, the oyster was the favorite of the tavern and town set. And nineteenth-century cookbooks were more than generous in instructing cooks to "enrich" a modest gumbo with a hundred oysters, and add at least two quarts of them to a soup.

Perhaps this American fondness for oysters was in imitation of the craze that swept Paris and London, the twin capitals of the world known for taste and fashion. Maybe it was the inevitable adaptation of French, Italian, and Spanish cuisines to ingredients that were plentiful in the various "regions" of the country. Possibly the taste for oysters was attributable, at least in part, to the fact that many native beds of oysters were depleted as early as the 1770s and the difficult, time-consuming process of seeding and cultivation made the "oystermen" a breed apart and gave their "harvest" additional value. And there just might be another reason.

Reflections

While the androgynous oyster's own sense of romance is open to question, it is certainly no accident that the names associated with oyster lore and legend are the names of many of the world's great lovers. From rakishly Rabelaisian quips to the current psychophysiological mass market studies of human sexuality, the cult of oysters as aphrodisiacs is a story unto itself, and like all stories, it grows more suspect with each telling.

The possibilities of attribution are limitless, and wishful thinking is always open to question. If opening an oyster shell is a symbol for seducing a beautiful woman, are not all metaphors created in the imagination? If oysters on the half shell resemble female and male genitalia, isn't the comparison in the eye of the beholder? To wink and blink about Casanova's appetite for oysters and women and to

talk about it in some circles is a bit gamey. And for those sporting individuals who acquire "double entendres" at an awesome rate to add a little antic behavior to the cocktail party scene, there are certainly more than a few words associated with oysters, beginning with foot and *huitre*, to make the evening memorable. But what's one person's thrill may be another's tedium.

For a generation that has lived through the 1960s, 1970s, and 1980s, there is something dated and déclassé about this sort of twittering, something demeaning to both "love food" and lover. Eating a serving of oysters on the half shell and drinking a glass of Champagne may be the beginning of an affair of the heart, but it is also a culinary affair between a food that is an acquired taste and a person who has painstakingly cultivated it. And to regard oysters as a means to an end, as a magic potion for lovemaking, may well be a disservice to a food that is its own delectation and its own reward.

A closer look and a context might be helpful. And no one person has provided it with greater insight and style than M. F. K. Fisher: "Our three basic needs, for food and security and love are so mixed and mingled and entwined that we cannot straightly think of one without the others. . . ." A meal shared with someone one loves is a celebration; initiating someone into pleasures one has known is intensely human.

There is no doubt that eating a first oyster is a kind of coming of age, a rite of passage from the security of the familiar tastes associated with childhood to the unknown world of adult experience. It is a frightening and a joyous moment that prose cannot really describe as well as poetry can. Anne Sexton saw the dozen of oysters before her arranged on the plate like numbers on a clock, like time, and she looked from her father's satisfaction with his "clear as tears" martini and platter of oysters to her own plate of "twelve eyes . . . running with lemon and Tabasco." Like all difficult experiences, the first swallow was disconcerting, "a large pudding" going down. But by the time that "one o'-clock" and two were eaten, there was laughter and "I was fifteen/ and eating oysters/ and the child was defeated./ The woman won."* The initiation was complete.

Unique in a group of foods that includes truffles, lobster, artichokes, mangoes, passion fruit, and a score of other "love" foods, oysters are food for the initiated few. Often compared to a seductive woman, there is a mystery, a subtlety, a quality that defies explanation about them. No other food evokes such strong feelings of utter bliss or revulsion; no other food has been written about more eloquently or more trivially.

The history of oysters is definitely a riches to rags to riches story. As the favorite food of emperors and kings, oysters were transported with great difficulty and at great expense, devoured at banquets, synonymous with decadence and excess. Oysters were also the staple of the poor, the main ingredient in an astonishingly nutritious stew, roast, and pottage made to stave off hunger. Today, the story has come full circle. The days of plentiful, inexpensive oysters belong to the romantic days of America's past.

Oysters, along with caviar and *foie gras*, are in a class apart, the *pièce de résistance* in the menus of inspired chefs and the ultimate *tour de genie* at parties given by the most discriminating hostesses.

And a cookbook devoted to oyster cookery ought to reflect something of the exclusivity and versatility of its subject, should suggest the balance and harmony of a meal, and even the combinations of ingredients that complement the delicacy of the main ingredient.

Ruminations

This is a "come into my kitchen I want my oysters to meet you" kind of cookbook, written for the cook who needs no coaxing to purchase a half dozen or half peck of oysters at the local fish market, take the oyster knife out of the top drawer, and shuck away. For whether served on the half shell with a bit of lemon or fried, baked, and grilled as a substantial dinner entrée, the fascination with the many possible ways of preparing oysters never wanes for the person who enjoys pampering family and friends with elegant, delectable dishes.

But this is also a cookbook written to seduce the hesitant into the wonderful world of oyster cuisine possible to everyone within the perimeters of the kitchen. The oyster enthusiast need not limit his enjoyment of oysters to expensive restaurants or dockside oyster bars. Oysters are trucked and flown to virtually every part of this country and are available twelve months of the year. Shucking is definitely neither a male nor an Amazonian prerogative; the skill can be learned quickly; practice makes short work of opening oysters. And the following six chapters, beginning with appetizers and ending with entrées, are a compendium of both traditional and innovative ways to prepare and serve oysters, complete with

*Anne Sexton, "Oysters," from *The Book of Folly*, Houghton Mifflin Co., 1973.

pertinent suggestions that are linked to specific cooking techniques.

Only one thing is necessary in oyster cookery, and that is a knowledge of and a certain respect for the ingredients used. Oysters differ tremendously in size, plumpness, and taste. Because an oyster pumps more than a hundred gallons of water a day through its mouth and gut and assimilates mostly sodium chloride and minerals, it will taste of salt and metals. Its taste will be a concentration of its last habitat.

Coppery, tinny, sweet, clean, intense—are all favorable descriptions and a matter of the strong personal preference of the oyster devotee. These same qualities have a different importance for the cook and signal caution. Some of the following recipes are especially suitable to the mild flavor of warm-water Gulf oysters, whereas New England and Long Island oysters are ideal in those recipes requiring raw oysters. It's always important to know the saltiness, texture, and taste of the oysters one is preparing, and to avoid, if possible, oysters that are not firm to the touch and indistinguishable in flavor. In every recipe the quality of the oysters used determines the success of the dish.

There is, I hope, something for everyone in this book—legend and lore, old recipes, traditional recipes updated, unusual combinations of ingredients, menu suggestions, and the assurance that oyster cuisine is very much on-going and going-on into the twenty-first century.

And now on to *Oysters: A Culinary Celebration.*

You are eating the sea, that's it!

—ELEANOR CLARK,
The Oysters of Locmariaquer

Four years ago—she remembered
distinctly—a meal had begun
with soup or oysters or
lobster cocktail or an avocado with
Roquefort dressing.
Something. But now, it seemed,
after large basins of Martinis-on-
the-rocks (a drink she considered
parvenu, as opposed to the classic
Martini), you sat right down to
the main course or it was
served to you on your lap.
Nobody alluded to the vanished
first course; it was like a relation
that had died and could
not be mentioned.

—MARY MCCARTHY,
Birds of America

Appetizers

There is simply no telling if civilization will survive without a first course, but life would certainly be lackluster without the proper prelude to a meal. An appetizer is somewhat like the tantalizing first chapter of a novel that captivates a reader's attention and compels him to turn page after page to the happy or not-so-happy end. Or perhaps it's as engaging as the beginning of a love affair—so much more scintillating than the day-to-day familiarity that eventually leads to a less-than-inspired good-bye. No doubt about it, first impressions are either infatuating or provoking; they can never be bland. And menus are very much the same. What diner has not glowed with delight, drinking a glass of fine Champagne and savoring a chilled briny oyster on the half shell?

Custom and history have served the oyster well and annotated such goings-on as a feast given in 50 B.C. The menu began with "sea urchins and raw oysters in profusion, giant mussels, and sea carp served on asparagus." And there was an account of the serving of roast mutton with oysters, "as a first course at the feast of the East India Company at Merchantailors' Hall, London, on January 20, 1622." Consider, also, that in Preston, England, from 1771 to 1841, there flourished the "Oyster and Parched Pea Club," whose members pledged to provide and open a barrel of oysters at exactly half past seven every Monday night during the winter season.

Perhaps it need not even be mentioned that Casanova ate at least fifty oysters per day and Louis XIV never ate less than a hundred when they appeared on the royal menu. Brillat-Savarin's observation sums it all up nicely:

I remember that in the old days any banquet of importance began with oysters, and that there were always a good number of the guests who did not hesitate to down one gross apiece (twelve dozen, one hundred and forty-four). I always wondered what the weight of this little appetizer would be, and finally I confirmed the fact that one dozen oysters (including their juice) weigh four ounces, which makes the gross amount to three pounds. I feel quite sure, then, that these same guests, who were not at all deterred from dining well after their oysters, would have been completely surfeited if they had eaten the same weight of meat, even if it had been the delicate flesh of a chicken.

The possibilities are endless, and, it seems, have always been. Every language has a special word for the small portions of food that contribute stylistically to a meal but are literally *hors d'oeuvre*, "outside the work" of the meal. The Mandarins of ancient China called them *ti wei ping* and boasted over one thousand. The Athenians enjoyed their numerous *dolmas*; in Rome, *gustatio* came to mean a minimum of fifty tasters.

Appetizers often identify a cuisine and, because they are served in small portions, exhibit more of the innovative aspects of culinary style than the main course, where combinations of ingredients and flavors are sustained for more than a bite or a nibble. A French *hors d'oeuvre* may be a few hot stuffed mussels or a chilled rémoulade of celery root. An order of Clams Oregano or sliced Settecento Genoa salami with a cool wedge of honeydew melon or half of a fresh fig may be fit-ting Italian *antipasti*. A "fresh from the stream to the smoke house" platter of trout or selection of wurst can be a simple *Vorspeise* in Germany. And then there is potted shrimp in England, a *zakuski* of jellied calves' feet in Russia, and a cracked wheat salad for a Syrian *maza*.

But, despite the distinctive features of international cuisine, there are a few "constants," a few ingredients that tempt the palate with more insistence than Vegetables a la Grecque or Chicken Satay. They are the gifts from the sea—oysters, caviar, smoked salmon, lobster, shrimp, and lump crabmeat.

Today, the menus of famous restaurants perpetuate the idea that the crisp, briny flavor of an oyster enhances the appetite. And even though the traditional favorites—Oysters Rockefeller, Bienville, and Casino—have surrendered some of their popularity to the lighter and purer tastes cultivated by the practitioners of nouvelle American cuisine, fresh oysters dressed with lime juice and slivered ginger, or with a simple shallot sauce, and grilled oysters served with leeks in a pure buttery sauce are proof positive that oyster cookery does and will always reflect the taste of the moment as well as the past.

This first chapter begins with some "authentic" recipes for serving oysters as an elegant sit-down beginning to a dinner party. Freshly shucked and quivering from the sea to a bed of ice, or properly sauced and piping hot from the oven, these oyster appetizers require plates and forks and are difficult to juggle at stand-up parties or even cocktail buffets. At a sit-down dinner, Champagne or an appropriate French Chablis can be leisurely sipped, lemon wedges, cracked pepper, and side dishes of sauce can be passed, and empty shells can be whisked away with the serving plates—all with great ease for the server and guests.

In spite of all this emphasis on serving oysters in their own shells or, as is often done on the Continent, in seafood cocktail glasses, there are a few recipes that will accommodate the hostess with a penchant for serving oysters during an informal "drinks" hour. Miniature turnovers, tartelettes, and profiteroles are attractive, delicious, and easy to serve, and there is even a dip that works well with crudités, crackers, and chips. Finger foods, including canapés, will spark up any cocktail party and whet the appetite.

Suggestions

- An appropriate appetizer complements the rest of the meal in every way but does not repeat any of the main ingredients, sauces, herbs, or preparation methods of the other courses. An elaborate first course such as oysters au Vin de Champagne can nicely introduce a grilled rack of lamb or sirloin steak, whereas raw oysters on the half shell would be wonderful with a stuffed chicken breast served with Sauce Suprême.
- Six raw oysters per person are usually served as a first course. However, because of their size, an appropriate serving of Kumamoto oysters would be 8 or 10. If the oysters are larger than 3 inches and they are baked or broiled with a rich sauce or dressing, 3 or 4 per person are usually adequate.
- Raw oysters served on the half shell must always be perfectly fresh and shucked as close to serving time as possible. It is not advisable to serve bulk or frozen oysters raw. There is nothing that can equal a just-harvested oyster served immediately, but, if that is not practical, fresh oysters can be kept cup-side-down in the refrigerator for at least two weeks, or shucked and then frozen for later use in cooked dishes with a minimum loss of taste. Oysters used as a hot appetizer or finger food can be shucked in advance and refrigerated, or can be purchased by the jar or by the pint, which may be stored in the freezer if necessary.

- Oyster shells, like scallop shells, can be reused any number of times. It is convenient to have a supply on hand if the dish can be made with bulk or frozen oysters.
- Oysters can never be undercooked, but can be ruined by overcooking, which toughens them and diminishes their flavor. When baking an oyster appetizer, use a hot oven, from 400° to 450°, unless the other ingredients dictate a lower temperature. When broiling, place the pan 4 inches from the heat and cook for less than 5 minutes. Some recipes can be prepared most efficiently by baking for a short time and then melting or browning the topping under the broiler for a minute or two. When poaching an oyster, cook it only until plump or until its edges begin to curl, and remove from heat.
- Because of the irregular shape of the deep shell, lining a baking or broiling pan with rock salt is recommended to steady the shells and retain both the liquor and heat. Crumpled heavy-gauge aluminum foil will accomplish the same thing, but the amount of heat retained is minimal and not quite worth the effort. Shells can be placed directly on a baking sheet or broiler rack and prepared with a minimum amount of spilling. The shells will retain enough heat to ensure a hot appetizer.

- Sauces for many of the hot appetizers and finger foods can be prepared in advance. Some of the recipes can also be assembled and refrigerated several hours before baking. If the prepared shells are cold, bring to room temperature before heating.
- Estimating servings of finger foods is somewhat determined by the variety of foods being served. Usually 3 per person are sufficient if the hostess has prepared three or four different kinds.
- Many of the recipes prepared as appetizers can also be served as the main course at a luncheon or late evening supper by adjusting the amount served.
- In general, French Chablis, and not most American Chardonnays which tend to be too rich and intense, pairs well with oysters, but, increasingly, the Loire Valley Sauvignon Blancs, Sancerres, Pouilly-Fumés, and Muscadets have become favorite accompaniments in raw bars and dining rooms across the country. And there have always been and will continue to be a few connoisseurs who will insist on Champagne or sparkling wine. On balance, specific ingredients and combinations of flavors will suggest specific wines, and these selections are included in the text.

Seven o'clock having struck, the rustle of a woman's costly robe is heard as the portieres part and our hostess moves forward to survey the table while placing the beautiful and costly dinner cards. Diamonds flash in her hair, about her neck, and on the corsage of her wonderful gown. Diamonds in front of her, diamonds at back of her, diamonds on top of her sparkle and dazzle as she goes to the salon to receive her guests.

Champagne is cooling in cracked ice, all the wines are ready, oysters on the halfshell, resting in silver plates of wondrous workmanship, garnished with artistically cut lemon, await the point of the tiny fork.

—MARY E. CARTER,
Millionaire Households:
And Their Domestic Economy, 1903

COLD APPETIZERS

On the Half Shell
A Sextet of Sauces for Raw Oysters
Oysters Granité
Oysters with a Splash
Unblushing Oysters
Oyster-Spinach Rolls on the
Half Shell With Mustard Sauce
With Golden Caviar
Oysters in Aspic
Oysters and Sausages

HOT APPETIZERS

Oysters Florentine (Rockefeller)
Parmigiano
Verde
Oysters Bienville
Imperial
au Vin de Champagne
aux Ecrivisses
Oysters Roffignac
Oysters Casino
Oysters 1826
Oysters Forestiére
Cider House Oysters
Gingered Oysters
Oysters Bourguignon
Stuffed Oysters
Stuffed Oysters Antillian Style

FINGER FOOD

Angels on Horseback
Galloping Oysters
Fritto Misto
Savory Oyster Asparagus Squares
Stuffed Mushroom Caps
Oyster Beignets
Acras
Oyster Profiteroles
Oysters Parnassus
Oysters Scandia
Wanton Wontons
Whistling Oyster Dip

CANAPÉS

COLD

Casino Canapés
Oysters Lucullus
Oysters Lucca
Oysters Otero

COLD OR HOT

Mushroom Oyster Rounds
Tunny Smoked Oyster Rounds

HOT

Zesty Oyster Canapés
Broiled Oyster Canapés
Oyster Puffs

COLD APPETIZERS

Oysters on the Half Shell

The ardent oyster lover, pure and undefiled by the allure of *haute cuisine*, demands his oysters pure and undefiled by any other flavor, seasoning, herb, or accompaniment that rivals the briny taste of the sea. So here is not only the obligatory recipe for savoring oysters, but also the one that perfectly expresses the author's own personal conviction that in oyster cookery less is better than more. The perfect accompaniment would be a glass of Muscadet or Pouilly-Fumé, wines grown, for the most part, in chalky soil with sedimentary deposits of the maritime provinces, thus establishing with more insistence than ever a connection with the sea.

SERVES 1

6   oysters
2   cups crushed ice
$^1/_4$ lemon (optional)
     Freshly cracked black pepper
     Wine vinegar (optional)

1. Scrub oyster shells under running cold water.
2. Shuck the oysters immediately before serving and strain any liquor that spills from the shells into a container.
3. Arrange the oysters in the deep shells on a bed of ice, and pour the strained liquor into the shells.
4. If desired, serve with a wedge of lemon, a bit of cracked pepper, or a splash of good-quality vinegar.

A Sextet of Sauces for Raw Oysters

Epicurean cooks sharpen with cloyless sauce his appetite.

—SHAKESPEARE,
Antony and Cleopatra

If guests are less-than-confirmed devotees of raw oysters, the gracious host or hostess, mindful of the words that Shakespeare wrote about sauces many years ago, will offer one or two of them whenever raw oysters are served either on the half shell or on a bed of lettuce chiffonade in stemmed glassware appropriate for seafood cocktails as was the custom at Delmonico's way back then.

Ranging from a simple Mignonette dressing to a zesty Rémoulade, the following sauces will please some palates more than others. In all of them, the ingredients speak for themselves and, along with personal taste, should dictate the choice. Each recipe yields about a cup of sauce. Mix thoroughly and serve well chilled.

MIGNONETTE SAUCE

1/4   *cup finely chopped shallots*
1   *cup red wine vinegar*
2   *teaspoons freshly ground white pepper*

Variation:
1/4   *cup finely chopped shallots*
1   *cup dry white wine*
2   *Tablespoons chopped chives*
1   *teaspoon freshly ground white pepper*

SPICED CHILI SAUCE

1   *cup chili sauce*
1/4   *cup lemon juice*
2   *teaspoons Worcestershire sauce*
1   *teaspoon dry mustard*
    Tabasco to taste

TOMATO AND HORSERADISH SAUCE

1   *cup chili sauce*
2   *Tablespoons prepared horseradish*
2   *Tablespoons lemon juice*
1   *Tablespoon dry Sherry*
2   *Tablespoons finely chopped celery*

Variation:
1   *cup tomato ketchup*
1/4   *cup red wine vinegar*
4   *Tablespoons prepared horseradish*

DILL SAUCE

1/2   *cup sour cream or crème fraîche*
1/2   *cup mayonnaise*
1   *Tablespoon dry Vermouth*
2   *Tablespoons chopped fresh dill weed*
1   *teaspoon finely chopped parsley*

RÉMOULADE SAUCE

1½	cups mayonnaise
2	Tablespoons Dijon mustard
1	teaspoon anchovy paste
¼	cup chopped cornichons
1	Tablespoon capers
¼	cup minced fresh parsley
¼	cup minced fresh chervil

> *Why should anyone need a recipe? Oysters are best fresh, cold, raw and plain.*
>
> —PHYLLIS C. RICHMAN

RÉMOULADE SAUCE NEW ORLEANS

¼	cup olive oil
½	cup Creole mustard
½	cup tomato ketchup
1	Tablespoon white wine vinegar
2	Tablespoons lemon juice
1	teaspoon grated lemon rind
1	teaspoon paprika
2	Tablespoons horseradish
1	Tablespoon Worcestershire sauce
1	teaspoon Tabasco
¼	cup minced celery
2	Tablespoons finely chopped scallions
1	Tablespoon finely chopped parsley
	Freshly ground black pepper

Good Beginnings

Although oysters are usually served icy cold on the half shell and as *au naturel* as possible, the following ideas for presenting these versatile shellfish add an innovative footnote to the fine art of using the oyster as a first course.

OYSTER GRANITÉ

SERVES 4

The idea of slacking one's thirst or cooling one's passion with flavored ice is not new. Alexander the Great indulged in it after a hard day's work sacking Persia. And a little later in time, Nero stationed runners along the Appian Way to pass along buckets of snow from the mountains to his banquet hall where the ice was flavored with fruit and honey. But a new twist to the peculiarly granular texture of traditional Italian *granita* or *granité* is serving oysters topped with this grainy version of oyster liquor. Serve with Muscadet.

24   *freshly shucked oysters and strained liquor*
      Dry white wine
      Freshly cracked black pepper
      Dash of freshly squeezed lemon juice

1. Make the *granité* by combining the strained oyster liquor with wine, lemon juice, and black pepper according to taste.
2. Pour into a shallow 9- by 13-inch baking pan, and freeze until mixture is set. Meanwhile, place the opened oysters in the refrigerator loosely covered with plastic wrap.
3. To serve, arrange the chilled shucked oysters on a plate; scrape the *granité* with a spoon or fork to create small shavings. Spoon over oysters and serve immediately.

OYSTERS WITH A SPLASH
(*Serve with iced Vodka*)

SERVES 4

24   *oysters*
1   *ruby red grapefruit*
1   *white grapefruit*
1   *blood orange*
1   *navel orange*
$1/2$ *cup mango vinegar*
2   *teaspoons lemon zest*
      Dash of freshly cracked pepper

1. Scrub and open the oysters, sever the bottom adductor muscle, drain off the liquor, and keep oysters on the half shell chilled.
2. Peel the citrus fruits with a sharp knife, cut out slices without membrane, and halve or quarter the slices if large. Remove seeds and place fruit in a bowl. Squeeze the juice from the membrane into the bowl, and discard. Add the flavored vinegar, zest, and pepper to the bowl.
3. Place 6 oysters on the half shell on each plate and spoon some of the citrus mixture over the oysters. Serve well-chilled.

UNBLUSHING OYSTERS

SERVES 2

With a little foresight this marinated oyster appetizer can be whisked out at the last moment and introduce a dinner for 2 at eight. Small and saline Kumamoto oysters are ideal, especially when served with a high-quality Alsace Riesling.

I received a letter from the California Avocado Advisory Board which stated unblushingly, "Since we so fondly think of our avocado as an aphrodisiac, and have such experts as Mae West [sic] explaining its proof positive in this area . . . we certainly do wonder, how do you know it isn't?"

—WAVERLEY ROOT, Food

12	shucked and drained small oysters
¹/₂	cup sliced pearl onions
¹/₂	cup sour cream
	Pinch of sugar
	Freshly cracked pepper
1	avocado
1	Tablespoon lemon juice
	Salt
2	select leaves of Boston or Bibb lettuce
¹/₄	cup julienned sweet red pepper

1. Blanch the onions for a minute, plunge in cold water, drain, and cut into paper-thin slices. Mix with sour cream, sugar, and a generous amount of pepper. Add the drained oysters and marinate at least 24 hours before serving.
2. Cut the avocado in half, remove the pit, and peel. Brush surfaces with lemon juice. And salt lightly. Arrange each half on a lettuce leaf and fill with the marinated oysters.
3. Garnish with a toss of julienned red pepper and serve.

OYSTER-SPINACH ROLLS ON THE HALF SHELL

SERVES 4

Wrapped in blanched spinach leaves and teased with the subtle flavor of smoked salmon or caviar, these miniature *rouleaux* are eye-catching appetizers. Serve them either with a mustard sauce or topped with your favorite caviar, and they taste as wonderful as they look. Double the recipe and either variation on a theme will make a luscious luncheon dish. Serve with a crisp Muscadet.

SPINACH-OYSTER ROLLS WITH MUSTARD SAUCE

24   *shucked oysters and deep shells*
12   *select spinach leaves*
4   *slices smoked salmon*
1   *cup mustard mayonnaise*
      Lemon wedges

Mustard Mayonnaise:

1   *cup mayonnaise*
1   *Tablespoon Dijon-style mustard*
1   *Tablespoon dry Sherry*

1. Drain the oysters. Wash and dry deep shells.
2. Stem and wash the spinach leaves. Drop one leaf at a time in boiling salted water. Remove almost immediately and refresh in cold water. Drain and pat dry. Cut each leaf in half along the central vein, discarding the vein unless using salad spinach.
3. Spread out the leaves, right-side-down, and arrange an oyster and a piece of salmon at the stem end of each half. Roll up jelly-roll style.
4. Place each roll, seam-side-down, on a shell and spoon mustard mayonnaise over it.
5. Serve with lemon wedges.

WITH GOLDEN CAVIAR

SERVES 4

24   *shucked oysters and deep shells*
12   *select spinach leaves*
8   *ounces sour cream*
8   *ounces golden whitefish caviar*
      Lemon wedges

Vinaigrette Sauce:

1   *Tablespoon finely chopped capers*
1   *Tablespoon finely chopped shallots*
3   *Tablespoons red wine vinegar*
$2/3$ *cup extra virgin olive oil*
      Freshly ground pepper to taste

1. Remove oysters from the shells and drain. Scrub and dry the deep shells.
2. Marinate the oysters in vinaigrette for at least 30 minutes.
3. Wash spinach leaves. Drop one leaf at a time in boiling salted water. Remove in a minute and refresh in cold water. Drain and pat dry. Cut each leaf in half along the central vein, discarding the vein.
4. Spread out the leaves, right-side-down, and arrange an oyster at the stem end of each piece. Sprinkle with pepper and roll up jelly-roll style.
5. Thin sour cream with a bit of vinaigrette and put a generous spoonful in the bottom of each shell. Add the spinach roll, seam-side-down, and spoon a little more sour cream over each one. Garnish with a generous topping of golden caviar. Serve with lemon wedges.

OYSTERS IN ASPIC

SERVES 6

This is a half-shell presentation that will sparkle at any special dinner, and the few steps of work involved will be amply rewarded by the delicious results. Why not serve with a well-chilled Champagne?

My last meal would be cooked at home in the company of a friend or two with whom I like to cook, and we would start with French Chablis and Cotuit oysters, accompanied with very thinly sliced homemade rye bread, lightly buttered.

—JULIA CHILD, "DINNER TO END ALL DINNERS," *Food and Wine,* January 1983

26	shucked oysters, deep shells, and liquor
2	cups Champagne
1	package gelatin
1	teaspoon butter
1	finely chopped shallot
$^1/_4$	cup whipped heavy cream
3	ounces crème fraîche
$^1/_4$	teaspoon Tabasco
$^1/_2$	teaspoon sea salt
	Freshly ground white pepper
1	bunch of watercress
	Lemon wedges

1. Rinse and dry the deep shells, and strain oyster liquor, measuring out 1 cup. Finely chop 2 oysters and set aside.
2. In a saucepan reduce Champagne down to 1 cup, add oyster liquor, and simmer. Remove from heat and cool slightly.
3. Dissolve gelatin in 2 tablespoons of warm water. Ladle some of the wine broth; into the gelatin, stir until smooth, and return the mixture to the broth; stir. Pour into a bowl and place over ice to chill.

4. In a small saucepan melt the butter and lightly sauté the shallots until soft. Add the 2 chopped oysters, whipped cream, and *crème fraîche.* Stir until smooth, and add seasonings.
5. Assemble by placing the deep shells on a tray. Spread a spoonful of cream mixture into the bottom of each shell. (Refrigerate if not a firm consistency.) Place a well-drained oyster over the cream mixture, and garnish with a few small watercress leaves.
6. Coat each oyster with a tablespoon of Champagne gelatin. Refrigerate until set, and repeat the process until each half shell is enclosed in gelatin.
7. To serve, arrange 4 prepared oyster shells on a bed of watercress, and add a lemon wedge.

OYSTERS AND SAUSAGES

SERVES 6

The complementary pairing of hot spicy sausages with ice cold oysters is especially worth the effort because it "kicks off" a beach party or a tailgate bash with every assurance of success. Keep the oysters packed in ice until the sausages are spitting on the grill. Then shuck the oysters and let the guests decide the order for themselves—oyster-sausage, or sausage-oyster. Be sure to have an ample supply of both and some bottles of Weissbier.

36	*freshly shucked oysters*
	Mignonette Sauce with Wine (see p. 15)
28	*sausages (recipe below or any good-quality pork sausage)*

Sausage:

5	*pounds lean pork butt or shoulder*
2	*teaspoons salt*
1	*teaspoon white pepper*
1¹/₂	*teaspoons brown sugar*
¹/₂	*teaspoon freshly grated nutmeg*
¹/₂	*teaspoon powdered ginger*
¹/₄	*teaspoon dried sage*
1	*egg*
¹/₄	*cup rum*
10	*feet sausage casing*

You can make a whole lunch of oysters if you eat them the way they do in Bordeaux. Buy a dozen oysters. Fry some link sausages. Take a bite of burning hot sausage, then soothe your mouth with a cool oyster. Twelve times. . . .

—Dr. Edouard
de Pomiane,
*French Cooking in
Ten Minutes or Adapting
to the Rhythm
of Modern Life,*
1930

1. Cut the pork into 1-inch cubes, be sure it is well chilled, and coarse-grind in a food processor fitted with the steel blade.
2. Mix in all the seasonings, egg, and rum.
3. Using a sausage stuffer, fill the casing, making each sausage about 4 inches long. Twist and tie. Refrigerate for 24 hours uncovered.
4. Cover with water and parboil the sausages for 5 minutes; sauté in butter or grill over wood charcoal, turning frequently, until they are crisp outside and juicy within.
5. Shuck and serve the oysters on ice with sauce on the side. Serve the sausages on a hot platter or directly from the grill.

HOT APPETIZERS

OYSTERS FLORENTINE
(Oysters Rockefeller)

Perhaps no other oyster appetizer has become as legendary as Oysters a la Rockefeller or subject to as much conjecture and duplication. Based on a recipe for Snails Bourguignon, the sauce was adapted to oysters by a number of enterprising New Orleans chefs and restaurateurs more than a century ago because oysters were less expensive and more readily available than snails.

Over the years, Jules Alciatore, the founder of the original Antoine's, and his successors have disclosed some of the "18" ingredients—chopped celery, minced shallots, fresh chervil and tarragon, crumbs of dry bread, Tabasco, and Herbsaint, a cordial made of southern herbs including anise— but the family-owned restaurant has consistently kept other ingredients "unknown." Whether the green color of the sauce is achieved by a combination of parsley, chervil, watercress, chives, and tarragon or, perhaps, by spinach will always be a "house secret."

Even today, the famous first course recipe remains somewhat elusive and, as usual, in matters relating to personal taste, the various ingredients of the recipe are dictated by preference. But the special affinity that oysters and spinach have for each other is a given in oyster cookery. And many of the recipes called Oysters Rockefeller would more accurately be named Oysters Florentine because spinach has become the main ingredient in the sauce.

The following recipes represent the major adaptations of the appetizer that has become synonymous with affluence. Whether bread crumbs or melted cheese is preferred or whether the oyster is bedded on a spoonful of creamed spinach and then napped with a glorious Béchamel or Mornay sauce, a dash of Pernod will most certainly heighten the flavor. And a glass of Macon or a flute of fine Champagne will raise the level of this first course to a celestial feast.

Variations on
a Theme

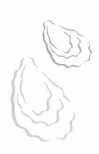

SERVES 4

OYSTERS FLORENTINE PARMIGIANO
While this recipe seems to be a straightforward saucing of fresh oysters with a simple spinach mixture, the addition of Pernod, anchovies, and Parmesan cheese adds a dash and daring that make it memorable.

24	*shucked oysters, liquor, and deep shells*
1	*pound fresh spinach*
8	*Tablespoons butter*
$^1/_2$	*cup chopped parsley*
2	*chopped anchovy fillets*
1	*Tablespoon Pernod*
$1^1/_2$	*teaspoons Worcestershire sauce*
$^1/_2$	*cup fresh bread crumbs*
	Salt and freshly ground pepper
	Tabasco
1	*cup freshly grated Parmigiano-Reggiano*

OVEN TEMPERATURE: 450°

1. Drain the oysters and set aside in bottom shells. Strain and reserve the liquor for the spinach mixture.
2. Rinse, wilt, drain, and chop the spinach.
3. Melt the butter in a saucepan. Stir in the spinach, parsley, and anchovies. Gradually add the Pernod, Worcestershire sauce, and bread crumbs.

4. Coarsely purée the mixture in a food processor or blender, thinning with oyster liquor if necessary.
5. Season to taste with salt, pepper, and Tabasco.
6. Place the oysters in the shells on a baking sheet. Spoon the spinach mixture over the oysters and top with cheese.
7. Bake from 5 to 10 minutes until the cheese is melted and light brown.

OYSTERS VERDE

SERVES 4

A subtle blend of green vegetables and herbs makes this recipe as pleasing to the eye as it is to the palate. The food processor will make light of the work, but chopping the vegetables by hand will add an interesting texture to the taste and appearance of the dish. Serve with an Alsace or Oregon Riesling.

24	*shucked oysters in deep shells*
$1/2$	*cup finely chopped Chinese cabbage*
$1/4$	*cup finely chopped shallots*
$1^1/2$	*cups chopped fresh spinach*
1	*cup chopped watercress*
$1/2$	*cup finely chopped parsley*
2	*Tablespoons chopped fresh basil*
5	*Tablespoons butter*
2	*finely chopped anchovy fillets or 1 teaspoon anchovy paste*
2	*Tablespoons dry white wine*
	Salt and freshly ground pepper
	Cayenne pepper
$1^1/2$	*cups shredded Gruyère*

OVEN TEMPERATURE: MEDIUM BROIL

1. Wash, drain, and finely chop the vegetables and herbs. Keep separate.
2. Melt the butter in a saucepan, and sauté the Chinese cabbage and shallots until soft. Add the spinach, watercress, parsley, and basil. Cook until the vegetables and herbs are wilted but not faded in color. Add the anchovies and wine. Season to taste with salt, pepper, and cayenne.
3. Arrange the oysters in the shells on a baking sheet. Spoon the vegetable mixture over the oysters, and top generously with cheese.
4. Broil from 3 to 5 minutes until the cheese is bubbling and golden.

OYSTERS BIENVILLE

Whether designated to sing the praises of legendary patriots and citizens, famous chefs, or prominent patrons, the dishes that have made New Orleans the haunt of epicureans remain the "original" oyster appetizers, possibly never improved upon, but always subjected to countless imitations.

Named in honor of the Frenchman who founded the "crescent city" in 1718, Oysters Bienville has not escaped the epigone's fancy. So, it is not surprising that the sauce associated with this well-known dish has come to include crabmeat and shrimp, bacon and mushrooms, and even Champagne as an added fillip instead of the usual white wine of the original recipe.

Giving away nothing to Rockefellers and Roffignacs in piquancy, this first course is a favorite of all those who love seafood and are willing to take the time and effort to present it with a bit of improvisation. Reinforce Bienville's indebtedness to France with a glass of Chassagne-Montrachet.

24	*shucked oysters, liquor, and deep shells*
³/₄	*cup chicken or fish stock (see p. 58)*
4	*Tablespoons butter*
¹/₄	*cup finely chopped mushrooms*
¹/₄	*cup finely chopped shallots*
2	*Tablespoons flour*
2	*egg yolks*
¹/₂	*cup light cream*
1	*cup chopped cooked shrimp and/or back-fin crabmeat*
3	*Tablespoons dry Sherry*
	Salt and freshly ground pepper
	Cayenne pepper
1	*cup buttered bread crumbs*

OVEN TEMPERATURE: 450°

1. Drain the oysters and set aside in the bottom shells. Strain and reserve ¼ cup of the liquor. Add it to the stock and heat in a small saucepan.
2. Melt the butter in another saucepan and sauté the mushrooms and shallots until soft. Stir in the flour and cook until straw yellow. Remove from heat and whisk in the stock mixture. Return to heat and cook, stirring constantly, for at least 5 to 8 minutes.

3. Whisk egg yolks and cream in a bowl. Whisk in ½ cup of the hot sauce, a spoonful at a time. Then slowly beat in the remaining sauce. Transfer the enriched sauce to the saucepan. Over moderate heat, bring to a boil and lower heat.
4. Add the shrimp, crabmeat, and Sherry. Season to taste.
5. Arrange the oysters in the shells on a baking sheet. Spoon the seafood mixture over the oysters and top with buttered crumbs.
6. Bake from 5 to 10 minutes until the sauce is bubbling and the bread crumbs are lightly browned.

OYSTERS IMPERIAL

SERVES 4

The generous use of cream and Cognac in this sauce elevates it to the category that French gastronomes usually reserve for caviar, *foie gras,* and *saumon fumé—hors d'oeuvre riches.* It's quite special. Serve it with Puligny-Montrachet, a white Burgundy with a reputation, to really boost it into the stratosphere.

24	shucked oysters, liquor, and deep shells
³/₄	cup heavy cream
2	Tablespoons butter
1½	Tablespoons flour
³/₄	cup chopped cooked shrimp
½	cup chopped cooked crabmeat
½	cup chopped cooked lobster meat
2	Tablespoons Cognac
½	teaspoon fresh lemon juice
	Salt and freshly ground white pepper
	Tabasco
1	cup buttered bread crumbs

"A loaf of bread,"
the Walrus said,
"Is what we chiefly need:
Pepper and vinegar
besides
Are very good
indeed—
Now, if you're ready,
Oysters dear,
We can begin to feed."

—LEWIS CARROLL,
Through the Looking Glass

OVEN TEMPERATURE: 450°

1. Remove the oysters from the shells, drain, and set aside in a bowl. Strain and reserve ¼ cup of liquor for the cream sauce. Dry the shells and arrange them on a baking sheet.
2. Heat the oyster liquor and cream in a small saucepan.

3. Melt the butter in another saucepan. Stir in the flour and cook until straw yellow. Remove from heat and whisk in the cream mixture. Return to heat and cook, stirring constantly, at least 5 to 8 minutes.
4. Add the shrimp, crabmeat, and lobster, and stir in Cognac and lemon juice. Season to taste with salt, pepper, and Tabasco.
5. Spoon some of the sauce into each shell. Add an oyster and cover with remaining sauce. Top with buttered bread crumbs.
6. Bake from 5 to 10 minutes or until the bread crumbs are a golden brown.

OYSTERS AU VIN DE CHAMPAGNE

SERVES 4

Lighter in texture than the other Bienville recipes, the subtle combination of Champagne and crabmeat makes this a wonderful first course before a grilled rack of lamb or boeuf entrecote. The Champagne used in this appetizer and, of course, served with it needs to be dry and delicate like a Taittinger.

24	shucked oysters, liquor, and deep shells
1	cup Champagne
2	Tablespoons finely chopped shallots
2	cups heavy cream
	Salt and freshly ground pepper
1	cup flaked cooked back-fin crabmeat
1	Tablespoon lemon juice

OVEN TEMPERATURE: 425°

1. Remove the oysters from the shells, reserving the liquor. Scrub and dry the shells, and place them on a baking sheet. Pat the oysters dry and set them aside in a bowl.
2. Boil the Champagne and shallots in a saucepan until the liquid is reduced by half.
3. Strain the oyster liquor, add to the wine, and reduce by half.
4. Add the cream, reduce again, and season to taste. There should be about 2 cups of sauce.
5. Stir some of the sauce into the crabmeat and spoon the mixture into the shells. Place an oyster on each shell and sprinkle with lemon juice.
6. Bake for about 2 minutes until the oysters are heated, nap with the remaining sauce, return to the oven, and heat until sauce bubbles.
7. Serve immediately.

OYSTERS BIENVILLE AUX ECRIVISSES

Not exactly plebeian fare, but definitely zestier than the other Bienvilles, this appetizer can also double as a luncheon treat when served with a simple tossed salad and a glass of California Sauvignon Blanc.

24	*shucked oysters, liquor, and deep shells*
4	*Tablespoons dry white wine*
³/₄	*cup light cream*
2	*slices bacon*
2	*Tablespoons butter*
¹/₂	*cup chopped cremini mushrooms*
1	*minced garlic clove*
¹/₄	*cup chopped onion*
2	*Tablespoons flour*
1	*cup chopped cooked crayfish and/or shrimp*
2	*Tablespoons chopped parsley*
	Salt and freshly ground pepper
1	*Tablespoon lemon juice*
	Paprika

OVEN TEMPERATURE: 450°

1. Drain the oysters and set aside in bottom shells. Strain and reserve ¼ cup of the liquor for the sauce.
2. Heat the oyster liquor, wine, and cream in a small saucepan.
3. Cut the bacon into very small pieces, and cook in a microwave oven or fry until brown. Drain the bacon bits, reserving 1 tablespoon of fat.
4. Melt the butter in a saucepan with the bacon fat, and sauté the mushrooms, garlic, and onions until soft. Stir in the flour and cook at least 3 minutes. Remove from heat and whisk in the hot liquids. Return to heat and cook, stirring constantly, for at least 5 minutes.
5. Add the bacon, crayfish and/or shrimp, and parsley. Adjust the seasoning, using lemon juice if desired.
6. Arrange the shells on a baking sheet and distribute the sauce over the oysters. Sprinkle with paprika.
7. Bake from 5 to 10 minutes until the sauce is bubbling.

OYSTERS ROFFIGNAC

SERVES 4

Whether Oysters Roffignac properly honors an early nineteenth-century mayor of New Orleans or is simply one of the most distinctive oyster recipes on the menu of the illustrious Roffignac restaurant matters very little. What is important about this appetizer is the introduction of red wine into the seafood and oyster sauce.

The dark color of the dish before it is baked may be somewhat disconcerting but, when it mellows in the oven, the result appeals to both the eye and the palate. Serve with a Dolcetto or a light- to medium-bodied California Cabernet Sauvignon.

Oyster dear to the gourmet,
beneficent Oyster, exciting
rather than sating,
all stomachs digest you,
all stomachs bless you!

—SENECA

24	*shucked oysters, liquor, and deep shells*
$1/2$	*cup fish or chicken stock (see p. 58)*
$1/4$	*cup dry red wine*
8	*Tablespoons butter*
$1/2$	*cup finely chopped wild mushrooms*
$1/2$	*cup finely chopped onions or scallions*
1	*finely chopped garlic clove*
2	*Tablespoons flour*
1	*cup chopped cooked shrimp*
	Salt and freshly ground pepper
	Cayenne pepper
	Paprika

OVEN TEMPERATURE: 450°

1. Drain the oysters and set aside in bottom shells. Strain ¼ cup of the oyster liquor, mix with the stock and wine, and heat in a small saucepan.
2. Melt the butter in another saucepan, and sauté the mushrooms, onions, and garlic until tender. Stir in the flour and cook at least 3 minutes. Remove from heat and whisk in the hot liquids. Return to heat and boil, stirring constantly, until the sauce thickens. Simmer at least 5 to 8 minutes.
3. Add the shrimp and season to taste with salt, pepper, cayenne, and paprika.
4. Arrange the shells on a baking sheet and spoon the sauce over the oysters.
5. Bake from 5 to 10 minutes until the sauce has heated through and mellowed in color.

OYSTERS CASINO

With a tip of the hat to a classic clam recipe, the combination of bacon, onions, and sweet red and green peppers doubles as a delectable oyster appetizer. There are many variations: if it suits, top with buttered bread crumbs, grated cheese, or tease with a jigger of Sherry or Vermouth, and garnish with lemon and parsley.* A Fino or Manzanilla Sherry would be a fine accompaniment.

24	*shucked oysters in bottom shells*
12	*slices bacon*
4	*Tablespoons butter*
1/4	*cup finely chopped shallots or scallions*
1/4	*cup finely chopped green pepper*
1/4	*cup finely chopped red pepper*
2	*Tablespoons dry Sherry*
	Salt and freshly ground pepper
	Tabasco to taste
1	*cup buttered bread crumbs*
1/2	*cup freshly grated Gruyère*

OVEN TEMPERATURE: 450°

1. Cut the bacon slices into eighths and cook in a microwave oven for 1 minute, or fry over low heat until the edges begin to curl. Remove with a slotted spoon and drain. Dice the bacon and set aside.
2. Heat 2 tablespoons of the bacon fat and the butter in a skillet. Sauté shallots and green and red pepper until tender. Stir in Sherry and bacon, and season to taste.
3. Arrange the oysters in bottom shells on a baking sheet. Spoon the sautéed vegetables over the oysters. Mix buttered bread crumbs and cheese together and top the oysters with the mixture.
4. Bake from 5 to 10 minutes until the crumbs are golden brown.

*Oysters Kirkpatrick are made with tomato ketchup added to the bacon, peppers, and cheese mixture, and are named in honor of chef Ernest Arbogast who devised the recipe at the Palace Hotel in San Francisco.

OYSTERS 1826

Whether Daniel Webster savored Boston's Union Oyster House oysters this way, or simply swooshed down a dozen or two of the famous bivalves with a tumbler of brandy and water, will never really be known. But this adaptation of the restaurant's special oysters perpetuates the fame of the oldest restaurant in continuous service in America. A glass of Pilsner would be in order, but a proper Bostonian would insist on a Samuel Adams lager.

24	*shucked oysters, liquor, and bottom shells*
6	*slices bacon*
4	*Tablespoons butter*
2	*Tablespoons finely chopped sweet green and red peppers*
$^1/_4$	*cup finely chopped Spanish onion*
$^1/_2$	*cup finely chopped button mushrooms*
$^1/_2$	*cup crumbled potato chips*
$^1/_2$	*cup fresh bread crumbs*
	Salt and freshly ground pepper
	Lemon wedges

OVEN TEMPERATURE: MEDIUM BROIL

1. Drain the oysters and set aside in bottom shells. Strain and reserve ¼ cup of the liquor.
2. Cut the bacon into small pieces and cook in a microwave oven for 1 minute or fry over low heat until golden. Drain, and set aside.
3. Melt the butter in a saucepan and sauté the peppers, onion, and mushrooms until tender. Add the oyster liquor, and bring to a boil. Stir in the potato chips and enough bread crumbs to absorb the liquid. The mixture should be the consistency of a stuffing. Add the bacon pieces and correct the seasoning.
4. Arrange the oysters in bottom shells on a baking sheet. Distribute the bacon and crumb mixture over the oysters.
5. Broil until a light crust forms over the topping.
6. Serve immediately with lemon wedges.

OYSTERS FORESTIÉRE

SERVES 4 A creamed mushroom sauce over oysters is a natural melding of two distinct but quite compatible flavors. And while the color of the sauce may be somewhat drab, the buttered bread crumb and parsley topping does wonders for this recipe, as will a glass of California Chardonnay.

24	*shucked oysters, liquor, and bottom shells*
³/₄	*cup light cream*
4	*Tablespoons butter*
¹/₄	*cup finely chopped shallots*
1¹/₂	*cups chopped wild mushrooms (porcini, morel, parasol, or meadow)*
2	*Tablespoons flour*
2	*teaspoons Dijon mustard*
¹/₄	*cup dry Sherry*
	Salt and freshly ground pepper
	Tabasco
1	*cup buttered bread crumbs*
2	*Tablespoons finely chopped parsley*

OVEN TEMPERATURE: 450°

1. Drain the oysters and set aside in bottom shells. Strain and reserve ¼ cup of liquor.
2. Heat the cream and liquor in a small saucepan.
3. Melt the butter in another saucepan and sauté the shallots and mushrooms until tender. Stir in the flour and cook until bubbling. Remove from heat and whisk in the warm cream. Return to heat and boil, stirring constantly, for 5 to 8 minutes.
4. Add the mustard and Sherry, and season to taste with salt, pepper, and a bit of Tabasco.
5. Arrange the oysters in the bottom shells on a baking sheet. Spoon the creamed mushroom sauce over the oysters. Top with a mixture of buttered crumbs and parsley.
6. Bake for at least 5 minutes until the bread crumbs begin to brown.

CIDER HOUSE OYSTERS

An "R" month of briny well-chilled oysters and a "just-picked" bushel of apples make this a tempting late October appetizer. Build a roaring fire in the fireplace, spice up the air with the aroma of hot cider, or open a bottle of dry Vouvray, and a weekend at the seashore is a bit of Eden.

24	*shucked oysters and deep shells*
1	*cup fresh bread crumbs*
3	*crisp tart apples*
6	*Tablespoons butter*
$^1/_4$	*cup finely chopped onion*
$^1/_4$	*cup finely chopped celery*
$^1/_4$	*cup hard cider*
1	*Tablespoon finely chopped summer savory, or sage*
$^1/_4$	*cup finely chopped walnuts*
	Salt and pepper

OVEN TEMPERATURE: 400°

1. Drain the oysters and quarter if small, or cut into eighths if large in size. Put the oysters in a bowl and stir in enough bread crumbs to bind. Scrub and dry the shells.
2. Peel, core, and coarsely chop the apples.
3. Melt the butter in a saucepan and lightly sauté the apples, onion, and celery. Add cider. Remove from heat and stir in the oyster and bread crumb mixture. Add herbs, walnuts, and season to taste.
4. Arrange the shells on a baking sheet and mound enough of the mixture in each shell to fill it.
5. Bake for about 10 minutes or until the mixture begins to brown around the edges of the shell.

GINGERED OYSTERS

Often called a spice lover's spice, ginger adds a zing to any recipe. Try it combined with *crème fraîche*, rather than the more traditional yogurt, and the result is nothing short of wonderful. Serve with a dry Alsace Gewurztraminer.

24	*shucked oysters and bottom shells*
4	*ounces fresh ginger root*
	Pinch of saffron
1	*teaspoon butter*
¼	*cup finely chopped scallions*
2	*cups chicken stock (see p. 59)*
	Freshly ground white pepper
1	*cup crème fraîche*

OVEN TEMPERATURE: 350°

1. Remove the oysters from the shells, drain, and set aside. Scrub and dry the shells and arrange them on a baking sheet.
2. Peel and finely grate the ginger root. Wrap the pulp in a double thickness of cheesecloth, squeeze the juice into a bowl, and discard the pulp. There should be about 2 tablespoons of juice. Add the saffron and allow to mellow for at least 1 hour.
3. Melt the butter in a saucepan, and sauté the scallions until soft.
4. Reduce the chicken stock to ½ cup; add the ginger mixture and season to taste.
5. Remove from the heat and stir in the scallions and *crème fraîche.*
6. Spoon the sauce into each shell, add an oyster, and divide the remaining sauce over the top.
7. Cover loosely with a sheet of heavy-gauge foil, and bake about 15 minutes until the sauce is bubbling.

OYSTERS BOURGUIGNON

This tempting oyster appetizer is an adaptation of a classic French recipe for

Escargots de Bourguignon. Serve with a fine Aligote, a loaf of crusty bread to catch up the extra melted butter, and receive a standing ovation.

Any of the following "compound butter" variations that are made with a different combination of herbs and spices create an easy but palate-provoking napping sauce . . . and a practical one. Keep in the refrigerator or freezer and simply use whenever needed.

24   *shucked oysters and deep shells*
8   *sprigs parsley*
$^1/_2$ *bunch watercress*
3   *shallots*
8   *garlic cloves*
4   *anchovy fillets*
$^1/_4$ *cup blanched almonds*
$^1/_2$ *pound butter*
1   *Tablespoon Pernod*
3   *drops Tabasco*
2   *Tablespoons lemon juice*
        Freshly ground pepper

OVEN TEMPERATURE: 450°

1. Drain the oysters and set aside. Wash and dry the shells and arrange on a baking sheet.
2. Wash and remove the stems from the parsley and watercress. Drain and blot dry. Peel the shallots and garlic cloves.
3. Place the parsley, watercress, shallots, garlic, anchovies, and almonds in the work bowl of a food processor and pulse with the steel blade for about 2 or 3 seconds.*
4. Cut the butter into 8 pieces and add a piece at a time until the mixture is smooth.
5. Add the Pernod, Tabasco, lemon juice, and a pinch of pepper, process for a second more, and correct seasoning.
6. Spoon some of the butter mixture into the shells, cover with an oyster, and top with more of the butter mixture.
7. Bake about 5 minutes until the sauce begins to bubble around the edge of the shell.

*If a coarser texture is preferred, ingredients may be chopped with a knife. At Steps 4 and 5, blend everything together with a fork.

Leek Butter Sauce: Melt 8 tablespoons of butter, add 2 medium-sized leeks that have been carefully washed, dried, and cut into fine julienne, and sweat for 1 or 2 minutes. Add a splash of cream and lemon juice, and season with a dash of Tabasco. Spoon over the oysters and bake until the oysters begin to plump.

Tomato Basil Garlic Butter Sauce: Melt 8 tablespoons of butter, add 1 large clove minced garlic, and sweat. Stir in 1 tablespoon tomato paste and add a squeeze of lemon and chiffonade of 6 basil leaves. Salt and pepper to taste. Spoon over the oysters and bake until the oysters begin to plump.

Fines Herbes Butter Sauce: Combine 3 tablespoons of each of the following herbs that have been finely chopped in a processor—chives, chervil, parsley, and tarragon. Add 8 tablespoons of butter, a dash of lemon juice, and salt and pepper to taste and spoon over the oysters. Bake until the sauce begins to bubble around the edge of the shell.

STUFFED OYSTERS

SERVES 4

To the traditionalist who believes that Thanksgiving and turkey with oyster stuffing are authentic Americana, the following recipe will raise eyebrows and pose questions, but Stuffed Oysters are a feast for all seasons and a token to those who like their oysters disguised a bit.

24	*shucked oysters, liquor, and deep shells*
8	*Tablespoons butter*
$^1/_2$	*cup finely chopped shallots*
$^1/_2$	*cup finely chopped celery*
1	*Tablespoon flour*
2	*Tablespoons dry Vermouth**
$^1/_4$	*cup finely chopped fresh sage*
1	*cup fresh bread crumbs*
1	*egg*
	Salt and freshly ground pepper
	Cayenne pepper
$^1/_4$	*cup melted butter*

OVEN TEMPERATURE: 375°

*If preferred, substitute Scotch whiskey or Cognac.

1. Remove the oysters from the shells, drain, and coarsely chop. Scrub and dry the shells and arrange on a baking sheet. Strain liquor and set aside.
2. Melt the butter in a saucepan, and cook the shallots and celery until tender. Stir in flour and cook for at least 3 minutes. Remove from the heat and stir in the Vermouth.
3. Combine the sage and bread crumbs and add to the shallot mixture.
4. Beat the egg and stir it into the stuffing with a fork. Add the oysters and some of the liquor if not moist enough. Adjust seasonings.
5. Brush the inside of the shells with butter, and spoon the oyster stuffing into the shells.
6. Bake for about 12 minutes until a light crust forms and the stuffing is thoroughly heated.

STUFFED OYSTERS ANTILLIAN STYLE

SERVES 6

While vacationing in the Caribbean, who has not been tempted to enjoy a seaside dinner preceded by a cool rum punch and a serving of *crabes farcies*, native land crabs stuffed with French bread and herbs? So easy to adapt to other shellfish, the recipe brims with flavor when made with oysters and served with a glass of Pilsner.

18   shucked oysters and liquor
6   slices sourdough bread
1   cup dry white wine
4   finely chopped shallots
1   minced garlic clove
1   minced seeded jalapeño pepper
$^1/_2$ teaspoon allspice
2   teaspoons Domenica W.I. hot pepper sauce
    Salt and freshly ground pepper
    Fresh bread crumbs
$^1/_2$ cup melted butter
    Lime wedges

OVEN TEMPERATURE: 375°

1. Remove the oysters from shells, drain, coarsely chop, and set aside. Mix the oyster liquor and white wine in a glass bowl. Scrub, rinse, and dry the shells, and assemble them on a baking sheet.

2. Cut the bread into ½-inch cubes and soak in wine mixture.
3. Combine the shallots, garlic, chili pepper, allspice, and hot pepper sauce in another bowl. Squeeze the liquid out of the bread cubes, and add bread and oysters to the pepper mixture. Correct seasoning, adding salt and pepper if necessary.
4. Fill the shells with the stuffing. Cover with a thin layer of bread crumbs, and spoon some melted butter over each one.
5. Bake until the bread crumbs are golden brown. Serve with lime wedges.

FINGER FOOD

SERVES 8

ANGELS ON HORSEBACK

Better known in Victorian England as an after-dinner "savoury" to clear the palate and prepare it for Port, these bacon-wrapped oysters skewered on a cocktail pick make excellent party fare. An interesting counterpart is Devils on Horseback, prunes stuffed with chutney, wrapped in bacon, skewered, and broiled in similar fashion. Serve both for a drinks hour that's truly Paradise Lost and Paradise Regained. Pilsner or Oregon Chardonnay does justice to both.

24	*shucked medium-sized oysters*
1	*cup dry white wine*
1	*minced garlic clove*
	Freshly ground pepper
12	*slices bacon*
24	*buttered toast rounds (optional)*

OVEN TEMPERATURE: HIGH BROIL

1. Drain the oysters and marinate them in wine, garlic, and pepper for 1 hour.
2. Cut the bacon in half and cook in a microwave oven for about 1 minute, or pan-fry until the edges begin to curl but the bacon is still flexible. Drain well.
3. Wrap each oyster in bacon and secure with a damp cocktail pick.
4. Place the oysters on a broiler pan and broil on each side until the bacon is brown and crisp.
5. Serve with the cocktail pick, or the pick can be removed and the oyster placed on a buttered toast round.

GALLOPING OYSTERS

Galloping rather than just trotting along, this recipe is a sophisticated version of an appetizer the Australians call "Oysters on Horseback." It takes time and a commendable display of dexterity to assemble, but it is well worth the effort. Open a bottle of Alsace Pinot Gris or Pilsner to accompany these little marvels.

24   *shucked oysters and liquor*

Marinade:
2   *Tablespoons sugar*
$^1/_4$ *cup cider vinegar*
$^1/_4$ *cup rice wine vinegar*
$^1/_4$ *cup Sherry*
$^1/_4$ *cup vegetable oil*
2   *teaspoons peeled, finely chopped ginger root*
1   *chopped dried chipotle chili*
12   *whole water chestnuts*
12   *slices bacon*

OVEN TEMPERATURE: HIGH BROIL

1. Drain the oysters and pat dry. Reserve ¼ cup of the oyster liquor for the marinade.
2. Mix the oyster liquor, sugar, vinegars, Sherry, oil, ginger, and chili together in a bowl and add oysters.
3. Cut each water chestnut into 4 round slices, add to the marinade, and refrigerate overnight.
4. Cut the bacon slices in half, and partially cook them in a microwave oven or skillet, but keep the bacon pliable. Drain on absorbent paper.
4. Place an oyster between 2 slices of water chestnut and wrap with bacon. Secure with damp cocktail picks.
5. Arrange the skewered oysters on a broiler pan and broil on each side until the bacon is crisp and sizzling. Serve immediately.

FRITTO MISTO

SERVES 4

What french fries and cherry cokes were to the drugstore gatherings of bobby-soxers in the 1940s, these serving platters of crispy deep-fried herbs and oysters are to the turn-of-the-century martini crowd. Serve with— what else?—an Italian Pinot Grigio.

24   *small oysters, shucked and drained*
Herbs, whole, including stems: parsley, sage, cilantro, chervil,
     mint, basil, dill, tarragon
Peanut or canola oil
Salt

Batter:
1   *cup flour*
³/₄   *cup water*
1   *teaspoon baking powder*

1. Using a fork, stir enough water into the flour to form a batter the thickness of heavy cream. Add baking powder.
2. Heat oil in a fryer to 350°. Dip the oysters into the batter, fry immediately, remove when golden brown, and drain on absorbent paper. Keep warm. Repeat the process with the herbs.
3. Salt to taste and serve immediately with a dipping sauce if desired.

SAVORY OYSTER ASPARAGUS SQUARES

YIELD: 42 SQUARES

Although this recipe can easily be adapted to spinach or broccoli, making it with asparagus is such a total *coup de partie* that the other possibilities may never become realities. The delicate flavor of fresh asparagus is so compatible with the oysters and Monterey Jack cheese that whenever asparagus is available is exactly the right season to serve these simple, do-ahead treats. Serve with a rich Sancerre.

1   *pint oysters*
1   *pound fresh asparagus*
2   *Tablespoons butter*
1   *finely chopped small onion*
1   *garlic clove*
5   *eggs*

$^1/_3$	cup dry bread crumbs
$^1/_2$	pound freshly grated Monterey Jack cheese
$^1/_2$	cup finely chopped parsley
1	teaspoon chopped fresh thyme
	Salt and freshly ground pepper
	Tabasco

OVEN TEMPERATURE: 350°

1. Drain and coarsely chop the oysters and set them aside.
2. Trim and peel the asparagus. Split the stalks once or twice lengthwise and cut into 1-inch pieces. Blanch in boiling salted water and drain, reserving some of the liquid.
3. Melt the butter in a skillet and sauté the onion and garlic until tender. Discard the garlic. Stir in about 2 tablespoons of the asparagus liquid.
4. Beat the eggs in a large bowl until frothy. Stir in bread crumbs, the butter and onion mixture, asparagus, cheese, and parsley. Add the oysters and thyme. Season to taste with salt, pepper, and Tabasco.
5. Pour into a buttered 9- by 13-inch shallow baking pan and bake for about 45 minutes until the edges begin to brown and a knife inserted tests clean.
6. Cool for about 3 minutes and cut into 1½-inch squares. Serve warm, at room temperature, or chilled, whichever is preferred.

STUFFED MUSHROOM CAPS

SERVES 8   If first impressions are lasting, this "drop-dead elegant" mushroom *hors d'oeuvre* and a glass of dry Champagne will make a party especially memorable. Or use 3 or 4 stuffed caps with a tumble of greens as a luncheon entrée.

$^1/_2$	pint oysters
24	large mushrooms
6	Tablespoons butter
1	minced garlic clove
1	finely chopped onion
$1^1/_2$	cups fresh bread crumbs
3	Tablespoons dry Sherry
1	Tablespoon chopped fresh chervil
	Salt and freshly ground pepper

OVEN TEMPERATURE: 400°

1. Drain and coarsely chop the oysters and set aside.
2. Wash and stem the mushrooms. Dry the caps on absorbent paper and chop the stems.
3. Melt the butter in a skillet. Brush the caps with some of the melted butter and set aside. Sauté the stems, garlic, and onion, and discard the garlic when the mushrooms and onions are tender. Add the bread crumbs, oysters, Sherry, and chervil. Correct the seasoning.
4. Mound each mushroom cap with the stuffing and arrange the caps on a baking sheet.
5. Bake about 5 minutes until the stuffing begins to brown.

OYSTER BEIGNETS

YIELD: 40

From the bayou comes another palate provoker—deep-fried oyster puffs just waiting to be savored with a creamy dipping sauce sparked with Creole flavor. Serve with a dry Alsace Riesling and a special party becomes a spectacular performance.

$^1/_2$	pint oysters including $^1/_2$ cup liquor
1	cup flour
1	teaspoon grated lemon zest
6	Tablespoons butter
$^1/_2$	cup milk
4	eggs
1	Tablespoon chopped chives or scallions
	Oil for deep-frying

Sauce:

$^1/_2$	cup sour cream
$^1/_2$	cup mayonnaise
$^1/_4$	cup finely chopped parsley
2	Tablespoons Dijon mustard
$^1/_2$	teaspoon cayenne
2	teaspoons drained capers

1. Make the sauce by mixing the ingredients together. Refrigerate.
2. Drain and coarsely chop the oysters, reserving the oyster liquor.

3. Combine flour and lemon zest in a small bowl.
4. Cut the butter into small pieces and heat with the milk and oyster liquor in a heavy 1½-quart saucepan, stirring until the butter has melted. Remove from heat and add the flour and zest all at once, beating vigorously with a wooden spoon until flour has been incorporated. Return to moderate heat and cook, stirring constantly, until mixture forms a mass and begins to film the bottom of the pan.
5. Remove from heat. Add 1 egg at a time, beating after each addition until the paste is well blended and completely smooth.
6. Fold in oysters and chives or scallions.
7. Drop by teaspoonfuls into hot fat and fry at 375° until golden. Cook a few at a time, and drain on absorbent paper. Beignets can be kept hot in a moderate oven if they are to be served immediately, or they can be made ahead and reheated at serving time.
8. Skewer on cocktail picks and serve with the sauce.

ACRAS

SERVES 4

These spicy little fritters will remind even the most jaded traveler of turquoise waters, overarching palm trees, and the Calypso beat of the Caribbean. Traditionally made with salt cod, the recipe invites improvisation. Anything goes if the spice is right. Serve with India Pale Ale.

1	*pint oysters and liquor*
¹/₂	*cup milk*
3	*Tablespoons melted butter*
2	*beaten eggs*
1¹/₂	*cups flour*
¹/₂	*teaspoon baking powder*
¹/₂	*teaspoon salt*
1	*seeded chopped jalapeño pepper*
3	*Tablespoons finely chopped scallions*
1	*Tablespoon chopped fresh parsley*
1	*finely chopped garlic clove*
¹/₂	*teaspoon thyme*
¹/₂	*teaspoon allspice*
	Freshly ground black pepper
	Vegetable oil for frying

1. Drain the oysters and chop coarsely. Strain the oyster liquor.
2. Whisk the oyster liquor, milk, melted butter, and eggs together in a small bowl. Sift flour, baking powder, and salt into a medium-sized bowl. Gradually pour the liquids into the flour, stirring slowly until incorporated. Cover and let the batter stand at room temperature for 2 or 3 hours.
3. Place the jalapeño pepper, scallions, parsley, garlic, thyme, allspice, and pepper in the work bowl of a food processor and pulse a few times. Add oysters and pulse once or twice. Add the oyster mixture to the batter. Cover and let stand for 30 more minutes.
4. Pour vegetable oil into a large heavy saucepan or deep-fryer to the depth of 3 to 4 inches and heat to 350°. Drop the batter by tablespoonfuls into the hot oil, using about a third of the batter. Fry, turning as necessary, until the fritters are evenly browned. Remove with a slotted spoon, drain on absorbent paper, and keep warm. Repeat the process until all the batter is used.
5. Serve immediately garnished with cilantro leaves.

OYSTER PROFITEROLES

YIELD: 36

Here is a nifty version of a French treat, complete with two different oyster fillings that definitely "stand up" to these versatile *pate a chou* miniatures. Try the zippy oyster, horseradish, caper, and vinegar filling to pique a guest's appetite. Or simply add the oysters to the enriched Béchamel sauce, add Sherry to the cooking liquid, and a jigger or two of Cognac to the sauce, and update a "Recipe of Quality," circa 1912. Now, as then, serve a glass of Muscadet with the profiteroles.

1	*pint oysters and liquor*
1	*cup chicken stock (see p. 59)*
¹/₂	*cup cream*
3	*Tablespoons butter*
3	*Tablespoons flour*
2	*egg yolks*
¹/₂	*Tablespoon white wine vinegar*
2	*teaspoons grated lemon zest*
1	*Tablespoon grated horseradish*
1	*Tablespoon capers*
	Salt and freshly ground pepper
	Cayenne pepper
36	*1¹/₂-inch pate a chou puffs*

OVEN TEMPERATURE: 400°

1. Drain and coarsely chop the oysters, reserving ¼ cup of liquor.
2. Heat the chicken stock and cream in a small saucepan.
3. Melt the butter in another saucepan. Stir in the flour and cook for 5 minutes or until bubbling. Remove from heat and whisk in the stock mixture. Return to heat and cook for about 5 minutes, stirring constantly.
4. Whisk egg yolks with the oyster liquor and vinegar. Whisk in ½ cup of the hot sauce, a spoonful at a time. Then slowly beat in the remaining sauce. Transfer the enriched sauce to the saucepan and, stirring carefully, bring to a boil.
5. Stir in the oysters, lemon zest, horseradish, capers, and season to taste with salt, pepper, and cayenne. Cook over low heat, stirring gently, until the mixture starts to bubble.
6. Fill the puffs shortly before serving time by removing the top, spooning the filling into the cavity, and replacing the top.
7. Heat the filled puffs in the oven for about 5 minutes and serve immediately.

OYSTERS PARNASSUS

YIELD: 48

Although the Greek chefs of yesteryear served up braised squid and octopus as well as grilled sea bass and red snapper to perfection, they resolutely spurned the oyster. If they had only thought to wrap it up in phyllo dough and serve it with a glass of Pouilly-Fumé or Sancerre, even Zeus would have been impressed, and Pegasus would surely have flown a tray of them to the summit of Parnassus.

1½   pints oysters and liquor
1   cup dry white wine
1¼   cups melted butter
2   Tablespoons chopped shallots
½   cup finely chopped celery
½   cup finely chopped parsley
1   teaspoon chopped fresh dill
2   eggs
3   ounces cream cheese
1   ounce Feta cheese

1   Tablespoon lemon juice
     Salt and freshly ground pepper
     Tabasco
1   cup fresh bread crumbs
12   sheets defrosted phyllo dough

OVEN TEMPERATURE: 375°

1. Poach oysters in the liquor and wine until they begin to plump. Drain and chop.
2. Heat 4 tablespoons of the butter in a skillet, sauté shallots and celery until tender. Stir in parsley and dill.
3. Beat the eggs in a bowl and blend in the softened cheeses. Stir in the sautéed vegetables and herbs, lemon juice, and oysters. Season to taste with salt, pepper, and Tabasco. Add enough bread crumbs to bind the filling.
4. While working, cover phyllo dough with a towel. Spread out 2 sheets at a time, brush with melted butter, and layer. Cut into 9 strips, 18 inches long and about 2 inches wide. Place a teaspoon of the filling on the bottom edge of the first strip. Fold the strip up, flag fashion, into a triangle. Brush top with butter and place on a baking sheet. Fill and fold the remaining strips, and repeat the process with 2 more sheets of dough. Turnovers may be chilled or frozen.
5. Bake on a buttered baking sheet 20 to 25 minutes until puffy and golden. If the pastries are frozen, allow extra baking time.

OYSTERS SCANDIA

Once these turnovers have been served at a cocktail party, a solitary tin of smoked oysters will never be the same. Keep one in the pantry at all times and experiment with either a sour cream or a cream cheese pastry dough and a dab of mustard before adding an oyster and opening a bottle of dry Vouvray.

1   3³/₄-ounce tin smoked oysters
1¹/₄   cups flour
2   cups grated sharp Cheddar cheese
¹/₄   pound butter
¹/₄   cup chopped chives
        Freshly ground black pepper
1   egg

*The only reason for
a cocktail party*

*For a gluttonous
old woman like me*

*Is a really nice tit-bit.
I can drink at home.*

—T. S. ELIOT,
The Cocktail Party

YIELD: 30

1. Make a dough of the flour, cheese, butter, chives, and a bit of pepper, and chill.
2. Roll the dough ⅛ inch thick, and cut into 3-inch rounds.
3. Use half an oyster, cut lengthwise, for each turnover. Place the oyster on the round. Fold over, seal, and crimp edges. Brush the top with egg beaten with 1 teaspoon of water.
4. Bake about 15 minutes until golden.

VARIATION

Fresh oysters may be substituted. Select 30 small oysters. Shuck, drain, and pat dry. Roll in 1 cup of flour, preferably corn flour, which has been seasoned with minced garlic. Proceed with turnovers. In Step 3, use the whole oyster and add a dash of Dijon mustard.

WANTON WONTONS

YIELD: 24

There is something so extravagant and seductive about these Asian dumplings that they should be served with sake or a light-bodied beer on special occasions only.

24	*small-sized oysters, shucked and drained*
24	*wonton skins*
	Blanched chives (optional)

Filling:

1	*Tablespoon peanut oil*
1	*cup finely shredded napa cabbage*
½	*cup finely chopped scallions*
½	*cup chopped bean sprouts*
1	*teaspoon peeled grated fresh ginger*
2	*Tablespoons chopped cilantro*
1	*teaspoon salt*
½	*teaspoon sugar*
½	*teaspoon light soy sauce*
1	*Tablespoon dry Sherry*
1½	*teaspoons cornstarch*
½	*teaspoon sesame oil*

YIELD: 2 CUPS

Dipping sauce:

1	Tablespoon peeled minced fresh ginger
2	finely chopped scallions
1/2	cup rice vinegar
3/4	cup soy sauce
1/4	cup sugar
1	Tablespoon sesame oil

1. Make the sauce by combining all the ingredients, and set aside.
2. Heat oil in a wok or sauté pan and add the cabbage, scallions, bean sprouts, ginger, and cilantro, and toss lightly until slightly wilted. Add seasonings, soy sauce, and cornstarch mixed with Sherry, and stir until filling begins to thicken. Stir in sesame oil and remove from heat. Cool completely.
3. Unwrap and cover the wontons with a damp towel. Fill one at a time by placing a heaping teaspoon of filling in the center of each wonton skin and adding an oyster to each. Moisten the edges of the wrapper, and gather up the corners. Pinch to seal or tie with a blanched chive.
4. Arrange the filled wontons on a parchment-paper-lined steamer base, making sure they are not touching. Cover and steam for about 8 minutes. Repeat the process until all are cooked.
5. Serve hot with the dipping sauce.

WHISTLING OYSTER DIP

The following recipe will summon almost everyone to a cocktail party at full speed. Be sure to adjust the amount of parsley so the dip will have a fresh green color and serve with chips, crackers, or tostadas and a glass of Pilsner.

12	shucked large oysters
1/2	cup dry white wine
3	ounces soft cream cheese
1 1/2	cups sour cream
2	Tablespoons finely chopped shallots
1/2	cup finely chopped parsley
1	Tablespoon capers
	Tabasco

1. Lightly poach the oysters in wine until they begin to plump. Drain and coarsely chop.
2. Combine cream cheese and sour cream in the bowl of a food processor or blender, and process for 1 minute. Add the shallots and parsley and process until blended. For a coarser mixture, the ingredients can be blended with a fork.
3. Spoon into a bowl and add oysters, capers, and Tabasco to taste. Cover and refrigerate for at least 4 hours.
4. Serve at room temperature.

CANAPÉS (Made for Champagne)

A beautifully decorated tray of canapés is an absolutely sensational way to flatter guests. And these miniature bread cutouts are also an ideal finger food, a bite or two easily eaten while standing with a drink in hand. Preparation may take a little time and a little doing, but it offers endless possibilities for a creative cook to entertain with panache.

For cold canapés, cut fresh bread into rounds, ovals, fingers, diamonds, or whatever shape the event or whimsy dictates. And then layer dibs and dabs galore. Or, if hot canapés are the order of the day, toast the cutouts on one side, turn over, and add a morsel or a glorious spread. Pop into the broiler and serve.

The following recipes are some of the traditional oyster canapés along with a few that offer a "twist and turn" slightly different from the "tried and true." While the specific name, Oyster Canapé, always properly designates a breaded fried oyster on a toast round that has been spread with a seasoned or herbed butter, the use of raw or smoked oysters in many of these recipes offers the option to serve the canapés either hot or cold.

He who plays host without giving his personal care to the repast is unworthy of having friends to invite to it.

—BRILLAT-SAVARIN, *"Aphorism XVIII"*

Cold Canapés

SERVES 6

Oysters are not really food, but are relished to bully the sated stomach into further eating.

—SENECA

Cold or Hot Canapés

SERVES 10

CASINO CANAPÉS

¹⁄₂	pint oysters
3	slices finely chopped bacon
2	Tablespoons butter
1	Tablespoon horseradish
4	Tablespoons finely chopped celery
2	Tablespoons finely chopped pimiento
	Mayonnaise
¹⁄₂	teaspoon lemon juice
18	pumpernickel bread ovals
	Chopped chervil

1. Drain the oysters and pat dry.
2. Cook bacon in the microwave oven or fry in a skillet until crisp and drain on absorbent paper.
3. Melt the butter in a skillet and lightly sauté the oysters. Drain and chop.
4. Combine the oysters, bacon, horseradish, celery, and pimiento with just enough mayonnaise to make a spreadable mixture. Add lemon juice.
5. Spread on the bread ovals and serve garnished with a bit of pimiento and chervil.

CANAPÉ VARIATIONS

Oysters Lucullus: Spread rounds of toast with steak tartare, place a raw oyster in the center of each, and garnish with beluga caviar.

Oysters Lucca: Spread oval slices of white bread with butter, top with a thin slice of smoked salmon, and place a small raw oyster in the center. Garnish with salmon roe and a sliver of lemon peel.

Oysters Otero: Spread rounds of white toast with butter, top with golden whitefish caviar, place a raw oyster in the center, and brush with Rémoulade sauce (see p. 16)

MUSHROOM OYSTER ROUNDS

¹⁄₂	pint oysters and liquor
³⁄₄	cup cream
2	Tablespoons butter
1	cup chopped mushrooms

2   *Tablespoons chopped shallots*
1½   *Tablespoons flour*
1   *Tablespoon chopped parsley*
1   *Tablespoon Cognac*
      Salt and freshly ground pepper
30   *bread or toast rounds*
6   *thinly sliced sautéed cremini mushrooms for garnish*

1. Drain and quarter the oysters. Strain and reserve ¼ cup of the liquor.
2. Heat the oyster liquor and cream in a small saucepan.
3. Heat the butter in a skillet and sauté the chopped mushrooms and shallots until tender. Stir in flour and cook until straw yellow. Remove from heat and whisk in the hot cream mixture. Return to heat and cook, stirring constantly, until the mixture thickens.
4. Stir in the oysters, parsley, and Cognac, and season to taste. Heat until the mixture starts to bubble.
5. Cool to room temperature and chop in a food processor. The mixture should be thick with a slightly coarse texture, not a smooth paste.
6. Spread on fresh white bread rounds, and garnish with thin mushroom slices if serving at room temperature. Spread on toasted bread rounds, garnish, and heat in the broiler for a minute or two if serving hot.

TUNNY SMOKED OYSTER ROUNDS

SERVES 12

1   *3¾-ounce tin smoked oysters*
1   *6½-ounce can tuna in oil*
3   *Tablespoons sour cream*
1   *teaspoon Dijon mustard*
2   *minced garlic cloves*
8   *Tablespoons unsalted butter*
½   *cup toasted chopped pistachios*
1   *Tablespoon lemon juice*
1   *Tablespoon chopped fresh summer savory*
      Salt and freshly ground pepper
36   *bread or toast rounds*

1. Drain the oysters and purée with tuna, sour cream, mustard, and garlic in a food processor or blender.

2. Cut butter into small pieces and add gradually to the mixture. Blend thoroughly.
3. Transfer to a mixing bowl and add pistachios, reserving 2 tablespoons for garnish; add lemon juice and savory, and season to taste.
4. Cover and refrigerate for at least 12 hours.
5. Allow stand at room temperature for 15 minutes before spreading on bread or toasted rounds. Sprinkle with chopped nuts.
6. If serving hot, run under the broiler for a minute or two.

Hot Canapés

ZESTY OYSTER CANAPÉS

SERVES 8

24	*shucked small oysters*
1/2	*cup olive oil*
1	*teaspoon chopped fresh tarragon*
1/2	*minced garlic clove*
1	*Tablespoon chopped parsley*
8	*Tablespoons butter*
1	*cup freshly grated Parmigiano-Reggiano Cornflake crumbs*
2	*teaspoons lemon juice*
24	*white bread rounds*

OVEN TEMPERATURE: 425°

1. Combine oil, tarragon, garlic, and parsley in a bowl and set aside for at least 2 hours.
2. Heat 2 tablespoons of butter in a skillet and brown the bread rounds lightly on both sides, adding more butter as needed. Drain the rounds on absorbent paper.
3. Drain oysters and pat dry. Roll the oysters in cheese, dip in the herb-oil mixture, and roll in crumbs.
4. Place the oysters on a lightly greased baking sheet and bake for about 5 minutes until they begin to plump.
5. Melt the rest of the butter and mix with lemon juice.
6. Place a hot oyster on each toasted bread round and drizzle with some of the hot lemon butter.

BROILED OYSTER CANAPÉS

SERVES 8

24	shucked small oysters
6	Tablespoons butter
$^1/_2$	teaspoon minced garlic clove
$^1/_2$	teaspoon dry mustard
2	Tablespoons minced parsley
1	teaspoon lemon juice
	Pinch cayenne pepper
1	teaspoon paprika
24	white bread rounds

OVEN TEMPERATURE: HIGH BROIL

1. Cream the butter with garlic, mustard, parsley, lemon juice, cayenne, and paprika in a food processor or with a fork.
2. Toast the bread rounds lightly on one side, remove from the oven, turn over, and spread with seasoned butter.
3. Drain and dry the oysters, and place one on each bread round. Sprinkle with additional paprika.
4. Broil about 2 minutes until the oysters begin to plump.

OYSTER PUFFS

SERVES 10

1	$3^3/_4$-ounce tin smoked oysters
8	ounces cream cheese
4	Tablespoons cream
1	chopped garlic clove
$^1/_4$	cup chopped shallots or scallions
$^1/_2$	teaspoon Worcestershire sauce
$^1/_2$	teaspoon lemon juice
30	white bread rounds

OVEN TEMPERATURE: LOW BROIL

1. Drain and coarsely chop the oysters.
2. Blend the cream cheese, cream, garlic, shallots or scallions, Worcestershire sauce, and lemon juice in a food processor until smooth.
3. Mix in the oysters with a spoon or rubber spatula. (Do not process.)
4. Toast the bread rounds on one side, turn over, top with oyster paste.
5. Place under the broiler for about 2 minutes until puffy and golden.

Beautiful soup! who cares for fish,
game, or any other dish?

Who would not give all else for two
pennyworth only of beautiful soup?

—Lewis Carroll,
Alice in Wonderland

When the cold winds begin to harp
and whinny at street corners and
wives go seeking among the
camphor balls for our last year's
overcoats, you will be glad to
resume your acqaintance with
a bowl of steaming bivalves,
swimming in milk, with little clots
of yellow butter twirling on the
surface of the broth. An oyster stew,
a glass of light beer and
a corncob pipe will keep your
blue eyes blue to any weather,
as a young poet of our
acquaintance puts it.

—Christopher Morley,
Travels in Philadelphia

Soups

The toddler in the playroom, the student home for lunch, the commuter with ten minutes until train time, the "regular" at the church supper, and the guest at an elegant dinner party—all appreciate a generous spoonful of "soup, wonderful soup." Whether served in a steaming tureen or a chilled glass bowl, soup can be many things to many people—a fond memory of Grandmother's kitchen, a piquant prelude to a holiday dinner, or a complete meal in itself.

No one country possesses the secret of a particular soup for very long, even though many chowders, bisques, pottages, and "stews" are associated with specific styles of cooking. If *bouillabaisse* originated in southern France, then Flemish fish soup, and Brazilian *bouquet do mar* are adaptations of it. And while the well-known chef Paul Prudhomme speaks of "chopped onions, celery, and green peppers" as the "holy trinity" of Cajun and Creole cookery, these ingredients are also liberally used in an Andalusian gazpacho and an Italian minestrone.

In the simple world of soup, borrowing is the name of the game. So, many of the recipes that follow are adaptations of soups for clams, mussels, and other kinds of seafood. In most instances, adding oysters simply expands the boundaries of oyster cookery. On the other hand, recipes for oyster stew are unique and traditionally have been so. All other ingredients are so minimal that the oyster literally *is* the soup, and it is essential to use freshly shucked oysters for the ultimate flavor. In all cases, from the lightest consommé to the heartiest chowder, the secret of preparing any kind of oyster soup is subtlety.

Beethoven was undoubtedly right when he said: "Only the pure of heart can make a good soup," and a sophisticated cook can present it with style. Bisques are enhanced when served from heirloom tureens, ladled into best china with a silver *cuiller a potage*; unadorned ceramic bowls work well with chowders. Pillivuyt lidded soup cups show off a velouté; an ample serving of oyster stew truly needs an adequate soup plate.

Soup is a total experience, and skill in presentation, natural instinct for garnishes, the artful use of herbs and spirits, and the test of taste will always be the cook's individual way of preserving the delicate and elusive essence of the sea captured in every oyster soup. The Spanish proverb says it well: "Of soup and love, the first is best," but, how can the two be separated?

Suggestions

- If homemade stock is not available, the following substitutes are workable:
  Fish Stock—bottled clam juice simmered with 1 cup each of water and dry white wine, vegetables, and an herb bouquet.
  Chicken Stock—chicken broth or bouillon simmered with dry white wine, vegetables, and an herb bouquet.
  Beef Stock—beef broth or bouillon simmered with red wine, vegetables, and an herb bouquet.
- If homemade stock is to be used only for oyster soup, omit salt or use it sparingly because oysters and their liquor vary in salinity.
- Homemade stock can be made in large quantities and frozen for later use, although some chefs believe that the flavor of the herbs can be reduced by freezing.
- Freshly shucked oysters make the best oyster stews, and fresh oysters, raw fish, and shellfish are highly recommended for all of the recipes. However, many of the soup recipes can be made with frozen or even canned seafood with some sacrifice of flavor.
- The following herbs and spices are particularly effective in oyster soups: chives, parsley, thyme, garlic, dill weed, celery seed, cayenne pepper, mace or nutmeg, paprika, and curry.
- The following spirits will enhance the flavor of an oyster soup: white wine, Sherry, dry Vermouth, Pernod, and Cognac.
- Traditionally, Tabasco sauce, Worcestershire sauce, and lemon juice are also suitable flavorings for oyster soups.
- Many oyster soups can be prepared in advance up to the final step, and then refrigerated or frozen. If whole oysters and other fresh seafood are used, they should be added immediately before serving. And it is always wise to taste after the oysters and their liquor are added because additional salt may be unnecessary.
- Soup may be served as a first course, as a luncheon entrée, or as a complete meal. In each case the quantity of the serving will be different. The suggested serving for each recipe is about 8 ounces per person, a generous amount for a first course and a minimal amount for a luncheon entrée. If the soup is a complete meal, the suggested amount will accommodate fewer people. Soup bowls also vary in the quantity of liquid they hold. Consequently, all of the suggested servings in the recipes are approximate.

STOCKS

Fish Stock
Chicken Stock
Vegetable Stock

SOUPS

Oyster Stew
Potage Crème d'Huitres
Oyster Stew aux Croûtes
Holiday Oyster Stew
Cream of Artichoke Soup
Plantation Pickuns
Oyster Bisque
Oyster Spinach Bisque
Green Pea and Oyster Bisque
Oyster Saffron Bisque
Oyster Chowder
Oyster Chowder Bonne Femme
Seafood Chowder
Chicken and Oyster Gumbo
Seafood Gumbo
Seafood Méditerranée
Cioppino
Leeward Island Oyster Soup
Shellfish Blaff
Pacific Rim Oyster Broth

STOCKS

In almost every instance, a superlative oyster soup, gumbo, or bisque depends on the stock used in its preparation. It is the implicit first step of every recipe, the initial challenge to the cook's judgment to use fresh ingredients and imagination in order to produce a satisfying soup.

Purists will opt for the classic recipe of milk or cream and oysters in their own liquor and will never be content with less than the authentic flavor of an oyster enhanced by anything more than dry white wine or Sherry. But fish stock is certainly the soul of many of the bisques and gumbos. And whenever a less intense seafood flavor is desired, chicken or vegetable stock is an excellent variation.

Homemade stocks derived from fish, chicken, and vegetables as well as the liquor of the oyster are to be preferred to canned broths or bouillon cubes and granules, which are usually laced with salt and monosodium glutamate. These processed "essences" and bottled clam juice can be prepared in a way that makes their use a reasonable substitute but never a convincing replacement for any of the stocks that follow.

FISH STOCK

YIELD: 2 QUARTS

4	pounds white fish bones and heads without gills
4	Tablespoons unsalted butter
2	chopped well-washed leeks, white parts only
2	chopped medium onions
2	chopped celery stalks
1	cup chopped mushrooms (optional)
2	quarts water
1	cup dry white wine

Herb bouquet:

2	whole cloves
1	bay leaf
	Pinch of leaf thyme
1	teaspoon fennel seed (optional)
1	garlic clove (optional)

1. Wash the fish parts thoroughly. Chop the bones to accommodate the size of the pot.

2. Melt the butter in a large enamel or stainless steel saucepan or stockpot and cook the vegetables, covered, over low heat until they are tender but not browned.
3. Add the fish parts, remaining ingredients, and enough water to cover. Bring to a boil and skim. Cover loosely and simmer for 30 minutes.
4. Strain through a double layer of cheesecloth; chill, and degrease the stock.
5. Taste the stock for intensity and, if necessary, reduce to strengthen the flavor.

CHICKEN STOCK

YIELD: 1 1/2 QUARTS

3	*pounds chicken parts (raw backs, necks, bones)*
1	*chopped medium onion*
3	*chopped celery stalks*
1	*chopped well-washed leek*
2	*chopped medium carrots*
2	*quarts water*

Herb bouquet:

1	*garlic clove*
6	*parsley sprigs*
1	*bay leaf*
1	*teaspoon thyme*

1. Place all the ingredients in a large stockpot and cover with at least 1 inch of water. Bring to a boil and skim. Cover loosely and simmer gently for about 2 hours.
2. Strain, chill, and degrease the stock.
3. Taste for flavor. If necessary, reduce to desired intensity.

VEGETABLE STOCK

YIELD: 2 QUARTS

6	*medium onions*
6	*scallions with greens*
10	*celery stalks*
4	*medium carrots*
3	*tomatoes*
6	*lettuce leaves*
1	*pound mushrooms*

1	bunch watercress (optional)
4	Tablespoons butter
3	quarts water

Herb bouquet:
1	bay leaf
4	parsley sprigs
1	teaspoon fresh thyme (optional)
12	peppercorns

1. Wash unpeeled vegetables thoroughly, and coarsely chop.
2. Melt the butter in a large saucepan or stockpot and sauté the onions, scallions, and celery until tender.
3. Add water and herb bouquet, bring to a boil, cover, and simmer gently for about an hour.
4. Strain, chill, and skim the stock.
5. Taste for intensity and reduce, if necessary, to enhance the flavor.

SOUPS

SERVES 4

OYSTER STEW

So many circumstances of time, place, and company occur to make a particular dish memorable in every way. M. F. K. Fisher has written about an oyster stew "the best in the world . . . mildly potent, quietly sustaining, warm as love and welcomer in winter." Its preparation is worth retelling:

"Three copper saucepans were used and carefully tended by a young man who warmed butter in one, placed freshly shucked oysters in the other, and heated a pint of milk in the third. When the butter frothed, he poured it over the oysters, stirring them round and round in the pan for about a minute. Then he poured in the hot milk, adding a little red pepper, salt, and a few drops of Sherry, and served it." No "stewing" here, just total absorption in the task at hand for a minute or two. It's the secret of a good oyster stew. Serving it with a Chablis Premier Cru is another.

36	shucked oysters and liquor
1	quart light cream
8	Tablespoons butter
	Salt
	Worcestershire sauce

Paprika
Tabasco

1. Remove the oysters from the shells; strain and reserve 1 cup of the liquor.
2. Heat the liquor and cream in a saucepan.
3. Melt the butter in another saucepan. When it froths, add the oysters and stir gently until they are hot and the edges begin to curl.
4. Stir in the cream mixture, season to taste, and serve immediately.

SERVES 4   POTAGE CRÈME D'HUITRES

Connoisseurs of oyster stew will probably always be convinced that less is better than more. But an imaginative cook will seize the opportunity to be creative by introducing a compatible flavor or an interesting texture. Chopped leeks, shallots, scallions, or celery are congenial additions and so are many herb and spice garnishes. And who doesn't remember spooning or crushing some of those familiar oyster crackers or pilot biscuits into the steaming bowl? The possibilities are limitless and, in many cases, a matter of family tradition, as is accompanying this version with a top-quality Graves Blanc.

36   shucked oysters and liquor
3   cups milk, half-and-half, or cream
3   Tablespoons butter
3   Tablespoons flour
1   teaspoon fresh lemon juice
*   Salt and freshly ground pepper*
*   Cayenne pepper*
¹/₂   cup sautéed morel or chanterelle mushrooms for garnish

1. Remove the oysters from the shells, drain, and set aside. Strain the liquor, combine with the milk or cream, and warm in a saucepan.
2. Melt the butter in a heavy-bottom saucepan. Stir in the flour and cook over moderate heat until the roux is straw color. Remove from the heat and stir in the hot cream mixture. Return to heat and cook, stirring constantly, until the soup thickens. Simmer at least 5 to 10 minutes.
3. Add the oysters and continue to cook until the oysters plump. Add lemon juice and salt and pepper to taste.

4. Season with a dash of cayenne pepper, and divide the sautéed mushrooms among the 4 bowls for garnish.

OYSTER STEW AUX CROÛTES

From the earliest "Invalid's Tea Tray" recipes for Oyster Toast to the "pale fried sippets" recommended as accompaniments to creamy oyster stew in Victorian England, *croûtes* have been an integral part of oyster cookery.

The *croûte* may be a simple slice of thick white toast. Or, in the truly French manner, bread cases are made by hollowing out the centers of thick bread slices. All surfaces are lightly brushed with melted butter and the *croûtes* are toasted until golden in a hot oven. Either version will reinforce the comfort of an oyster stew served in an old-fashioned soup plate with a glass of Meursault at the ready.

24	shucked oysters and liquor
$\frac{1}{2}$	cup dry white wine, or $\frac{1}{4}$ cup dry Vermouth
2	Tablespoons finely chopped shallots
2	Tablespoons finely chopped celery
$1\frac{3}{4}$	cups heavy cream
2	egg yolks
	Salt and freshly ground pepper
1	Tablespoon lemon juice (optional)
4	French bread croûtes

1. Remove the oysters from the shells and set aside. Strain the liquor.
2. Boil the liquor, wine, shallots, and celery in a 1½-quart saucepan until the liquid is reduced to about ½ cup. Add 1½ cups of cream and simmer 5 minutes.
3. Whisk the egg yolks and the remaining ¼ cup of cream in a bowl. Whisk in ½ cup of the hot liquids, a spoonful at a time. Then slowly beat in the remaining liquids. Transfer the enriched soup to the saucepan, bring to a boil, and reduce heat.
4. Add the oysters, salt and pepper to taste, and lemon juice, if desired. Cook the soup, stirring carefully, until the edges of the oysters start to curl, but do not boil.
5. Place a *croûte* in each soup plate and ladle the stew over it.

When I want to vary the fish soup, I often serve a sauce rouille [literally rust sauce because of paprika], which is an easily made mayonnaise-type preparation with potatoes and garlic.

—Pierre Franey, More 60-Minute Gourmet

SERVES 6

If there is a dinner of roast turkey with pecan and rice stuffing, rum-glazed sweet potatoes, and damson plum tarts in the oven, the ingredients for this holiday oyster stew should be ready and waiting. One spoonful says it all—either Happy Thanksgiving or Merry Christmas. And if there's a bottle of California Viognier under the tree, it would be a perfect time to open it.

1	*quart oysters and liquor*
4	*Tablespoons butter*
1/4	*teaspoon anchovy paste*
1	*Tablespoon Dijon or English mustard*
2	*cups finely chopped celery*
1	*quart heavy cream*
1/4	*cup dry Sherry*
	Salt and freshly ground pepper
1	*cup cooked wild rice*

1. Melt the butter in a large saucepan and stir in anchovy paste and mustard. Add the celery and cook until tender.
2. Stir in the cream and bring to a boil.
3. Add the oysters, liquor, and Sherry, and heat until the edges of the oysters begin to curl. Salt and pepper to taste.
4. Serve in warm best soup dishes garnished with a heaping tablespoon of wild rice.

CREAM OF ARTICHOKE SOUP

SERVES 4 This lightly creamed soup of artichokes, mushrooms, and oysters should create a spurt of interest in the everyday miracles that are possible when fresh ingredients and wines are used innovatively. Dare to be different and serve with a glass of Amontillado Sherry. *Chacun à son gout*, is the rule, but this recipe will please almost everybody.

1	*pint oysters and liquor*
2	*large artichokes*
3	*cups chicken stock (see p. 59)*
$^1/_2$	*pound chopped mushrooms*
2	*Tablespoons finely chopped parsley*
	Pinch of mace or nutmeg
	Pinch of thyme
	Pinch of cayenne pepper
3	*Tablespoons butter*
1	*garlic clove*
3	*Tablespoons finely chopped scallions*
2	*Tablespoons flour*
1	*cup light cream*
	Salt and freshly ground pepper

1. Quarter the artichokes and remove the chokes and stems.
2. Bring the chicken stock to a boil in a 2-quart saucepan. Add the artichokes, cover, and simmer for 20 minutes. Add mushrooms, parsley, mace, thyme, and cayenne. Cover and simmer for another 20 minutes.
3. Remove artichokes, scrape the pulp from the leaves and chop bottoms, and return the pulp and bottoms to the stock.
4. Melt the butter in another large saucepan and sauté the garlic and scallions until tender. Discard the garlic.
5. Stir in the flour and cook until the roux is straw yellow. Remove from the heat and stir in about 2 cups of the hot stock. Return to heat and simmer, stirring constantly, until the mixture thickens. Stir in the remaining stock and vegetable mixture and simmer at least 15 minutes. At this point the soup may be refrigerated or frozen.
6. Stir the cream into the soup and bring to a boil. Add the oysters and liquor and heat until the edges of the oysters begin to curl.
7. Season to taste with salt and pepper, and serve immediately.

PLANTATION PICKUNS

SERVES 4 Devised to grace the buffet table of a southern plantation, this creamy peanut and oyster soup will add a bit of antebellum nostalgia to any dinner party, especially if accompanied by a glass of Amontillado Sherry. It may be served with unsalted peanuts, minced parsley, or crumbled bacon, but its smooth texture and remarkable blend of flavors are quite successful without any garnish except the oysters that make it so memorable.

1	*pint oysters and liquor*
2¹/₂	*cups chicken stock (see p. 59)*
¹/₂	*cup heavy cream*
2	*Tablespoons butter*
2	*Tablespoons chopped onions or scallions*
3	*Tablespoons flour*
¹/₃	*cup creamy peanut butter*
2	*Tablespoons dry Sherry*
1	*teaspoon chopped fresh summer savory*
	Salt and freshly ground pepper
	Sour cream (optional)
	Crumbled bacon (optional)

1. Drain the oysters, reserving ½ cup of the liquor.
2. Heat the oyster liquor, chicken stock, and cream in a saucepan.
3. Melt the butter in another saucepan and sauté the onions or scallions until translucent. Stir in the flour and peanut butter and cook about 5 minutes. Remove from the heat and whisk in the hot stock mixture. Return to heat and add the Sherry and savory. Simmer at least 15 minutes.
4. Add oysters and cook until the edges of the oysters begin to curl. Correct seasoning.
5. Serve with a dollop of sour cream and crumbled bacon if desired.

OYSTER BISQUE

SERVES 8 Sinfully extravagant are the only words for the following recipe. It captures the essence of all the oysters and vegetables that go into its making and then releases them in a deceptively simple velouté. Ladle it into fine china and add a freshly shucked oyster or two to each bowl for an elegant touch. This particular bisque demands a rich California Chardonnay or creamy Champagne.

1½	pints oysters and liquor
1	pint fish stock (see p. 58)
1½	cups dry white wine
2	chopped onions
2	chopped celery stalks
2	chopped peeled carrots
2	lemon slices
1	Tablespoon chopped parsley
12	peppercorns
	Pinch of thyme
	Pinch of mace or nutmeg
5	Tablespoons butter
5	Tablespoons flour
2	egg yolks
3	cups heavy cream
	Dry Sherry
	Salt
	Cayenne pepper

1. If oysters are large, cut in half or quarter.
2. Combine oysters, liquor, stock, wine, vegetables, lemon, parsley, and seasonings in a large saucepan. Bring to a boil, reduce heat, and simmer, uncovered, for 45 minutes.
3. Strain through a fine sieve or cheesecloth-lined strainer. Discard the solid ingredients, and measure 5 cups of the liquid. If there is less, add stock or substitute clam juice.
4. Melt the butter in a heavy-bottom large saucepan. Stir in flour and cook until pale yellow. Remove from the heat and whisk in the hot liquid. Return to heat and boil, stirring constantly, and cook a minimum of 5 to 10 minutes.
5. Whisk egg yolks and ½ cup of cream in a bowl. Whisk in ½ cup of the hot soup, a spoonful at a time. Then slowly beat in 2 more cups of the hot soup. Pour the egg mixture into the saucepan and, stirring carefully, bring to a boil and remove from heat. Bisque may be refrigerated or frozen.
6. Reheat the bisque and stir in the remaining 2½ cups of cream, Sherry, salt, and cayenne to taste. Garnish with freshly shucked oysters if desired.

OYSTER SPINACH BISQUE

SERVES 8

While a history of the liaison between spinach and oysters is still to be written, it is a culinary "match" that seems destined to go on forever. Little wonder that this bisque is a February favorite. The stalwart green color and no-nonsense flavor make it a wonderful Lenten supper, especially when served with a loaf of homemade rye bread, a rustic Port Salut, and a glass of dry Vouvray—not exactly penitential, but properly subdued.

1	*quart oysters and liquor*
4	*Tablespoons butter*
1	*cup chopped onions*
1	*cup chopped celery*
2	*garlic cloves*
1	*quart chicken stock (see p. 59)*
1	*cup dry white wine*
1	*pound stemmed and chopped fresh spinach*
	Salt and freshly ground pepper
3	*cups heavy cream*
	Dry Sherry
	Pinch of nutmeg
	Worcestershire sauce
	Seasoned croutons (optional)

1. Drain the oysters, reserving 1 cup of the liquor.
2. Melt the butter in a large saucepan and sauté the onion, celery, and garlic for a few minutes; discard the garlic.
3. Add the oyster liquor, stock, and wine to the saucepan and cook uncovered until the mixture is reduced to about 4 cups.
4. Add the oysters and spinach, and season with salt and pepper. Heat until the edges of the oysters start to curl.
5. Cool the mixture slightly and purée in a food processor or blender. The bisque may be refrigerated or frozen.
6. Reheat over moderate heat but do not permit the bisque to boil. Stir in the cream, Sherry, and seasonings to taste. Serve with croutons if desired.

SERVES 8

There is something almost playful about the combination of ingredients in this bisque. The result is a bright and smiling luncheon treat or a whimsical transition from a cocktail hour to an entrée of roast lamb surrounded by parsleyed new potatoes and glazed carrots. Add jonquils to the centerpiece for a perfect early spring dinner. And serve with a fresh Alsace Sylvaner that has the aroma of springtime and some minerality in its bouquet.

1	*quart oysters and liquor*
6	*Tablespoons butter*
1/2	*cup finely chopped onion*
3	*cups shelled green peas, or 2 10-ounce packages frozen peas*
2	*cups milk*
2	*cups fish stock (see p. 58)*
1/2	*cup dry white wine*
	Salt and freshly ground pepper
1/4	*cup chopped chives (optional)*

1. Melt 2 tablespoons butter in a large saucepan and sauté the onions until soft.
2. Add the peas and milk. Cover, and simmer gently until the peas are tender.
3. Stir in the stock and wine. Bring to a boil, and add the oysters and liquor. Heat until the oysters begin to curl. Stir in the remaining 4 tablespoons of butter.
4. Allow the mixture to cool slightly and purée in a food processor or blender.
5. Return to the saucepan, season with salt and pepper to taste, and heat thoroughly.
6. Serve immediately because keeping the bisque warm over an extended period of time will diminish the bright green of the peas.
7. Garnish with blanched fresh peas or chopped chives.

OYSTER POTAGE

Take some boild pease, strain them and put them in a pipkin with some capers, some sweet herbs finely chopped, some salt, and butter; then have some great oysters fryed with sweet herbs and grosly chopped, put them to the strained pease, stew them together, serve them on a clean scowred dish on fine carved sippets, and garnish the dish with grated bread.

—ROBERT MAY,
*The Accomplisht Cook,
or the Art and Mastery
of Cooking,* 1660

OYSTER SAFFRON BISQUE

SERVES 8 Second only to beets in sugar content, carrots seem an unlikely ingredient for an oyster bisque, but spiced with saffron, the southern Mediterranean influence on this dish is unmistakable and unique. The recipe and a chilled bottle of Hermitage will definitely do the trick for the hostess who likes to be different.

24   shucked oysters and liquor
3   medium carrots
4   Tablespoons butter
1   cup chopped celery
1   cup chopped onion
1½   quarts vegetable stock (see p. 59)
1½   cups diced potato
½   lemon
1   teaspoon saffron
1   cup heavy cream
    Salt and freshly ground white pepper
    Chopped chives

1. Drain oysters, reserving the liquor.
2. Peel the carrots and chop 2 of them for the soup. Cut the remaining carrot into fine julienne strips and blanch in boiling salted water. Refresh in cold water, drain, and reserve for garnish.
3. Melt the butter in a large saucepan and sauté the chopped carrot, celery, and onion until tender.
4. Add the oyster liquor, stock, potato, lemon, and saffron. Bring to a boil, cover, and simmer for 15 minutes.
5. Remove the lemon, and purée the vegetable mixture in a food processor or blender.
6. Transfer the puréed vegetables back to the saucepan, add the cream, and bring to a simmer.
7. Add the oysters and heat until the edges begin to curl. Season to taste.
8. Garnish with julienned carrots and chives, and serve immediately.

OYSTER CHOWDER

SERVES 4

A tureen of this simple but delicious chowder on a buffet table and a carafe of light California Chardonnay capture the essence of the new comfortable style of entertaining. Vary the recipe and make it with fresh corn-off-the-cob and heavy cream for an unforgettable vegetable and oyster combination.

LATE
AUTUMN DINNER

Oyster Chowder

Crown Roast of Pork
with Wild Rice

Acorn Squash with
Apple and Raisin Stuffing

Endive and
Watercress Salad

Chestnut Roll

Opus One Cabernet

1	*pint oysters and liquor*
1	*cup creamed corn*
1	*cup milk*
2	*ounces finely diced salt pork*
$^1/_2$	*cup finely chopped onion*
1	*cup finely chopped celery*
1	*cup diced potato*
1	*cup water*
1	*Tablespoon finely chopped parsley*
	Salt and freshly ground pepper

1. Drain the oysters and reserve liquor.
2. Heat the corn and milk in a 2-quart saucepan. Set aside.
3. Blanch the salt pork in boiling water for 5 minutes. Pour off the water and sauté the salt pork until crisp. Remove the cracklings with a slotted spoon and reserve for garnish.
4. Sauté the onion and celery in the pork drippings until tender. Add the potato, oyster liquor, and water, and bring to a boil. Cover and simmer until the potato is tender but firm.
5. Combine the potato mixture with the corn and milk. Add oysters, parsley, and salt and pepper to taste. Heat thoroughly, stirring carefully, until the oysters are plump. Serve immediately garnished with cracklings.

OYSTER CHOWDER BONNE FEMME

SERVES 6

This traditional "homey" soup can be served with or without oysters. With, it is definitely company fare and a subtle variation on the New England chowder theme. Without, that extra touch of class is missing.

1	*pint oysters and liquor*
6	*Tablespoons unsalted butter*
1	*coarsely chopped medium onion*

4	coarsely chopped medium leeks
3	cups diced potato
1	cup water
2	cups vegetable or chicken stock (see p. 59)
	Salt
1	cup heavy cream
2	teaspoons chopped fresh parsley or chives

1. Melt 3 tablespoons butter in a large saucepan. Sauté the onion and leeks until tender.
2. Add the potato, water, stock, and ½ teaspoon salt. Bring to a boil and simmer, covered, until potatoes are cooked but firm.
3. Add the oysters, liquor, and cream. Heat until the oysters ruffle. Stir in the remaining 3 tablespoons of butter and adjust salt.
4. Ladle into warmed serving bowls and sprinkle with parsley or chives.

SEAFOOD CHOWDER

SERVES 6

Even though the Puritans might frown a bit at the sheer luxury of this seafood chowder, there is simply no more sophisticated way to begin "Dinner at Eight." Medium- to full-bodied Champagne and Wedgwood service are *de rigueur*.

1	pint oysters and liquor
1	quart water
2	cups diced potato
1	cup dry white wine
1	pound white fish fillets, flounder or halibut
1	pound raw shrimp, or 1 pound bay scallops
3	Tablespoons butter
1	cup finely chopped shallots
3	Tablespoons flour
1¹/₂	cups heavy cream
	Cognac
	Salt and freshly ground pepper
	Cayenne pepper
	Chopped fresh parsley

1. Drain oysters, reserving liquor.
2. Combine oyster liquor and water in a 3-quart saucepan and bring to a boil. Add potatoes, cover, and simmer until the potatoes are cooked but still firm.
3. Use some of the liquid and wine to poach the fish fillets in a shallow sauté pan. As soon as they turn opaque, remove the fillets, cover with waxed paper, and keep warm. Return the poaching liquid to the saucepan.
4. Add shrimp or scallops to the saucepan and poach for 2 minutes. Remove shellfish with a slotted spoon. Peel and devein the shrimp. Keep the shrimp or scallops warm with the fillets.
5. Reduce the poaching liquids over high heat to about 1 quart.
6. Melt the butter in a heavy-bottom 2-quart saucepan, and sauté the shallots until tender. Stir in the flour and cook until pale yellow. Remove from the heat and stir in the hot poaching liquid and potato water. Return to heat and cook, stirring frequently, for at least 15 minutes.
7. Stir in the oysters and cream. Heat until the oysters are plump. Add 1 or more tablespoons of Cognac, and adjust seasoning with salt and peppers.
8. Distribute the fillets and shrimp or scallops into heated bowls and ladle the hot chowder over them. Garnish with parsley and serve immediately.

CHICKEN AND OYSTER GUMBO

SERVES 8

Through the years, Creole cooks, working in the homes of Spanish, Italian, French, and Anglo families, acquired recipes and ways of preparing food that they, in turn, handed down to their sons and daughters. Cajun and Creole cooking, therefore, is a jumble of culinary styles.

Cooks and chefs made gumbos with almost any seafood, meat, or poultry available, but they usually seasoned them with peppers, herbs, and the powder of wild sassafras they borrowed from the Indians, and called filé. Added to a bowl of gumbo just before serving, filé flavors, slightly thickens, and gives a fine dark color to this legendary soup. And a tall glass of Pilsner adds just the right Bourbon Street note.

1	*pint oysters and liquor*
2	*quarts chicken or vegetable stock (see p. 59)*
1	*cut-up frying chicken*

1	cup flour
4	Tablespoons butter
2	Tablespoons oil
1	cup chopped celery
1	cup chopped onions
1/2	cup chopped sweet red pepper
1/2	pound diced ham
2	cups peeled and chopped tomatoes
1/2	pound sliced fresh okra, or 1 10-ounce package frozen okra
	Paprika
	Salt and freshly ground pepper
2	Tablespoons filé powder (optional)
4	cups cooked long-grain rice

1. Drain the oysters and set aside. Combine the oyster liquor and stock in a large saucepan and simmer for 15 minutes.
2. Coat the chicken pieces with flour, reserving 5 tablespoons for the roux.
3. Melt half of the butter and oil in a large heavy-bottom cast-iron pot, and lightly sauté the celery, onions, and red pepper until soft. Remove and reserve.
4. In the same pot fry the chicken until the pieces are dark brown. Set aside.
5. Lightly fry the ham; remove with a slotted spoon and set aside.
6. Add the rest of the oil and butter to the pot, heat and with a wooden spoon stir 5 tablespoons of flour into the pot, and cook over moderate heat, stirring constantly, for about 15 minutes or until the roux is a deep hazelnut color. Pour hot stock into the roux gradually, stirring to prevent lumps, and gradually add all of the stock.
7. Return the chicken pieces and vegetables to the pot, add the tomatoes and okra, and simmer for about 30 minutes. Remove chicken pieces, bone, and discard the skin. Return chicken to the pot.
8. Add the ham and oysters and continue to simmer until the edges of the oysters begin to curl. Season to taste with paprika, salt, and pepper.
9. Stir in the filé powder, if used, and remove from heat.
10. Serve the gumbo over rice in individual bowls.

SEAFOOD GUMBO

SERVES 8 Although some of the famous restaurants in New Orleans serve almost twenty different kinds of gumbo,* seafood gumbo remains a favorite—the one that "tastes just like my mother made when I was growing up in Louisiana." Just turn on the jazz and open a bottle of Heineken.

1	pint oysters and liquor
$^1/_2$	pound white fish fillets
1	pound raw medium shrimp
$^1/_2$	pound crabmeat
$^1/_2$	pound fresh okra, or 1 10-ounce package frozen okra
4	Tablespoons butter
1	minced garlic clove
1	cup chopped onions
$^1/_2$	cup chopped green pepper
$^1/_2$	cup chopped celery
2	quarts fish stock (see p. 58)
$^1/_3$	cup dry Vermouth
1	bay leaf
	Pinch of thyme
$^1/_2$	cup butter or corn oil
$^1/_2$	cup flour
$1^1/_2$	cups peeled and chopped tomatoes, or canned plum tomatoes
$^1/_2$	pound sliced smoked sausage (optional)
$^1/_2$	teaspoon cayenne pepper
1	teaspoon Worcestershire sauce
	Salt and freshly ground pepper
2	Tablespoons filé powder
4	cups cooked long-grain rice

1. Drain the oysters, reserving the liquor. Quarter the fillets; shell and devein the shrimp; pick over crabmeat, removing shell bits and cartilage, and set aside.

2. Trim and cut the okra in 1-inch pieces. Melt 2 tablespoons of butter in a large saucepan and sauté the okra until lightly browned. Remove with a slotted spoon and drain the pan.

*The African Bantu name for gumbo is *okra*, usually one of the vegetables used in the soup. The mucilaginous texture of okra thickens any kind of liquid it is cooked in. Use it with tomatoes because their acidity cuts the gluey texture and complements the taste of the vegetable.

3. Melt the remaining butter in the same saucepan, add the garlic, onions, pepper, and celery, and cook until wilted. Set aside vegetables.
4. Pour the oyster liquor, stock, and Vermouth into a saucepan. Add the bay leaf and thyme, cover, and bring to a boil.
5. Heat the butter or oil in a large heavy-bottom enamel cast-iron pot, add the flour, and stir constantly over moderate heat for about 15 minutes or until the flour turns a rich brown. Gradually incorporate the hot stock into the roux and simmer.
6. Remove the bay leaf. Add all the vegetables, including the tomatoes, smoked sausage, cayenne pepper, and Worcestershire sauce. Partially cover and simmer for 1 hour.
7. Add the fish and shellfish, and simmer until the shrimp turn pink and the edges of the oysters begin to curl. Season to taste with salt and pepper.
8. Stir in the filé powder, and remove from heat.
9. Serve the gumbo over a mound of rice in individual bowls.

SEAFOOD MÉDITERRANÉE

SERVES 6

The swirl of vermicelli into this simple seafood recipe is a bonus, and it absolutely guarantees a hearty supper after a busy day. If there is a supply of fish stock in the refrigerator or freezer, the soup can be simmering during the cocktail hour and served minutes after the seafood is added. A dry brisk white wine from the seacoast of southern France called Cassis would be more than appropriate.

24	*shucked oysters and liquor*
6	*Tablespoons olive oil*
3	*chopped medium leeks*
1	*cored and chopped medium fennel bulb*
1	*chopped medium onion*
1	*chopped garlic clove*
6	*cups fish stock (see p. 58)*
2	*cups peeled and chopped tomatoes, or chopped canned tomatoes*
$1/_2$	*teaspoon saffron*
1	*teaspoon orange zest*
1	*teaspoon thyme*
1	*teaspoon rosemary*
24	*raw medium shrimp*

$^1/_2$	pound cooked lobster meat
1	cup cooked vermicelli
	Salt
	Cayenne pepper

1. Heat the oil in a large saucepan and sauté the leeks, fennel, onion, and garlic until tender.
2. Add the fish stock, tomatoes, saffron, orange zest, thyme, and rosemary, and bring to a boil. Cover and simmer about 30 minutes.
3. Strain the broth through a double layer of cheesecloth. Return to the saucepan and bring to a boil.
4. Peel and devein the shrimp.
5. Add the oysters, shrimp, lobster, and vermicelli to the pot and heat until the edges of the oysters start to curl. Season lightly with salt and cayenne.
6. Adjust the seasoning and serve immediately.

CIOPPINO

SERVES 8

The search for the perfect "one-dish" meal stops here. A mélange of seafood, vegetables, herbs, spices, and a reserve Pinot Noir from California will make it a perfect Sunday night supper, especially if there's a loaf of homemade bread on the sideboard, and good friends at the table.

1	pint oysters and liquor
12	mussels in shell
$^1/_2$	pound white fish fillets
6	ounces lobster meat, or 6 small tails in shell
$^1/_2$	pound raw medium shrimp
6	ounces crabmeat
3	Tablespoons olive oil
2	chopped medium onions
1	finely chopped garlic clove
10	ounces tomato purée
2	cups peeled and chopped tomatoes, or canned tomatoes
1	quart water
2	cups red wine, Zinfandel, or Pinot Noir
$^1/_2$	cup finely chopped parsley
1	teaspoon basil

1	teaspoon oregano
2	Tablespoons sugar
	Salt and freshly ground pepper

1. Scrub and rinse the mussels, removing the beards. Cut the fillets and lobster meat into bite-sized pieces. Shell and devein the shrimp; remove cartilage from crabmeat.
2. Heat the oil in a 3-quart saucepan and sauté the onions and garlic until tender. Add the purée, tomatoes, water, wine, herbs, and sugar. Season lightly with salt and pepper. Cover and simmer for 1 hour.
3. Add the mussels and lobster tails, and simmer 2 minutes.
4. Add the fillets, shrimp, crabmeat, lobster meat (if used), and oysters. Heat until the oysters begin to curl. Adjust seasonings and serve at once.

LEEWARD ISLAND OYSTER SOUP

SERVES 6

Explorers who followed in Columbus's wake found a plentiful cache of conch and oysters in the waters off many of the Caribbean islands. So it's entirely appropriate to imagine a recipe or two that might have pleased their palates, especially if accompanied with a California Sauvignan Blanc or a simple glass of Continental Pilsner.

3	dozen shucked oysters and liquor
2	cups fish stock or clam juice (see p. 58)
7	cups water
2	cups long-grain rice
4	Tablespoons unsalted butter
3	peeled diced carrots
3	washed slivered leeks
2	peeled diced yams
1	thinly sliced celery rib
1	cup coarsely chopped green cabbage
$^1/_2$	pound rinsed and stemmed callaloo leaves (spinach or Swiss chard may be substituted)
1	seeded chopped jalepeño pepper
4	Tablespoons finely chopped parsley
	Salt and freshly ground pepper
6	sprigs of fresh thyme

1. Remove the oysters from shells, and set aside. Strain the oyster liquor, and add fish stock or clam juice to make 2 cups of stock.
2. Heat 4 cups of water to boiling in a medium saucepan. Add rice, reduce heat, cover, and simmer until water is absorbed and rice is tender. Remove from heat, keep covered, and set aside.
3. Melt butter in a large saucepan over medium heat. Add carrots, leeks, yams, celery, cabbage, callaloo, and pepper. Reduce heat and sweat until the vegetables are tender. Stir in parsley.
4. Add stock plus 3 cups water to vegetables and bring to a boil; simmer for 10 minutes.
5. Add the oysters to the vegetable soup; cook until the edges curl. Season to taste.
6. Divide the rice into 6 serving bowls and ladle the soup over the rice. Garnish with a sprig of fresh thyme.

SHELLFISH BLAFF

SERVES 6

Hey mon, ready for some real Caribbean cooking? Share in the spirit of this soul-satisfying cuisine with a bowl of one of the islands' most delicious soups and a tall glass of Weissbier. It's like bringing the ambience of a seaside restaurant and a garden run riot with palm trees and bougainvillaea into your own dining room.

24	shucked oysters and liquor
$^1/_2$	pound shelled deveined large shrimp
$^1/_2$	pound bearded mussels
1	pound spiny lobster tails
3	cups dry white wine
2	Tablespoons fresh lime juice
2	finely minced garlic cloves
$^1/_2$	teaspoon salt
$1^1/_2$	cups water
1	whole Scotch bonnet pepper

Herb Bouquet:
3	whole cloves
2	sprigs parsley
2	garlic cloves
$^1/_2$	teaspoon whole green peppercorns

1	bay leaf
6	thick garlic croûtes
	Salt and pepper
$^1/_2$	cup chopped scallion for garnish

1. Remove the oysters from the shells, reserving the liquor. Place the oysters, shrimp, mussels, and lobster tails in a large shallow dish. Add 1 cup of the wine, lime juice, garlic, and salt. Cover and refrigerate for ½ hour.
2. Strain the oyster liquor and add water to make 2 cups of liquid. Mix with the remaining 2 cups of wine in a heavy noncorrosible saucepan, add the whole pepper and herb bouquet, and bring to a boil. Adjust the heat to maintain a slow simmer and cook until the liquid is reduced by half. Remove the pepper and herb bouquet.
3. Remove the shellfish from the marinade, and add the marinade to the reduced broth. Bring to a simmer.
4. Toast thick slices of French bread, rub with garlic, and brush with olive oil. Place a *croûte* in the center of each heated shallow soup plate.
5. Add the shrimp, scallops or mussels, lobster, and oysters to the broth, cover, and poach until the edges of the oysters begin to curl and the shrimp turns pink. Remove the shellfish to a hot platter. Keep warm. Adjust the seasoning of the broth.
6. Divide the shellfish among the bowls, and spoon the broth over each. Garnish with chopped scallions and serve.

SERVES 4

After years of enjoying *Crassostrea gigas*, otherwise know as the Pacific oyster, another native of Japan, the Kumamoto, has become the most sought-after oyster in the country. Now cultivated and harvested in Washington State and California, the small and deep-cupped, ridged-shelled Kumamoto is ideal for raw savoring, and it is completely at home lightly poached in an Asian broth. Enjoy with a glass of sake.

24	*shucked Kumamoto oysters and strained liquor*

Broth:

1½	*quarts chicken stock (see p. 59)*
	Oyster liquor
1	*Tablespoon rice wine vinegar*
1	*Tablespoon light soy sauce*
½	*teaspoon ground white pepper*
½	*cup chopped onion*
1	*Tablespoon minced garlic*
1	*Tablespoon minced fresh ginger*
2	*stalks lemongrass, cut into ¼-inch pieces*

4	*ounces rice vermicelli*
2	*ounces bean sprouts*
6	*ounces snow peas, ends trimmed, strings removed, and julienned*
2	*Tablespoons chopped cilantro*
	Salt and freshly ground white pepper
	Sesame oil

1. Make the broth by placing the broth ingredients in a 2-quart saucepan. Bring to a boil, cover, and steep for 1 hour. Strain and return to heat.
2. Soften rice noodles in hot water for 15 minutes, then boil for about 45 seconds, drain.
3. Blanch bean sprouts and snow peas separately, and rinse in cold water.
4. Divide the rice noodles among 4 shallow soup bowls, spoon bean sprouts and snow peas over the noodles, add 6 oysters to each bowl, and ladle hot broth into the bowls. Stir a drop of sesame oil into each bowl. Sprinkle cilantro over the broth, and serve immediately.

I can think of no better way to have been initiated into
the world of Christmas than this one.

OLYMPIA OYSTER STEW

It seems to me that the milk we had with cream at the top was richer and more
satisfying for cooking than much we have now. I know that if I do an oyster stew
today, I use light cream or half-and-half plus heavy cream. So I advise you to do
the same with this delectable stew. Naturally if you don't live where the delicious
little Olympia oysters are available, use others or use clams or even scallops.

For each person heat 1 cup half-and-half and heavy cream mixed according to
your taste. Add the oyster liquor and for each person use about 1/2 cup or a few
more oysters. It is plainly and simply a matter of your own taste. Heat the milk
and oyster liquor and put a good dollop of butter in the dishes in which your stew
is to be served. Add to the stew a dash of Tabasco, salt to taste, and lastly the
oysters. Let them cook just long enough to give them a chance to heat through
and curl slighly at the edges. Serve the stew very hot with paprika and
plenty of buttered toast.

The utter simplicity of these flavors makes it a classic dish.
If you are on the Pacific Coast in the Northwest or the part of
California where the Olympias are available, do make a stew for yourself
or find a good restaurant where it is carefully and lovingly made.

—JAMES BEARD

*Chiffonade applies to leafy
vegetables, spinach, sorrel, or
lettuce, cut into shreds the width
of a matchstick. The simplest way
of doing this is to roll up a wad
of leaves and cut them across
with a sharp knife or scissors
into thin slices. They will unroll
into shreds. The lengths will
be uneven, but this does not
matter usually as a chiffonade is
such a tumble of greenery.*

—JANE GRIGSON,
Vegetable Book

I need no oyster
to be in love with you,
Nor, when I roister,
raw roots to chew. . . .

—A. P. HERBERT, *Love Song*

Salads & Vegetables

Over the past decade, salads and vegetables have come a long way from faded, overcooked, tedious, but-they're-so-good-for-you accompaniments to a meal. And, for many reasons. Vegetarianism is now popular, even chic. Fear of additives, preservatives, and chemicals motivates many amateurs to perfect their own gardening skills. And the influence of ethnic cuisines sends Americans into shops in search of the perfect wok for stir-frying and the most efficient food processor to slice, shred, julienne, and purée.

Urban dwellers and suburbanites alike are discovering that tending a garden of one's own or taking a deliberate detour to a country roadside stand—where bunches of brilliant dahlias and drying sea lavender mingle with baskets of zucchini, onions, peppers, and tomatoes—is a celebration of life. Indeed, the experience is a continual reminder "of the order of Nature itself: first freshness, then flavor and ripeness, and then decay." For that is the way M. F. K. Fisher describes her own efforts to purchase and prepare fruits and vegetables during the season of their "explosive rush toward ripeness and disintegration." And, doing so under the sunny skies of Provence, her effort was its own reward.

Vegetables do keep one in tune with the natural world. Anticipating the arrival of the first, tender, green asparagus in spring, the first peas of summer, the sun-flavored tomatoes of early fall, and the wholesome harvest of squash, potatoes, and onions is more meaningful because it is anticipated. And the memory more satisfying because gratefully remembered. With such a wealth of fresh ingredients to work with, how can anyone fail?

Let there be no more soggy salads prepared hours in advance, or gelatinous, artificially flavored molds, or "tarted-up" frozen vegetables. The "fresh connection" from garden to table is here to stay, and has opened the door to a dazzling array of first course, luncheon, buffet, and side dishes. There are new and exciting possibilities with each ripe tomato, snappy bean, opulent eggplant, and bouncy bouquet of salad greens.

The recipes in this chapter are limited to those "composed" salads and vegetable dishes that simply work well with oysters. The cooking methods, blending of flavors and textures, and presentation are basically the same ones that are used in all vegetable cookery. Preserving the integrity of each ingredient and the judicious use of seasonings, herbs, and spices are essential for their success. Many of the salads and vegetable dishes are accompaniments—special fare for a special dinner. Some of the recipes will do nicely for a luncheon or a simple family meal. All of them are truly "gifts" from the sea and garden.

Suggestions

- Freshly shucked oysters are essential for some of the salad and vegetable recipes, and bulk oysters can be used for others if oysters in the shell are not available. Frozen oysters are not recommended for any of the salad recipes.
- Fresh vegetables are a must for all of the recipes. If necessary, frozen vegetables can be used, but there is always some sacrifice of flavor. Vine-ripened tomatoes are essential for all the recipes that call for tomatoes.

- Vegetables retain their color, nutrients, and flavor when blanched in a microwave oven. Simply follow the instructions found in a basic manual regarding the amount of water and time.
- Herbs for salads should be fresh if possible because dried herbs have a slightly musty flavor.
- Tossing a salad at table is recommended because it ensures the essential fresh quality and it also designates the importance of a salad course.
- Adding the dressing to the greens and various ingredients of a salad implies using only as much dressing as desired. A lightly dressed salad is frequently preferred to a more generously dressed one.
- Extra virgin olive oil, either a quality wine, herb, or flavored vinegar, and a carefully selected mustard are some of the essentials of a "good" salad dressing.
- Homemade mayonnaise is always preferred to a commercial brand.
- Chilled plates are a nice touch when serving cold salads.
- Many of the recipes are for salads and vegetables that accompany an entrée. Care should be taken that all the courses of the meal complement rather than duplicate each other.

SALADS

As Accompaniments
Spinnaker Salad
Oyster Cucumber Boats
Eggs on the Half Shell
Venus's Own Salad
Love Apple Salad

As Main Courses
Oyster Mousse
Bermuda Triangle Salad
Oyster Nicoise
Bamboo Hut Oyster Salad
Seashell Salad
Insalata Romana
Posh Potato Salad
Pier I Salad

VEGETABLES

Artichokes
Gratin
Stuffed

Asparagus
Sauced

Broccoli
Mousse

Corn
Casserole
Soufflé

Eggplant
Stuffed

Fennel
Sautéed

Mushrooms
Ragout

Onions
Stuffed

Peppers
Warm Roasted

Potatoes
Mashed
Casserole
Kugel

Salsify
Oyster Bake

Spinach
Gratin

Squash
Spaghetti Squash
Zucchini Shells

Tomatoes
Baked
Fried

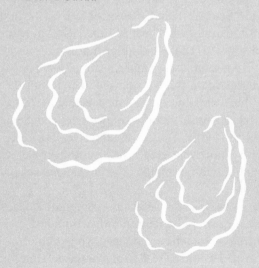

OH! IS
FOR OYSTER
SALAD

Seafood salads, once the special province of lobster, lump crab, shrimp, and the more plebeian tuna, now happily include squid, mussels, and even oysters. Perhaps it is a logical development because marinating oysters to preserve them has a somewhat eclectic history of its own.

One of the earliest Roman cookbooks, *The Apicius Book,* underscores the difficulties involved in keeping oysters fresh and mentions eating "oysters, well-seasoned with pepper, lovage, egg yolks, vinegar, broth, oil, and wine [sometimes honey]"—an interesting vinaigrette. Another Roman gastronomer describes a typical first course as "oysters, salt or pickled fish, raw onions and lettuce with various piquant sauces." And through the years "pickled" oysters customarily were eaten with brown bread, vinegar, onions, and pepper.

In America, the Indians cooked oysters and, when the colonists finally began eating them themselves rather than feeding them to their livestock, they used them in stews and stuffings. But in the South, "pickled" oysters became a common dish. *The Recipe Book of St. Anne's Parish,* Annapolis, Maryland, suggests serving "pickled" or ripe oysters in a salad. And by the turn of the last century, such names as "'Katzenjammer Salad," "Salad Tartare," and "Spanish Salad" were being used to designate the way a sauced or dressed oyster was "heaped" upon a bed of lettuce, cress, or celery.

Experience proves that pickling or marinating an oyster for a longish period of time does not always make it completely palatable, and with contemporary refrigeration there is no need to do it. But the use of a basic oil, vinegar, and herb dressing on raw or poached oysters can create a delectable salad, especially if the other ingredients complement the flavor and the texture of the oyster. Tangy tomato aspic, flavorful potato salad, pasta combined with crunchy vegetables bring out the oyster in oyster. It may not be a new idea but, with a slightly different zig and zag, oysters in salad can be provocative.

Whether a classic green salad or a composed salad, this palate pleaser should be given unshared attention rather than just tucked in between the soup and entrée or somehow managed while dinner plates are being collected. The hostess would do well to plan a special time for a salad and make it a feast in itself. In order to do this, the salad must definitely make a statement. Ingredients should be absolutely fresh, the dressing simple, well blended, and custom-made. Above all, the timing must be perfect because only so much can be prepared in advance.

Anyone can follow directions for a soup or a casserole; a salad requires intuition and flair—a cook who respects, even loves, all the ingredients involved. If greens wilt, tomatoes run, watercress dangles, or croutons limp before the salad is served, there is no remedy. If the oysters are not quite literally "quivering" right out of their shells, flavor will be lost. It's a pass-fail situation, the test of a sensitive cook, and very often the best indicator of a successful meal.

Salads as Accompaniments

SPINNAKER SALAD

As colorful as a spinnaker and just as racy, this salad is an attention getter. Use perfect asparagus, let the oysters billow over the stalks in their savory dressing, and serve a chilled Sancerre or Pouilly-Fumé.

Most people spoil garden things by over boiling them. All things that are green should have a little crispness, for if they are overboil'd they neither have any sweetness or beauty.

—HANNAH GLASSE,
Art of Cookery, 1747

12	*shucked small oysters*
2	*pounds fresh asparagus*
2	*ounces Roquefort cheese*
³/₄	*cup sour cream*
	Salt and freshly ground white pepper
1	*large sweet onion*
	Cayenne pepper
1	*cup peeled, seeded, diced tomatoes*

1. Remove the oysters from the shells, pat dry, and chill. Reserve the liquor for another use.
2. Wash, trim, and peel the asparagus. Blanch in boiling salted water for 1 minute. Refresh in ice water, drain, and chill.
3. Mix the Roquefort cheese with a small amount of sour cream, and gradually add the rest of the cream. Season to taste.
4. Slice the onion into paper-thin slices.
5. Arrange the asparagus stalks on chilled plates, place 2 oysters over the asparagus, top with onion rings, and spoon dressing over the salad.
6. Garnish with a dash of cayenne pepper and a tablespoon of diced tomatoes.

SALADS & VEGETABLES 87

OYSTER CUCUMBER BOATS

SERVES 4

The alliance of oysters and cucumbers in this "place" salad has the mermaids singing. With the availability of Continental cucumbers, it can be served all year long, but it is particularly tantalizing when homegrown cucumbers are ready to be picked. If a glass of wine suits your fancy, a light Graves would be perfect.

12	shucked small oysters
2	small cucumbers or a large one cut in half
	Salt
1	bunch watercress
2	slices diced smoked salmon
$^1/_4$	cup chopped chives
4	lime wedges (optional)

Dressing:

$^2/_3$	cup plain yogurt
1	Tablespoon lemon juice
2	teaspoons white wine vinegar
	Freshly ground pepper

1. Remove the oysters from the shells, drain, and pat dry. Reserve the liquor for another use.
2. Halve the cucumbers lengthwise. Remove the seeds and some of the pulp, leaving a ¼-inch shell. Sprinkle with salt, invert, and drain on absorbent paper for about 30 minutes. Pat dry.
3. Stem watercress and measure out ½ cup of leaves. Place the oysters, watercress leaves, smoked salmon, and chives in a bowl.
4. Mix the dressing and add to the oysters and salmon; season to taste with salt and pepper.
5. Fill each cucumber half with the oyster salad and serve on a bed of watercress with lime wedges if desired.

EGGS ON THE HALF SHELL

SERVES 8

With the array of glorious appetizers currently tempting cooks, deviled eggs have become somewhat outdated. But, stuffed with chopped oysters and a variety of fillings and presented on a tumble of greens, they can raise eyebrows on a buffet table. Serve with a light California Chardonnay.

HOW TO BARREL UP OYSTERS, SO AS THEY SHALL LAST FOR SIX MONETHS SWEET AND GOOD, AND IN THEIR NATURAL TASTE

Open your oisters, take the liquor of them, and mix a reasonable proportion of the best white wine vinegar you can get, a little salt and some pepper, barrell the fish up in a small caske, covering all the Oysters in this pickle.

—SIR HUGH PLAT, *Delightes for Ladies,* 1609

$^1/_2$	pint oysters and liquor
$^1/_2$	cup dry white wine
12	hard-boiled large eggs
	Salt and pepper

Fillings:

I

1	cup sour cream
1	teaspoon Dijon mustard
1	teaspoon Worcestershire sauce
1	teaspoon capers
	Chopped dill weed
	Tabasco
	Garnish: Snipped dill

II

1	cup yogurt
2	teaspoons minced celery
2	teaspoons minced chives
1	teaspoon minced green olives and pimiento
1	teaspoon Pommery mustard
	Tabasco
	Garnish: Slivers of green pepper

III

1	cup mayonnaise
2	Tablespoons chopped fresh chives, parsley, chervil
1	teaspoon dry mustard
	Cayenne pepper
	Garnish: Small shrimp

IV

1	cup mayonnaise
$^1/_2$	teaspoon curry powder
1	teaspoon chopped pickled ginger
1	teaspoon soy sauce
	Lemon juice
	Garnish: Chopped fresh cilantro

OYSTERS
A L'ALEXANDRE
DUMAS

Place in a sauce-bowl a heaped teaspoonful of salt, three-quarters of a teaspoonful of very finely crushed white pepper, one medium-sized, fine, sound, well-peeled, and very finely chopped shallot, one heaped teaspoonful of very finely chopped chives, and half a teaspoonful of parsley, also very finely chopped up. Mix lightly together, then pour in a light teaspoonful of olive oil, six drops of Tabasco sauce, one saltspoonful of Worcestershire sauce, and lastly one light gill, or five and a half tablespoonfuls, of good vinegar. Mix it thoroughly with a spoon; send to the table, and with a teaspoon pour a little of the sauce over each oyster just before eating them.

—FILIPPINI OF
DELMONICO'S,
The Table, 1891

SERVES 8

1. Poach oysters in liquor and wine until the edges curl. Drain and coarsely chop.
2. Shell the eggs. Cut them in halves, and sieve the yolks into a bowl.
3. Select one of the fillings, mix the ingredients in a medium bowl, and add to the yolks. Season lightly with salt and pepper.
4. Gently stir in the oysters, and spoon the filling into a pastry bag fitted with a large tube.
5. Pipe the filling into the reserved halves and garnish.
6. Arrange the eggs on a bed of salad greens and serve.

VENUS'S OWN SALAD

Glowing with the color of the sun, chilled oysters emerge from their shells glistening in aspic and crisp vegetables. Season the aspic to taste, add a bit of chicken stock if desired, and these oysters will turn an ordinary meal into a love feast. Serve with an Alsace Pinot Blanc.

12	*shucked oysters*
24	*deep 3-inch shells*
1	*envelope plain gelatin*
$^1/_4$	*cup dry Vermouth*
8	*ounces seasoned tomato juice or V-8 juice*
1	*teaspoon lemon juice*
	Tabasco
1	*Tablespoon finely chopped red onion*
1	*Tablespoon finely chopped celery*
1	*Tablespoon finely chopped sweet red pepper*
1	*Tablespoon finely chopped green pepper*
1	*Tablespoon finely chopped chervil*
	Frisée

1. Cut the oysters in half and drain well, reserving the liquor for another use. Scrub and dry the shells.
2. Soften the gelatin in Vermouth.
3. Bring the tomato and lemon juice to a boil in a small saucepan. Add the gelatin and stir until it has completely dissolved. Season with Tabasco.
4. Chill the aspic until it begins to set. Stir in the onion, celery, peppers, and chervil.

5. Place half an oyster in each shell and cover with aspic. Chill until the aspic is set.
6. For individual servings, arrange 3 shells on a bed of frisée.

LOVE APPLE SALAD

Select only medium-sized perfect tomatoes for this salad, and they'll be as tempting as Eve's apples probably were in Paradise. The stuffing is simple and certainly congenial to a few changes here and there. It could be seductive, especially with a bottle of light California Sauvignon Blanc.

$^1/_2$	pint oysters and liquor
$^1/_2$	cup dry white wine
4	medium tomatoes
$^1/_2$	cup finely chopped celery
2	Tablespoons finely chopped sweet red pepper
2	Tablespoons finely chopped Belgian endive
2	Tablespoons chopped watercress
$^1/_4$	cup finely chopped chives, parsley, tarragon, chervil
1	finely chopped hard-boiled egg

Dressing:

2	Tablespoons white wine vinegar
1	teaspoon lemon juice
$^1/_2$	teaspoon dry mustard
$^1/_2$	teaspoon paprika
2	finely chopped scallions
1	garlic clove
	Salt and freshly ground pepper
$^1/_2$	cup extra virgin olive oil

1. Mix the vinaigrette by stirring together the vinegar, lemon juice, mustard, paprika, scallions, and garlic clove. Slowly whisk in the oil. Season to taste. Allow the dressing to stand for at least 30 minutes. Discard the garlic clove.
2. Poach the oysters in their own liquor and white wine. Drain, coarsely chop, and marinate the oysters in some of the dressing for at least 30 minutes.

"The whole plant is of ranke and stinking savour," says GERARD'S HERBALL *under the heading "Apples of Love," which of course means "tomatoes," in reference to the aphrodisiac reputation they then enjoyed.*

—WAVERLEY ROOT, *Food*

3. Cut off the tomato tops with a serrated knife and remove the pulp and seeds, taking care not to pierce the bottoms and sides. Salt lightly, invert, and drain on a rack or on absorbent paper.
4. Combine the oysters, celery, pepper, and endive in a large bowl. Toss lightly with enough dressing to moisten. The mixture should not be runny. Adjust salt.
5. Fill the tomato cavities with the oyster mixture and garnish with watercress.
6. Drizzle some of the excess vinaigrette on each plate, sprinkle with chopped herbs and hard-boiled egg, and place a stuffed tomato in the center of the plate.

Salads as
Main Courses

SERVES 6

OYSTER MOUSSE

Prepared in individual 4-ounce ramekins and garnished with a spoonful of chopped herbs and salmon roe, this oyster mousse is first-class fare. But a word of caution—puréed oysters may "gray" the mousse, so add chopped oysters just before jelling. Serve with a chilled California Chardonnay.

1	*pint oysters and liquor*
4	*cups fish or chicken stock (see p. 58)*
1/4	*cup dry Vermouth*
8	*ounces ocean scallops*
2	*Tablespoons chopped shallots*
1	*medium coarsely chopped carrot*
1	*coarsely chopped celery rib*
3	*fresh tarragon sprigs*
1/2	*envelope powdered gelatin soaked in 1 tablespoon water*
1	*Tablespoon lemon juice*
1	*cup whipping cream*
	Salt and freshly ground white pepper
1/2	*cup chopped herbs: parsley, chives, basil*
1	*ounce salmon roe*

1. Poach the oysters in the liquor, stock, and Vermouth until the edges begin to curl. Drain, coarsely chop the oysters, and chill.

2. Return the poaching liquid to the heat, poach the scallops for about 8 minutes, remove from broth, and set aside. Add shallots, carrot, celery, and tarragon, and simmer until reduced to 2 cups. Strain. While still warm, stir in the gelatin with its soaking liquid and stir until melted.
3. While broth is reducing, purée the scallops in a processor or blender, and chill.
4. Chill 6 ramekins, and whip the cream to medium stiffness.
5. Add oysters and lemon juice to the scallop purée and slowly stir the broth into the purée. Gently fold the whipped cream into the mixture. Season to taste.
6. Divide the mousse among the 6 ramekins, and chill for at least 2 hours.
7. Unmold by dipping the ramekin into hot water for a second, run a sharp knife around the edge of the ramekin, and invert on a chilled plate. Sprinkle chopped herbs around the mousse, and top the mousse with a bit of salmon roe.

BERMUDA TRIANGLE SALAD

SERVES 6

Three key ingredients—oysters, mushrooms, and watercress—are the secret of this "let's get away from it all" luncheon salad. If preferred, substitute young spinach leaves for watercress, but the slightly spicy flavor of its cloverlike leaves makes watercress a great taste balancer in these uncharted waters.

24	*shucked small oysters*
2	*bunches watercress*
1	*head frisée*
8	*slices bacon*
1/2	*pound thinly sliced button mushrooms*
1/2	*thinly sliced red onion*
2	*Tablespoons lemon juice*
1	*garlic clove*
2	*sieved hard-boiled egg yolks*
	Cherry tomatoes

Dressing:

1	*teaspoon dry mustard*
1/2	*teaspoon freshly ground pepper*
1/2	*teaspoon sugar*

*Pick over two dozen oysters,
dry them carefully and put
them on the ice. Rub the
yolks of six hard-boiled
eggs, with a fork, till they
are dry and mealy;
add a teaspoonful of melted
butter, two tablespoonfuls
of vinegar, a tablespoonful
of tomato catsup,
a little salt and a teaspoonful
of Gebhardt's Eagle Chili
powder; mix thoroughly,
squeezing in the juice from
half a lemon. Toss the
oysters up in this sauce and
serve them on shredded
celery garnished
with celery tops.*

—MAY E. SOUTHWORTH,
*One Hundred & One Ways
of Serving Oysters,* 1907

SERVES 4

2	teaspoons Dijon mustard
3	Tablespoons wine vinegar
	Worcestershire sauce
$1/2$	cup extra virgin olive oil
	Salt and pepper

1. Remove the oysters from the shells, drain, and pat dry. Reserve the liquor for another use.
2. Wash and trim the watercress. Pat the leaves dry and wrap in a towel or absorbent paper until ready to use. Repeat the process with the frisée.
3. Cook the bacon in a skillet or microwave oven until it is crisp; drain, crumble, and reserve for topping the salad.
4. Mix the ingredients for the dressing, and slowly whisk in the oil.
5. Rub the inside of a large bowl with a peeled garlic clove and lightly toss all the salad ingredients, including oysters, with some or all of the dressing. Adjust the salt, add pepper to taste.
6. Distribute the salad on chilled plates and sprinkle with crumbled bacon and egg yolks. Garnish with cherry tomatoes.

OYSTERS NICOISE

This salad can be a cornucopia of fresh and lightly cooked ingredients, and assembling it is certainly a cook's delight. The salad can be presented in a shallow, lettuce-lined glass or wooden bowl, each ingredient arranged in spokelike fashion from the center. Or the ingredients can be arranged on individual serving plates. Whichever arrangement is used, adding the lightly fried oysters to the center of the salad is the penultimate step to success. Serve with a crisp California Sauvignon Blanc.

16	shucked oysters
$1/4$	cup corn flour
	Salt and freshly ground pepper
2	whisked eggs
1	Tablespoon water
$1/2$	cup cornflake crumbs
8	cooked small new potatoes
2	sliced medium tomatoes
$1/2$	pound blanched green beans
3	Tablespoons butter

1	Tablespoon vegetable oil
$^1/_2$	head romaine lettuce
4	sliced hard-boiled eggs
$^1/_2$	thinly sliced red onion
8	flat anchovies
16	pitted ripe Greek olives

Dressing:

3	Tablespoons red wine vinegar
$^1/_2$	teaspoon salt
	Pinch of pepper
$^1/_2$	teaspoon dry mustard
1	Tablespoon fresh basil chiffonade
$^2/_3$	cup extra virgin olive oil

1. Drain the oysters, reserving the liquor for another use. Pat the oysters dry, and dredge in seasoned flour. Dip in eggs mixed with water, and roll in crumbs. Place on a plate lined with absorbent paper and chill for 1 hour.
2. Mix the vinegar with the salt, pepper, mustard, and basil. Slowly whisk in the oil.
3. Marinate the potatoes and beans in some of the dressing and set aside. Drizzle some of the dressing over the tomato slices and set aside.
4. Heat the butter and oil in a skillet and shallow-fry the oysters on both sides until golden. Drain.
5. Assemble the salad by lining a large salad bowl with leaves of romaine, tearing some leaves into smaller pieces. Arrange the vegetables and other ingredients, placing the oysters in the center. Drizzle with some of the dressing before serving.

BAMBOO HUT OYSTER SALAD

Somewhere between Egg Drop Soup and Peking Duck, this "cold" appetizer salad would be an tasty addition to an array of first courses at an Asian dinner. Or, if served at a luncheon, it could take its place with Shrimp Toast and Spring Rolls to pique the appetite but not overindulge it. A glass of dry Alsace Gewurztraminer would be the right touch.

1	*pint oysters and liquor*
$^1/_2$	*cup dry white wine*
1	*large sweet red pepper*
1	*cup chopped baby bok choy*
6	*ribs slivered Chinese cabbage*
1	*cup fresh bean sprouts*
$^1/_2$	*cup julienned jicama*
$^1/_4$	*cup chopped cilantro*
	Salt and freshly ground pepper
2	*Tablespoons roasted chopped peanuts*

Dressing:

1	*Tablespoon sesame oil*
3	*Tablespoons vegetable oil*
1	*teaspoon lemon juice*
$^1/_4$	*cup rice vinegar*
2	*teaspoons soy sauce*
1	*teaspoon fresh minced ginger*
	Pinch of sugar

1. Poach the oysters in the liquor and wine until the edges curl. Drain and set the oysters aside in a large bowl.
2. Broil the pepper, turning it to char all surfaces. Place in a bowl covered with plastic wrap to steam. Cool and remove the skin, core, and seeds, and dice.
3. Mix the dressing.
4. Combine the vegetables and herbs with the oysters, and toss the salad with enough dressing to coat; add salt and pepper if necessary. Garnish with nuts and serve on chilled plates.

SEASHELL SALAD

What could be more redolent of the depths of the sea than a clever combination of oysters and pasta seashells? A cool and casual luncheon dish or a gala buffet table treat, this salad will please almost every palate. Serve with a California Sauvignon Blanc.

1	*pint oysters and liquor*
1	*cup dry white wine*
2	*quarts water*
	Salt
1¹/₂	*cups maruzelle (seashells)*
	Butter or olive oil
¹/₄	*cup chopped stuffed olives*
3	*Tablespoons chopped green pepper*
¹/₂	*thinly sliced cucumber*
6	*thinly sliced radishes*
¹/₄	*cup chopped parsley, chives, basil*
	Salad greens
1	*sliced medium red tomato*
1	*sliced medium yellow tomato*

Dressing:

2	*Tablespoons lemon juice*
¹/₂	*teaspoon celery seed*
¹/₂	*teaspoon dry mustard*
¹/₄	*teaspoon freshly ground pepper*
1	*Tablespoon minced Spanish onion*
¹/₂	*cup mayonnaise*

1. Poach the oysters in the liquor and wine until the edges begin to curl, drain and pat dry. If large, cut in halves or quarters.
2. Bring salted water to a boil, add the pasta shells, and cook until tender but firm. Drain the pasta, toss with a small amount of butter or oil, and set aside.
3. Mix the dressing in a large bowl.
4. Stir in the olives, vegetables, herbs, and pasta. Add the oysters, and salt and pepper as needed. Chill until ready to use.
5. Serve in individual bowls garnished with baby lettuces and red and yellow tomato slices.

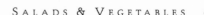

INSALATA ROMANA

Nuovo cucina at its most convincing, this salad can be made with almost any vegetable or combination of vegetables from the garden. Asparagus is celestial, but green peas, zucchini, and broccoli are inspired, if a little less divine. Serve with Italian Pinot Blanc.

1	pint oysters and liquor
1	cup dry white wine
1	pound asparagus
4	Tablespoons olive oil
1	garlic clove
¼	cup pine nuts
1	pound egg fettuccini or egg fusilli
¼	pound julienned ham
1½	Tablespoons balsamic vinegar
	Salt and freshly ground pepper
	Basil chiffonade

1. Lightly poach the oysters in the liquor and wine, drain, and set aside.
2. Trim, peel, and blanch the asparagus in boiling salted water. Refresh in ice water and cut into 1-inch pieces.
3. Heat the olive oil in a small saucepan and cook the garlic clove for 1 minute. Discard the garlic. Add pine nuts to the pan and toast lightly. Allow oil and nuts to cool slightly.
4. Cook the pasta in boiling salted water until tender and drain. Transfer to a large bowl and toss with olive oil and nuts.
5. Add the asparagus, ham, olives, oysters, and vinegar. Toss and adjust seasonings.
6. Serve at room temperature with a garnish of fresh basil.

As much depends upon the mixing as upon the proportions. The foolish pour in first their oil, then their vinegar, and leave the rest to chance, with results one shudders to remember. The two must be mixed together even as they are poured over the salad, and here the task but begins. For next, they must be mixed with the salad. To "fatigue" it the French call this special part of the process, and indeed, to create a work of art, you must mix and mix and mix until you are fatigued yourself, and your tomatoes or potatoes reduced to one-half their original bulk. Then will the dressing have soaked through and through them. Then will every mouthful be a special plea for gluttony, an eloquent argument for the one vice that need not pall with years.

—ELIZABETH ROBINS PENNELL,
The Feasts of Autolycus

POSH POTATO SALAD

SERVES 6

Fried oysters add a touch of sass to a delightfully seasoned potato salad and make it a luscious luncheon meal. Serve with a glass of chilled Macon or St. Veran, a rustic loaf of bread, and some sweet butter.

1	pint medium oysters and liquor
5	medium red potatoes
2	Tablespoons chopped parsley
2	Tablespoons chopped chives
1	Tablespoon chervil

Dressing:

¹/₂	cup white vinegar
1	teaspoon Dijon mustard
1	teaspoon celery seed
1	teaspoon sugar
	Salt and freshly ground white pepper
	Sour cream (optional)
1	cup corn flour
	Oil for deep frying

1. Drain the oysters, reserving ⅓ cup of the liquor. Refrigerate the oysters.
2. Boil the potatoes in salted water, drain, and cool slightly.
3. Mix the oyster liquor, the dressing ingredients, and ¼ teaspoon salt in a saucepan, and simmer for a few minutes.
4. Peel the warm potatoes and cut into ½-inch cubes. Sprinkle with parsley, chives, and chervil, and toss with the hot dressing. Marinate for a few hours. Adjust salt and pepper, and bind with sour cream if desired.
5. Dry oysters and roll in seasoned corn flour.
6. Deep-fry the oysters in 375°oil, or pan-fry over moderately high heat until both sides are golden brown. Drain on absorbent paper.
7. Serve the salad at room temperature, garnished with oysters.

PIER I SALAD

SERVES 8

Perfect as a side dish for a seashore picnic of grilled hamburgers, potato salad always waves a flag. But range a bit farther and serve it with swordfish kebabs and the skipper and crew will quickly "reach" for the finish line.

1$^1/_2$	pints oysters and liquor
1	cup dry white wine
2	pounds potatoes
	Salt
1	chopped medium red onion
2	cups chopped celery
$^1/_2$	cup chopped parsley
4	slices bacon
2	sliced hard-boiled eggs

Dressing:

$^1/_2$	cup mayonnaise
3	Tablespoons extra virgin olive oil
2	Tablespoons tarragon vinegar
1	teaspoon Dijon mustard
1	teaspoon sugar
$^1/_4$	teaspoon coarsely ground pepper

1. Poach the oysters in the liquor and wine until the edges start to curl. Drain and pat dry. If the oysters are large, cut in halves or quarters.
2. Boil the potatoes in salted water until centers can be pierced with a fork. Drain and cool slightly.
3. Mix the dressing and ½ teaspoon salt in a large bowl. Stir in the onion, celery, and parsley.
4. Peel and cut the warm potatoes into ½-inch cubes.
5. Add the potatoes and oysters to the salad and bind with more mayonnaise if necessary. Season to taste, and refrigerate at least 4 hours.
6. Cook the bacon in a skillet or microwave oven until crisp, drain, and crumble. Reserve the bacon for garnish, or stir into the salad just before serving.
7. Garnish with egg slices.

This pretty phrase, "la salade . . . qui réjouit le coeur," is often quoted and misquoted.

At the expense of being thought dully practical and unpoetical, I truthfully do not think it means that salads gladden the heart, but that they are light in the stomach and easily digested, and that they bring a feeling of easiness and comfort to the whole belly and especially to the poor overworked organ that perches on top of it, the human heart. Anything which does that is, of course, a gladsome thing.

—M. F. K. FISHER,
"The Translator's Glosses,"
The Physiology of Taste

VEGETABLES

Bounty of the Garden Basket

From the Food Halls of Harrods in fashionable Kensington to Quail Hollow on Cape Cod, everyone has a favorite market where tomatoes are so luscious, lettuce so fresh and crisp, in fact, all the fruits and vegetables so bursting with color and flavor that within minutes a shopping basket can be filled and rushed home to the kitchen.

And the market is all the more beguiling if it is a seasonal one. When afternoon shadows suggest fall and leaves turn a little, the aroma of pickling spices prevails in the back of the shop, and jars of "just-made" chutney, relish, and marmalade line the shelves. It's a special time of year and an inner voice says, "Please, stay a little longer," as the wind shifts from south to northeast by east.

It was during the waning days of summer and early fall that most of these vegetable and oyster recipes were tested. The oysters came from the Cotuit Oyster Company minutes away; the herbs and vegetables came from the garden or other gardens nearby. The results were so immediate, so tangible, that this particular cache of recipes can only be called the bounty of the garden basket.

Artichokes

The artichoke has been cultivated for centuries and has retained its identity as a "love food," the darling vegetable of the Renaissance, and the symbol of "Taste" in the visual arts. Not surprising, then, that like the oyster, the artichoke has remained "the pleasure of people who mind about good food." What can be more natural than a combination of the two? It could be called a marriage, but an *affaire de coeur* seems much more suitable for this compatible pair.

Individual servings of Artichoke Gratin and perfectly contained Stuffed Artichokes are nothing short of elegant with either a fish or chicken entrée.

ARTICHOKE GRATIN
(*Serve with a Hermitage Blanc*)

SERVES 6

1	pint small oysters and liquor
3	medium artichokes
1/2	lemon
	Salt
1/2	sliced onion

1	cup heavy cream
6	Tablespoons butter
2	Tablespoons flour
2	Tablespoons dry Sherry
2	Tablespoons minced parsley
2	minced garlic cloves
1	teaspoon chopped fresh basil
	Salt and freshly ground pepper
	Tabasco
$^1/_2$	cup fresh bread crumbs

OVEN TEMPERATURE: 375°

1. Remove the stems and lower leaves from the artichokes and rub the cut edges with lemon. Add 1 teaspoon salt, the piece of lemon, and the onion slices to 1½ inches of boiling water in a saucepan large enough to hold the artichokes upright. Cover and simmer for about 40 minutes, or until the bottoms are tender when pierced with a fork. Drain and cool the artichokes.

2. Remove the leaves and scrape them, saving the pulp; discard the bristly choke and dice the bottoms.

3. Drain the oysters, reserve ¼ cup of the liquor, and heat it with the cream in a small saucepan.

4. Melt the butter in another saucepan; spoon off and reserve 2 table-spoons for the bread crumbs. Stir in the flour and cook until straw yellow. Remove from the heat and whisk in the warm cream. Return to heat and cook, stirring constantly, until the mixture thickens.

5. Stir in the artichoke pulp and bottoms, Sherry, parsley, garlic, and basil, and simmer a few minutes. Remove from the heat and add the oysters. Adjust seasoning.

6. Spoon into 6 buttered scallop shells or ramekins and top with the buttered bread crumbs.

7. Bake about 15 minutes until the sauce is bubbling and the tops are golden brown.

STUFFED ARTICHOKES
(Serve with Pouilly-Fumé)

SERVES 6

$^1/_2$	pint oysters and liquor
6	extra large artichokes
2	Tablespoons lemon juice
	Salt
4	Tablespoons butter
3	Tablespoons finely chopped shallots
1	cup heavy cream
1	Tablespoon chopped fresh parsley
1	egg yolk
1	Tablespoon brandy
	Freshly ground pepper
	Tabasco
$^1/_2$	cup fresh bread crumbs
	Lemon wedges

OVEN TEMPERATURE: 375°

1. Trim and discard the stems and outer leaves from the artichokes, cut off the sharp tips of the remaining leaves, and rub all cut surfaces with lemon juice. Add remaining lemon juice to boiling salted water in a saucepan and cook the artichokes about 20 minutes, until they are tender when pierced with a fork. Drain, cool, and scoop out the bristly chokes, leaving an artichoke "cup" for filling. Keep warm.
2. Drain and chop the oysters, reserving the liquor.
3. Melt 3 tablespoons of butter in a heavy saucepan. Add the shallots, oyster liquor, ¼ cup of cream, and parsley, and simmer until the mixture is slightly reduced.
4. Whisk the egg yolk in a bowl with the remaining ¼ cup of cream. Whisk in the hot mixture, a spoonful at a time. Transfer the enriched sauce to the saucepan and, stirring carefully, bring to the point of boil.
5. Add the oysters and brandy. Add salt, pepper, and Tabasco to taste; stir in the bread crumbs, and cook until hot.
6. Fill the artichokes, dot with the remaining butter, and arrange in a buttered baking dish.
7. Bake about 15 minutes, and serve with lemon wedges.

Asparagus

Another vegetable that "manifestly provoketh Venus," asparagus is as legendary, luxurious, and love-inspiring as the artichoke. Although it can be prepared in a fraction of the time that it takes to cook its illustrious peer, asparagus, like the artichoke, can also be served with a little melted butter, a squeeze of lemon, or dressed more elegantly with a Hollandaise sauce. But asparagus has its own special allure. Napped with a light oyster and mushroom cream sauce, it works its magic in ways that even Madame Pompadour could never have imagined when she combined asparagus with eggs for her not-too-subtle purposes.

SAUCED ASPARAGUS

SERVES 4

20	shucked medium oysters and liquor
2	pounds asparagus
1	cup heavy cream
3	Tablespoons butter
1	Tablespoon finely chopped scallions
1½	Tablespoons flour
	Pinch of mace or nutmeg
1	cup well-washed sautéed morels
	Salt and freshly ground pepper

1. Trim, peel, and blanch the asparagus for 3 minutes in boiling salted water. Remove the stalks with a slotted spoon to a rack lined with a towel.
2. Remove the oysters from their shells, strain, and reserve ½ cup of the liquor.
3. Heat the oyster liquor and cream in a small saucepan.
4. Melt 2 tablespoons of butter in another saucepan and sauté the scallions until tender. Stir in the flour and cook until straw yellow. Remove from the heat and whisk in the cream. Return to heat, add the mace or nutmeg, and cook, stirring constantly, until the mixture thickens.
5. Stir the remaining tablespoon of butter into the sauce, and simmer for 5 minutes. Add the oysters and mushrooms. Season to taste, and heat until the edges of the oysters start to curl.
6. Reheat asparagus in butter and a touch of water. Arrange on a serving platter or on individual plates, and nap with the oyster and mushroom sauce.

Broccoli

Broccoli is simply a nifty vegetable to "team up" with chicken, pasta, eggs, or shellfish. Blanched for a minute or two, it has a delightful crunch; sautéed, the stems and florets retain their color, flavor, and crispness; stir-fried, it does wonders for a vegetable platter. For a little added drama, cast it as the main ingredient in a soufflé or mousse. It will perform magnificently at a matinee and steal the evening show.

BROCCOLI MOUSSE
(*Serve with Washington State Riesling*)

SERVES 8

1	*pint oysters*
1¹/₂	*pounds broccoli*
	Salt
5	*Tablespoons butter*
²/₃	*cup heavy cream*
¹/₂	*Tablespoon lemon juice*
4	*eggs*
	Freshly ground pepper
1	*cup blanched julienned carrots*
	Toasted almonds

OVEN TEMPERATURE: 375°

1. Wash, peel, and cut the broccoli stems into ½-inch pieces, setting aside 1½ cups of coarsely chopped florets. Blanch the stems in boiling salted water for 1 minute, drain, refresh in cold water, and drain again. Blanch and refresh the florets separately.
2. Melt 3 tablespoons of butter in a skillet, add the blanched stems, cream, and lemon juice, and cook over moderately high heat, stirring constantly, until the cream thickens and the broccoli is cooked.
3. Purée the mixture in a food processor or blender, adding the eggs one at a time.
4. Drain and chop the oysters; stir into the purée. Season to taste with salt and pepper.
5. Pour the mixture into a buttered 6-cup ring mold or individual custard cups, and place in a baking pan in 1 inch of boiling water.
6. Bake for 25 minutes, or until a knife tests clean.

7. Melt the remaining 2 tablespoons of butter in a saucepan and sauté the broccoli florets and carrots until they are thoroughly heated. Season to taste.
8. Unmold the mousse on a serving dish, fill the center with the vegetables, and garnish with toasted almonds. Or unmold individual cups and garnish with florets, carrots, and almonds.

Corn

Considered too "sweet" for Continental palates, corn is a New World "vegetable" and probably one of the largest grain crops in America. Edible in its "green stage," corn quickly perishes and really should be prepared as soon after picking as possible or its sweetness becomes starchy.

While many devotees believe that "just-picked" corn on the cob is the only way to eat this vegetable, the following recipes for a casserole and soufflé may give them second thoughts and, perhaps, if they also fancy oysters, second servings.

CORN CASSEROLE
(*Serve with light California Chardonnay*)

SERVES 6

1	pint oysters and liquor
6	Tablespoons butter
$^1/_4$	cup chopped onion
$^1/_2$	cup chopped green and red sweet peppers
2	cups scraped corn
	Pinch of sugar
$^1/_2$	teaspoon celery seed
	Salt and freshly ground pepper
1	egg
$^3/_4$	cup light cream
$^1/_2$	cup fresh bread crumbs

OVEN TEMPERATURE: 350°

1. Drain the oysters, reserving ¼ cup of the oyster liquor.
2. Melt the butter in a skillet, pour off and reserve 2 tablespoons for the bread crumbs, and sauté the onions and peppers until they are tender. Remove from the heat, stir in the corn, pinch of sugar, and celery seed, and season lightly with salt and pepper.

3. Whisk the egg, oyster liquor, and cream together in a bowl.
4. Spread a third of the crumbs on the bottom of a buttered 1½-quart baking dish; spoon some of the vegetable mixture and oysters over the crumbs. Repeat the layering, and pour the egg-cream mixture over the top. Sprinkle with the remaining crumbs and melted butter.
5. Bake about 20 minutes, until the casserole is thoroughly hot and the crumbs are golden brown.

CORN SOUFFLÉ
(Serve with Chateauneuf-du-Pape Blanc)

SERVES 4

½	pint oysters and liquor
1	cup milk
3	Tablespoons butter
3	Tablespoons flour
⅓	cup grated Gruyère
4	egg yolks
1½	cups scraped corn
¼	cup finely chopped chives
	Salt and freshly ground pepper
5	egg whites

OVEN TEMPERATURE: 350°

1. Drain oysters and chop, reserving the liquor.
2. Heat the oyster liquor and ¾ cup of milk in a small saucepan.
3. Melt the butter in another saucepan, stir in the flour, and cook until straw yellow. Remove from the heat and whisk in the hot milk. Return to heat and cook, stirring constantly, until the mixture thickens. Stir in the cheese.
4. Whisk the egg yolks and the remaining ¼ cup of milk in a large bowl. Whisk in ½ cup of the hot sauce, a spoonful at a time; then slowly beat in the remaining sauce.
5. Stir in the oysters, corn, chives, and salt and pepper.
6. Beat the egg whites to stiff peaks, stir a third of them into the oyster mixture, and fold in the remaining whites.
7. Pour into a buttered 2-quart soufflé dish or 4 individual dishes.
8. Bake for 40 minutes, and test with a knife. When the knife blade comes out clean, remove from the oven and serve immediately.

Eggplant

The Syrians and Turks claim to have a thousand ways to prepare eggplant, and southern Mediterranean cuisine reflects the versatility of this vegetable. So beautiful and exotic in appearance that it provoked John Gerard to write in his Elizabethan *Herball*, "those apples have a mischievous quality," the eggplant was viewed with some suspicion in many countries, including this one, until the turn of the century when such prestigious restaurants as Delmonico's began to serve it.

Today dishes like Moussaka, Caponata, and Ratatouille are commonplace, and the suitability of eggplant in the preparation of hearty stews, cold and hot appetizers, and one-dish meals is well known.

Try this variation of the classic Stuffed Eggplant recipe, and if there is a little extra stuffing left over it will do wonders for a rock cornish hen or a small roasting chicken.

STUFFED EGGPLANT
(*Serve with Brown Ale*)

SERVES 8

1	pint oysters and liquor
4	medium eggplants
	Salt
2	Tablespoons butter
1/2	pound finely chopped linguica or kielbasa
1	minced garlic clove
1	chopped small onion
1/2	cup chopped celery
1/2	cup chopped green pepper
1	cup chopped parsley
1	cup chopped cremini mushrooms
1	teaspoon Worcestershire sauce
1/4	teaspoon thyme
1	bay leaf
	Freshly ground pepper
1/2	cup chicken stock (see p. 59)
1 1/2	cups fresh bread crumbs
2	eggs
1/2	cup freshly grated Swiss cheese

OVEN TEMPERATURE: 350°

1. Cut the unpeeled eggplants in half lengthwise, and scoop out the centers, leaving ¼- to ½-inch shells. Cut the pulp into small cubes, and use 2 cups for the stuffing. Toss the cubes with salt and drain for 30 minutes.
2. Melt the butter in a large saucepan and sauté the sausage until it is partly cooked. Add the eggplant cubes, garlic, onion, celery, pepper, parsley, and mushrooms, and sauté until tender.
3. Drain the oysters, cut in half or quarter if large, and reserve ⅓ cup of the liquor.
4. Add the liquor, Worcestershire, thyme, bay leaf, and pepper to the sautéed vegetables. Cover and simmer for 30 minutes, adding stock if the mixture becomes dry. Remove the bay leaf.
5. Combine the oysters and 1 cup of bread crumbs with the vegetables, and stir in the well-beaten eggs. The stuffing should be moist but not runny. Adjust seasonings.
6. Fill the eggplant shells and sprinkle with a mixture of cheese and remaining crumbs.
7. Place the shells in an oiled baking pan and bake 30 minutes.

Fennel

Although the vegetable Florentine fennel, or *finocchio*, is another latecomer to American cuisine, Thomas Jefferson had two varieties of it in his vegetable garden at Monticello and was eloquent in its praise: "The fennel is beyond every other vegetable, delicious. It greatly resembles in appearance the largest size celery, perfectly white, and there is no vegetable equal to it in flavour"—a reputation to be envied, but deserved. Fennel can be used in soups, stuffings, and casseroles. It can be marinated or eaten raw with cheese for dessert, and its anise flavor makes it a super complement to seafood. In this simple recipe for sautéed fennel, and oysters, the addition of a dash of Pernod may well become an exclamation point.

SAUTÉED FENNEL

SERVES 4

½	*pint oysters*
1	*large fennel bulb with leaves*
1	*Tablespoon olive oil*
3	*Tablespoons butter*

1	large leek, white and light green parts, chopped
1	teaspoon fresh lemon juice
	Salt and freshly ground pepper

1. Drain the oysters, pat dry, and coarsely chop.
2. Cut the bulb in quarters and thinly slice against the grain, discarding the core. Finely chop about ¼ cup of the leaves.
3. Heat the oil and 1 tablespoon of butter in a large skillet, and sauté the leeks until tender (if necessary, add a bit of water). Remove with a slotted spoon and set aside.
4. Melt the remaining 2 tablespoons of butter and add the fennel to the skillet. Cook until the fennel is tender but still crisp.
5. Add the oysters, leeks, and lemon juice and cook, stirring gently, for about 5 minutes. Season with salt and pepper.
6. Stir in the chopped fennel leaves and serve immediately.

Mushrooms

Mysterious and multiple, mushrooms are as legendary as oysters, and like oysters can be prepared in innumerable ways. But this Mushroom Ragout really struts its stuff in terms of flavor and intensity, and adding oysters makes it even more interesting. Serve the ragout with Amontillado Sherry.

MUSHROOM RAGOUT

SERVES 4

12	shucked oysters
2	pounds assorted mushrooms (cremini, chanterelle, porcini, button, morel)
2	Tablespoons butter
¹/₄	cup minced onion
¹/₄	cup chopped celery
¹/₂	minced garlic clove
¹/₂	cup white wine
¹/₄	cup Madeira
2	cups chicken stock (see p. 59)
2	sprigs fresh thyme
	Salt and freshly ground pepper

1. Drain oysters, and set aside.
2. Prepare the mushrooms by rinsing the morels several times; brush the other mushrooms as needed.
3. Melt 1 tablespoon of butter in a saucepan and sauté the mushrooms until brown.
4. In another large saucepan, melt the remaining butter, and sweat the onions, celery, and garlic.
5. Add the Madeira and wine and reduce by three quarters. Add stock, thyme, and mushrooms, and reduce until the broth has concentrated flavor. Add oysters and heat until the edges curl. Add salt and pepper to taste. Serve *en cocotte.*

Onions

The less-than-glamorous stepsister of shallots, scallions, and leeks, the common onion can finally dress up and strut her stuff, providing, of course, her "stuff" is made of oysters. For years minced, chopped, sliced, and cast in a secondary role in thousands of soups and stews, the onion can be presented in more fetching attire. Just bake to a light golden color, and show off in the company of grilled veal chops or salmon steaks.

STUFFED ONIONS

SERVES 6

¹/₂	*pint oysters and liquor*
3	*large Spanish or Vidalia onions*
³/₄	*cup cream*
3	*Tablespoons butter*
1¹/₂	*Tablespoons flour*
2	*Tablespoons dry Sherry*
¹/₄	*cup toasted walnuts*
2	*Tablespoons chopped parsley*
	Lemon juice
	Salt and freshly ground pepper
	Buttered bread crumbs

OVEN TEMPERATURE: 375°

1. Drain the oysters, cut in half if large, and reserve the liquor.
2. Cut the onions into halves, peel outer layer, and cut a slice from the stem and root ends so the halves will stand upright. Hollow out the insides, leaving a ⅜-inch shell. Fine-chop the removed onion, and set aside ½ cup.
3. Steam the onion shells over boiling water until tender. Remove with a slotted spoon, place upside-down on a tray, and keep warm.
4. Heat the oyster liquor and cream in a small saucepan.
5. Melt the butter in another saucepan. Sauté the ½ cup of chopped onion. Stir in the flour and cook until straw yellow. Remove from the heat and whisk in the hot cream. Return to heat and cook, stirring constantly, until the mixture thickens. Stir in the Sherry and simmer for at least 5 minutes.
6. Add the oysters, walnuts, and parsley, and a squeeze of lemon juice. Season to taste with salt and pepper.
7. Fill the onion cavities, top with crumbs, and place the onions in a buttered, shallow baking dish, filled with an inch of water.
8. Bake for 30 minutes; add liquid if the dish becomes dry, and cover with foil if the onions brown too quickly.

Peppers

For a "pick a peck of . . ." think of peppers and oysters, and ordinary meals will "quick like a jingle" become extraordinary ones. Warm Roasted Peppers paired with poached oysters work well as a side dish or atop garlic- and olive-oil-brushed toasted slices of Italian bread as one of the offerings in a well-planned buffet. Serve with a light-bodied Ale.

WARM ROASTED PEPPERS

SERVES 6

24	*shucked small (Kumamoto) oysters*
1	*cup shallots*
2	*red sweet peppers*
1	*yellow sweet pepper*
1½	*Tablespoons oil*
	Salt and freshly ground black pepper
¼	*cup chopped basil*

Dressing:

1	*Tablespoon lemon juice*
2	*Tablespoons balsamic vinegar*
1	*Tablespoon Dijon mustard*
2	*Tablespoons extra virgin olive oil*

OVEN TEMPERATURE: 450°

1. Rub shallots and peppers with oil and place in a shallow pan. Roast in a hot oven or under the broiler until the skins are browned and blistered. Remove and steam in a container with a tight lid or in a plastic bag until cool.
2. Peel off skins. Keep the shallots whole but cut off the stem end of the peppers and open them. Flatten, remove the core and seeds, and cut in ½-inch strips. Lightly salt and pepper.
3. Using the oyster liquor, poach the oysters lightly. Add the oysters to the shallots and peppers and keep warm.
4. Mix the vinaigrette dressing by combining the lemon juice, vinegar, and mustard. Slowly whisk in the oil and season to taste.
5. Pour the vinaigrette over the oysters and peppers and lightly toss. Garnish with basil.

Potatoes

That [potato] which was heretofore reckon'd a food fit only for Irishmen, and clowns, is now become the diet of the most luxuriously polite.

—STEPHEN SWITZER, 1733

Associated with wars and famines, carried from South America to Europe and back again to North America, planted in presidents' gardens and outside the hovels of the poor, the potato is unique among vegetables. It has been fodder for animals, the food of prisoners and slaves, the delight of gourmets. And today the search is on for the perfect potato, one that has not been processed, packaged, or subjected to all the vagaries of convenience and fast food. The word is out—either grow your own potatoes or select them as carefully as asparagus, and suit the potato to the dish in terms of size, starch content, and flavor.

The following recipes are adaptations of dishes found in the tradition of potato cookery. From the Baltic "kugel" to the comforting casserole, these recipes have been partnered with oysters successfully. Potatoes are so neutral in taste and so exciting in adaptability that even the most conservative cook will soon recognize that the culinary potential of this alliance is limitless.

MASHED POTATOES

1½ pints oysters
4   cups mashed potatoes*
¼   cup sour cream
2   whisked eggs
1   Tablespoon water
1   cup heavy cream
2   Tablespoons butter
1½ Tablespoons flour
    Salt and freshly ground white pepper
    Lemon juice
½   cup sautéed button mushrooms
2   Tablespoons chopped parsley and chives

OVEN TEMPERATURE: 400°

1. Add sour cream to the mashed potatoes and pipe a layered 1-inch-thick wall of mashed potatoes inside the rim of a buttered 2½-quart baking dish or 6 individual gratin dishes. Brush the surface of the potatoes with a glaze of eggs mixed with water.
2. Bake in the upper third of the oven about 10 minutes, until the potatoes are golden; turn off the oven, leaving the door ajar.
3. Drain the oysters, reserving the liquor for another use.
4. Heat the cream in a small saucepan.
5. Melt the butter in another saucepan, stir in the flour, and cook until straw color. Remove from the heat and whisk in the cream. Return to heat and cook, stirring constantly, until the mixture thickens. Simmer at least 5 minutes.
6. Stir in the oysters, salt, and pepper to taste; heat until the edges of the oysters begin to curl. Add a squeeze of lemon juice and the mushrooms.
7. Pour the creamed oyster mixture inside the potato ring, garnish with parsley, and serve immediately.

*The potatoes can be boiled in stock; garlic or an herb bouquet may be added to the potato water for flavor.

POTATO CASSEROLE
(Serve with Pinot Blanc)

SERVES 6

1	pint oysters
1	cup crème fraîche
1	Tablespoon chopped fresh dill weed
4	Tablespoons butter
2	thinly sliced Spanish onions
	Salt and freshly ground pepper
4	boiled medium potatoes
1	cup coarsely grated Swiss cheese
$^1/_4$	cup chopped parsley or chives

OVEN TEMPERATURE: 350°

1. Drain the oysters and place in a bowl, reserving the liquor for another use.
2. Combine ½ cup of the *crème fraîche* with the dill, mix with the oysters, and marinate for at least 30 minutes.
3. Melt the butter in a skillet and sauté the onions until tender, seasoning with salt and pepper.
4. Peel the potatoes and cut them into ⅛-inch slices.
5. Spread some *crème fraîche* on the bottom of a 2-quart buttered gratin dish or casserole, layer with potatoes, onions, oysters, the marinade with additional *crème fraîche,* and some cheese. Repeat the layers until all the ingredients are used.
6. Bake about 25 minutes, and, if necessary, place under the broiler to brown the top. Serve garnished with parsley or chives.

POTATO KUGEL
(Serve with a light Sauvignon Blanc or a dry hard cider)

SERVES 8

$^1/_2$	pint oysters
6	medium potatoes
2	shallots
4	eggs
2	Tablespoons melted butter or chicken fat
2	Tablespoons flour
8	parsley sprigs

1/4   cup diced, lightly cooked bacon
        Sour cream
        Chopped chives

OVEN TEMPERATURE: 350°

1. Drain the oysters, pat dry, and chop.
2. Peel the potatoes and shallots and coarsely grate in a food processor.
3. Add the eggs, shortening, flour, and parsley to the work bowl, and process for a minute.
4. Spoon half of the potatoes into a buttered 2-inch-deep quiche dish. Distribute the oysters and bacon over the mixture, and cover with the remaining potatoes. Bake immediately or the potatoes will discolor.
5. Bake for about 40 minutes or until a golden-brown crust forms over the top. Allow the kugel to stand for a short time before cutting it into wedges.
6. Serve with a garnish of sour cream and chopped chives.

Salsify

Nineteenth-century cooking school teacher and cookbook writer Mrs. Sarah Tyson advised vegetarians to make a mock oyster soup from it; Fannie Farmer's *Original Boston Cooking-School Cook Book* (1896) listed two recipes for Creamed Oyster Plant and Salsify Fritters. Fast forward to the present and a variety of recipes are provided for both French- and Italian-inspired salsify dishes. Blanched and sautéed with prosciutto, batter-fried, or used in a creamy gratin, this versatile tuber continues to hint of the sea. Otherwise known as the oyster plant, it is beginning to come into its own again. Here salsify is paired with Olympia oysters in a gratin suitable as a side dish.

SALSIFY OYSTER BAKE
(*Serve with Muscadet*)

SERVES 6

1   pint Olympia oysters, drained, liquor reserved
1   pound salsify
3   Tablespoons lemon juice
3   Tablespoons butter
1/4   cup chopped scallions
2   Tablespoons flour

$^1/_2$ cup heavy cream
1   cup grated Swiss-type cheese
      Salt and freshly ground white pepper
$^1/_2$ cup fresh bread crumbs

OVEN TEMPERATURE: 400°

1. Wash, peel, and cut the salsify into ¼-inch slices. Put into water mixed with a tablespoon of lemon juice. Boil salted water, add a tablespoon of lemon juice and salsify, and cook for about 8 to 10 minutes. Drain, set aside, and reserve the cooking liquid.

2. Melt butter in a sauté pan, add scallions, and cook until tender. Stir in flour, and cook for about 5 minutes. Remove from heat; whisk in 1 cup salsify liquid combined with oyster liquor. Return to heat and cook for 10 minutes. Stir in cream and ½ cup cheese, remaining lemon juice, salsify, and oysters, and season with salt and pepper. If too thick, thin with salsify liquid and oyster liquor.

3. Butter a 1-quart gratin dish; pour the creamed mixture into the dish. Top with the remaining ½ cup of cheese mixed with bread crumbs. Dot with butter and bake for about 10 to 15 minutes or until the top browns.

Spinach

"On a bed of spinach" has come to have such lusty charm that the temptation to do it one more time cannot be overcome. Oh, *felix culpa*! The simple earthiness of a well-flavored layer of spinach, inlaid with oysters, and topped with cheese can only be called Oysters Jezebel. It's a perfect side dish to sautéed white-fleshed fish like sea bass.

SPINACH GRATIN
(*Serve with Graves Blanc*)

SERVES 6

24   shucked oysters and liquor
$3^1/_2$ pounds spinach
2   Tablespoons vegetable oil
4   Tablespoons butter
2   Tablespoons chopped shallots
2   teaspoons minced ginger root
      Salt and freshly ground pepper
$^1/_2$ cup heavy cream

$1^1/_2$ Tablespoons flour

$^1/_4$ cup dry white wine

4 ounces grated Italian Fontina cheese

OVEN TEMPERATURE: 350°

1. Remove the oysters from the shells, pat dry, and set aside, reserving ⅓ cup of the strained liquor.
2. Wash and stem spinach; spin dry.
3. Heat the oil and 2 tablespoons of the butter in a large saucepan. Add the shallots and ginger and cook about 1 minute. Add the spinach, toss to coat the leaves, and cook until the spinach is wilted. Season with salt and pepper, remove the spinach with a slotted spoon, and spread in a buttered gratin dish.
4. Heat the oyster liquor and cream in a small saucepan.
5. Melt the remaining 2 tablespoons of butter in another saucepan. Stir in the flour and cook until straw yellow. Remove from the heat and whisk in the hot cream mixture. Return to heat and cook, stirring constantly, until the mixture thickens. Add the wine, season with salt and pepper, and simmer at least 5 minutes.
6. Arrange the oysters on the spinach, pour the sauce over them, and top with the cheese.
7. Bake for 15 minutes; if necessary, place under the broiler to lightly brown the cheese.

At the beginning of the 14th century, [spinach] is listed in the household accounts of wealthy families, and at the end of that century the anonymous MENAGIER DE PARIS *reported that "there is a species of chard called* ES-PINACHE *which is eaten at the beginning of Lent."*

—WAVERLEY ROOT, *Food*

Squash

Maybe it's the autumn leaves turning pumpkiny orange and the abundance of summer and winter squash that bring the words *rustic* and *robust* to mind whenever these vegetables are displayed in mounds or heaped into oversized baskets. Perhaps it's simply the beneficence of the generous vines that makes one want to gather all the interesting shapes and colors of squash, and either use them or hoard them. The opportunities to do so are endless.

The zucchini that has slipped notice and grown a little larger than one might wish can always be cut crosswise, scooped out, and filled with a savory oyster stuffing. More stunning in presentation, but equally delicious, is a platter of sautéed spaghetti squash with a heavenly cream sauce. And then there's acorn, butternut, patty pan, and. . . . It's definitely a hoarding vegetable.

Dungeness, extra large (Washington)

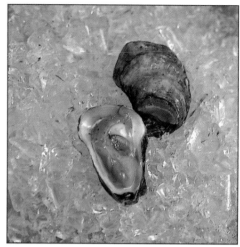

Caraquet (New Brunswick)

Royal Miyagi (British Columbia)

Prudence Island (Rhode Island)

Wellfleet (Massachusetts)

Sunset Beach (Washington)

Chincoteague, regular (Maryland, Virginia)

Chincoteague, extra large (Maryland, Virginia)

Blue Point (Northeastern United States)

Bras d'Or (Nova Scotia)

Malepeque, regular (Prince Edward Island)

Malepeque, extra large (Prince Edward Island)

Kumamoto (California)

Quilcene (Washington)

Belon, regular (Maine, New Hampshire)

Belon, extra large (Maine, New Hampshire)

SPAGHETTI SQUASH
(Serve with a Pouilly-Fumé)

SERVES 6

24	shucked oysters
1	large spaghetti squash
8	Tablespoons butter
	Salt and freshly ground pepper
1½	cups heavy cream
	Pinch of nutmeg
¼	cup grated Parmigiano-Reggiano
1	cup finely chopped fresh herbs: parsley, chives, basil, chervil
	Cayenne pepper

OVEN TEMPERATURE: 350°

1. Cut squash in half, remove seeds and stringy center, season, and bake cut-side-down in a pan filled with about an inch of water. It is done when it separates into strands but is not mushy.
2. When cool enough to handle, comb out long strands of the flesh with a fork. Place in a heatproof dish, mix with 4 tablespoons of butter, season, cover, and reheat in the oven before serving.
3. Remove the oysters from the shells and pat dry.
4. Combine the cream, remaining butter, and nutmeg in a heavy saucepan, and boil over medium heat until the sauce is reduced to about 1 cup. Remove from heat and whisk in the cheese until it melts.
5. Stir in the fresh herbs and oysters, and cook over low heat until the edges of the oysters start to curl. Season to taste.
6. Arrange the hot squash on a serving platter, pour the sauce over it, and serve immediately.

ZUCCHINI SHELLS

SERVES 6

1	pint oysters
2	medium-large zucchini
2	Tablespoons olive oil
¼	cup finely chopped sweet onion
¼	cup finely chopped cremini mushrooms
¼	cup finely chopped celery
¼	cup finely chopped sweet red pepper

$^1/_4$ cup chopped peeled seeded tomato
$^1/_4$ cup fresh herbs—basil, parsley, chives, thyme
       Salt and freshly ground pepper

OVEN TEMPERATURE: 350°

1. Select zucchini that are about 2 ½ to 3 inches in diameter. Cut into 2-inch slices and remove the centers from each slice with a melon baller or teaspoon, leaving a shell ¼ to ½ inch in thickness. Finely chop the scooped-out zucchini.
2. Put the shells into salted boiling water for 1 or 2 minutes, remove, place in cold water, remove, invert, and drain on absorbent paper.
3. Drain the oysters and coarsely chop. Reserve liquor for another use.
4. Heat the oil in a medium sauté pan and sauté the vegetables, including the chopped zucchini and herbs, until tender and the vegetable juices are reduced. Add the oysters, season to taste, and fill the zucchini shells with the vegetable mixture.
5. Place in a baking pan, and heat through for 10 to 15 minutes.

Why, then the world's mine oyster, Which I with sword will open.

—SHAKESPEARE, *The Merry Wives of Windsor*

Tomatoes

If there is a surfeit of vine-ripened tomatoes in the garden, this recipe will put them to good use. Baked tomatoes are so easy, so versatile, they brighten up any meal, and really show off oysters to advantage.

BAKED TOMATOES
(*Serve with Pilsner*)

SERVES 4

1	pint oysters and liquor
4	Tablespoons butter
2	Tablespoons chopped onion
$^1/_4$	cup chopped sweet red pepper
1	Tablespoon flour
2	Tablespoons full-bodied red wine
3	cups peeled, seeded, coarsley chopped tomatoes
1	teaspoon sugar
1	Tablespoon chopped fresh oregano
	Salt and freshly ground pepper
	Tabasco

OYSTERS AND TOMATOES

Two tablespoonsful of butter, one tablespoonful of flour, one slice of onion, one cup of stewed and strained tomato, one pint of oysters, salt and pepper. Cook the onion in the butter till light brown, add the flour and brown again, add the tomato and cook and stir until thick. Add the oysters, drained, and cook until they plump up. Serve on toast.

— WHAT WE COOK ON CAPE COD, compiled by Amy L. Handy, 1911

SERVES 6

½   cup fresh bread crumbs
2   Tablespoons freshly grated Parmigiano-Reggiano

OVEN TEMPERATURE: 375°

1. Drain oysters, pat dry, and set aside. Reserve ⅓ cup oyster liquor.
2. Melt butter in a saucepan. Pour off and reserve 2 tablespoons for the bread crumb and cheese topping. Sauté the onion and pepper until tender. Whisk in flour, and cook for 5 minutes. Stir in oyster liquor, wine, tomatoes, sugar, Tabasco, and oregano. Season to taste. Simmer uncovered until the mixture thickens.
3. Spoon some of the tomato mixture into a buttered shallow baking dish. Add oysters, and cover with the rest of the tomato mixture. Combine bread crumbs and cheese with the reserved melted butter and spread over the top.
4. Bake about 15 to 20 minutes until the top is golden brown.

FRIED GREEN TOMATOES
(*Serve with Weissbier*)

12   shucked medium-large oysters
½   cup stone-ground cornmeal
4   large green tomatoes
2   Tablespoons olive oil
1   Tablespoon butter
     Salt and freshly ground pepper

1. Remove oysters from shells, pat dry, roll in cornmeal, and set aside.
2. Wash tomatoes, dry, and thickly slice.
3. Heat the butter and oil (bacon fat may also be used) in a frying pan. Dip the tomato slices in cornmeal, shake off excess coating, and fry tomatoes on both sides until lightly browned. Add oil if necessary.
4. After tomatoes are fried, season with salt and pepper, and place in a warm oven while the oysters are fried. Season oysters.
5. Serve tomato slices topped with oysters. If used as a first course, a mayonnaise-based sauce could be used.

No matter how good the cooking is,
it's not worth eating
with the wrong people.
Call it the tea ceremony,
call it what you will,
breaking bread is a way of
making contact.
It's the mass;
and when we break bread
we say a barucha. It's part of
the dance between the man
and the woman,
the marvelous meal,
the bottle of wine—
the civilized way of saying
I want to eat with you,
I like you.

—ART BUCHWALD, *Cuisine,*
October 1983

Breads & Pastries

Bread can be leavened or unleavened, white or dark, round or baguette, thin as muslin or heavy and coarse textured, and there is always a reason for these differences. Often more revealing than an archaeological dig, the customs, folkways, even the utensils used in the preparation of bread tell the story of a people.

Baked, poached, fried, or steamed, bread has brought men to their knees in thanksgiving or supplication. The Chinese believed that wheat was a gift from heaven; the Anglo-Saxons offered to God the loaves baked from the first harvest. And Chaucer's pilgrims carried "Goddes Kechyl," a cake given as alms. Bread is eucharistic, a messianic bonding, "Take and eat for this is My Body." The antithesis to barrenness, it is also the symbol of the earth's fecundity. And bread is one of the ingredients for a perfect love feast, " A Jug of Wine, a Loaf of Bread, and Thou. . . ."

Bread has united men in the rites of communion and in battle (it is said that Norman soldiers demanded white bread for courage), in the partaking of saddlebag fare around a campfire, and, framed in a more contemporary idiom, in the sharing of a sandwich from a lunch box or picnic hamper. But bread has also divided men. The Jews eat unleavened bread as a reminder of their expulsion from Egypt. "To know the color of one's bread" was a Roman saying that cautioned men to keep their place in society. All through Europe, the darker the bread, the poorer the family. Mixing, kneading, and baking bread was simply a "peasant" thing to do.

In the New World things were different. From early colonial cabins and the settlers' covered wagons to today's gourmet kitchens, Americans have had a tradition of baking their own bread. And the efforts of pioneer women to bake bread in heavy iron pots buried deep in hot ashes and to transport "starters" in order to turn out nourishing loaves as soon as possible after camps were set up would be an amazing tale, and one worth telling.

Using cornmeal, wheat, barley, rye, or oats in the kitchens of Plymouth, Sturbridge, and Williamsburg, or improvising with whatever was available on a southern plantation or on the trail, colonial women and generations of their daughters have, quite literally, made America the "bread basket of the world." And that basket is filled with a dazzling list of hoe cakes, griddle cakes, steamed brown bread, beignets, rice flour, and sourdough breads.

And while one may envy the French their *boulangeries* on every street corner, the sniff and whiff of bread baking in one's own oven, of tarts and muffins cooling on racks, are as American as— dare it be said?—motherhood and apple pie. In the tradition of "homemade is best," a marble slab can replace the trencher table, stainless steel bowls and not earthenware crocks can hold the rising dough, and a convection rather than a clay oven can register 375°, but the search for the perfect loaf continues. The bread box and the pie basket are never empty, and those loaves, muffins, griddle cakes, and pie shells are the substance of this chapter.

Basically hearth-and-kettle in nature, the following recipes range beyond the usual breads and pastries to include biscuits, corn sticks, vol-au-vents, and quiches that become the "serving dishes" for a variety of oyster fillings. They are the possibilities an enterprising baker can conjure up when she eyes her dough rising or when she sends some flour and shortening whirling in the work bowl of a food processor. But they are possibilities with a difference. A hollowed-out loaf can be a box for fried oysters, ordinary rolls readily become "oyster rolls," crêpes, pancakes, and waffles can be embellished by an oyster sauce.

Bread has always sustained and nourished man. While some of these recipes are tradition-bound, others are distinctly different; but all of them feed a man's hunger if made with love.

A very exaggerated idea of the difficulty of breadmaking prevails amongst persons who are entirely ignorant of the process.

—ELIZA ACTON,
The English Bread Book, 1857

Suggestions

- For dietary reasons poached oysters may be substituted for fried oysters in some of the following recipes, although the suggested method of cooking suits the recipe most effectively.
- Recipes will definitely be tastier if made with homemade breads and pastries. The availability of specialty breads, frozen phyllo leaves, and puff pastry, however, can be helpful in preparing a given dish in a limited amount of time.
- Fresh bread removed from loaves and rolls makes excellent bread crumbs.
- If the top crust of a baked, filled loaf is too difficult to pierce with a knife, brush the crust with melted butter, cover with a damp towel, return to a warm oven for about 10 minutes, and then cut into the desired number of slices.
- Traditionally, pumpernickel or rye bread is the perfect complement to oysters, but various kinds of corn breads and sourdough bread are also very compatible with the flavor of smoked and raw oysters.
- After the final rolling, classic puff pastry can be cut into scallop shells, baked, and filled with a rich oyster sauce.

- Cheese, lemon zest, and congenial "shellfish herbs" like basil, parsley, chives, dill, marjoram, oregano, sage, tarragon, and thyme can be added to bread and pastry dough to sharpen the flavor of the recipe.
- Sour cream or buttermilk, additional eggs, honey or brown sugar, and the color of corn flour will alter the flavor and texture of corn bread. Water-ground white flint corn is supposed to produce a finer, sweeter loaf than most of the other varieties of corn flour. Kiln-dried, stone-ground yellow meal is often preferred by other bakers. Some recipes for corn bread call for both.
- The consistency of the filling and the quantity of the ingredients used to assemble a sandwich should guarantee ease in eating it.
- Watercress and other salad greens can be substituted for lettuce in most sandwiches.
- If a quiche is allowed to " rest" when removed from the oven, cutting it into serving pieces will be facilitated.
- If a quiche, pie, or tart is served as a supper course, the number of servings may be fewer than those suggested in the recipe.

BREADS

La Médiatrice
Not So "Po" Boy Loaf
Carnival Loaf
Scallywag Oyster Sandwiches
Rye, Please
Make Mine Danish
Croque Monsieur
Oysters Derring-Do
Beguiling Brioche
Foggy Bottom Oysters
Oysters Narragansett Bay
Oysters Benedict
Oysters Newport News
Merry Olde Oyster Pye

PANCAKES, WAFFLES, CRÊPES

Nip and Tuck Griddle Cakes
Waffles High Hampton
East India Company Crêpes
Oysters Hamilton Place
Chartwell Oyster Crêpes

PASTRIES

Oysters la Nacelle
Twelfth Night Oyster Tarts
Governor's Oyster Pie
Dockside Pizza
Quiche
Yankee Clipper Quiche
Kettle Cove Quiche

BREADS

La Médiatrice

SERVES 2

Whether it is associated with peacemaking, with poverty, or a treat for a frightened "po" boy matters very little. A hollowed-out, toasted bread with dozens of fried oysters inside is guaranteed to please a less-than-understanding wife, especially in the early hours of the morning.

A favorite way of preparing this classic loaf is to use a square or rectangular loaf, traditionally called a *pain de mie*. Within its crusty cavity, the fried oysters can be "boxed" handsomely and kept warm—ideal for a "kiss and make up" situation, especially if presented with a bottle of California Sauvignon Blanc.

Shredded lettuce, chili, tartar, or a special yogurt sauce may be used if desired. But if the "peace loaf" must be transported, serve the garnish or sauce on the side.

24	shucked large oysters
	Seasoned flour
1	whisked egg
1	Tablespoon water
	Fine bread crumbs
1	loaf bread
1/2	cup melted butter
	Oil for frying

Sauce (optional):

1	pint plain yogurt
1	minced garlic clove
2	Tablespoons grated onion
1	teaspoon chopped fresh dill
1/2	peeled, seeded, and diced cucumber
	Salt and freshly ground pepper

OVEN TEMPERATURE: 400°

1. Make the sauce by combining the yogurt, garlic, onion, and dill, and refrigerate. Just before serving, stir in the cucumber and season to taste.
2. Remove the oysters from the shells, drain, and pat dry. Dust with seasoned flour, dip in egg mixed with water, and roll in crumbs. Refrigerate at least 15 minutes before frying.

3. Slice the top crust from the loaf and scoop out some of the soft bread, leaving a generous shell. Brush the cavity and lid with melted butter, bake until golden, and keep warm.
4. Heat the oil to 375° and deep-fry the oysters a few at a time, until they are golden brown. Drain on absorbent paper and keep warm until all are fried.
5. Brush the inside of the loaf and lid with sauce if desired. Fill the loaf with the fried oysters, replace the lid, cut in half, and serve with bowl of sauce.

NOT SO "PO" BOY LOAF

Imagine Colchester oysters selling for eight pence a bushel two hundred years ago. Little wonder that "olde" recipe books pass along hints for "small economies in the kitchen" and provide directions for "Penny Loaves." Here are a few. Hollow out and fill a loaf with stewed oysters and a bit of lemon juice or fry the oysters in batter. And, as Elizabeth Smith suggests in the *Compleat Housewife* (London, 1727), toast the loaf in a pound of butter and season the oysters with "... a blade of mace, a little white pepper, a little horseradish and a piece of lean bacon, and a half a lemon."

The following recipe, slightly more expensive and elaborate than the earlier ones, is known in New Orleans as the "po" boy. It is highly recommended to assuage the fears of a frightened boy, or comfort the "boy" inside the man. If the latter, a glass of either British or American Brown Ale would be appropriate.

1	pint oysters and liquor
2	eggs
3	Tablespoons water
2	medium tomatoes
1/2	cup fine bread crumbs
8	slices bacon
1	Vienna loaf
1	cup dry white wine
2	Tablespoons butter
1	Tablespoon flour
	Hot pepper sauce
	Pinch of thyme

	Salt and freshly ground pepper
$^1/_2$	*thinly sliced green pepper*
$^1/_2$	*thinly sliced sweet onion*
4	*lemon wedges*

Dressing:

$^1/_2$	*cup mayonnaise*
1	*teaspoon Dijon mustard*
1	*teaspoon prepared horseradish*

OVEN TEMPERATURE: 400°

1. Separate the egg yolks from the whites, beat the yolks with 2 tablespoons of water, and beat 1 tablespoon of water into the whites.
2. Cut the tomatoes into 12 thin slices, dip in the egg yolk, coat with crumbs, and dry on a rack for 30 minutes. Reserve the remaining yolk mixture for use in the sauce.
3. Sauté the bacon in a skillet until crisp, and drain on absorbent paper.
4. Fry the tomato slices in the bacon drippings until brown on both sides; remove and drain.
5. Cut off the top of the loaf and scoop out the bread, leaving a ¼-inch shell. Brush the inside of the loaf and top with the egg whites. Bake top and bottom for about 10 minutes until they are golden.
6. Lightly poach the oysters in the liquor and wine; drain, reserving ⅔ cup of the poaching liquid.
7. Melt the butter in a saucepan, stir in the flour, and cook until light yellow. Remove from the heat and stir in the hot poaching liquid. Return to heat and cook, stirring constantly, until the mixture thickens.
8. Whisk the hot mixture into the reserved egg yolks, a spoonful at a time. Transfer the enriched sauce to the saucepan; season with a drop or two of hot pepper sauce and thyme. Stirring carefully, cook until bubbles form around the edge. Reduce heat.
9. Assemble the loaf by laying half the tomato slices on the bottom, spreading the oyster mixture, adding pepper and onion slices, and placing another layer of tomatoes and bacon. Replace the upper crust.
10. Wrap the loaf in foil and bake for 20 minutes.
11. Unwrap, cut off the ends, and slice with a serrated knife. Garnish with lemon wedges and serve the dressing on the side.

CARNIVAL LOAF

Ideal for a "Mardi Gras" buffet and a "trumpet-tooting" loaf for hundreds of other occasions, this picture-perfect stuffed oyster and spinach loaf can be prepared hours in advance, stored in the refrigerator, and heated in the oven about 45 minutes before serving. A round filled sourdough *boule* makes for a dramatic presentation, but a traditional Vienna loaf or baguette is equally festive. Serve with a toasty and moderate-bodied California Chardonnay.

1	pint medium oysters
6	slices diced bacon
1	10-inch boule
4	Tablespoons butter
1	minced garlic clove
3	eggs
3/4	cup mayonnaise
2	cups cooked chopped spinach
	Pinch of nutmeg
	Salt and freshly ground pepper
2	sliced medium tomatoes
1/2	cup freshly grated Parmesan cheese

OVEN TEMPERATURE: 350°

1. Drain the oysters, pat dry, and set aside.
2. Cook the bacon in a skillet until crisp and brown; drain on absorbent paper.
3. Slice off the top of the *boule*, and hollow out the center, leaving about a 1-inch shell. Process the soft bread in a blender for crumbs. Spread the inside and lid of the bread with butter creamed with the garlic.
4. Whisk the eggs in a bowl with the mayonnaise; add the spinach, bacon, nutmeg, salt, and pepper to taste.
5. Arrange half of the oysters on the bottom of the *boule*, cover with half of the spinach mixture, half of the tomato slices, a layer of crumbs, and half of the cheese. Repeat the layers, and replace the bread lid.
6. Wrap the loaf in foil and bake for 45 minutes.
7. Cut into 6 wedges with a serrated bread knife, and serve with a toss of watercress.

SEALED PACKAGE

Cut the top from a round loaf of bread and dig out all the crumb; butter the inside of the crust and brown in the oven. Fill with hot creamed oysters and put the cover back on. Cover the entire loaf with beaten egg yolk and put in the oven to glaze.

—MAY E. SOUTHWORTH,
One Hundred & One Ways of Serving Oysters, 1907

Scallywag Oyster Sandwiches

The picture-perfect and painstakingly decorated "open-faced" sandwiches that distinguish Continental cuisine are a tribute to the careful preparation that goes into the simplest snack. And while Americans do not usually serve "knife and fork" sandwiches, it might be a delightful thing to do, especially with oysters. Those "scallywags" are open to anything.

RYE, PLEASE
(*Serve with Graves Blanc*)

SERVES 4

24	*shucked oysters*
8	*slices rye bread*
4	*Tablespoons butter*
1	*teaspoon anchovy paste*
1	*cup grated Swiss cheese*
4	*Tablespoons bread crumbs*
1	*teaspoon grated lemon zest*
4	*lemon wedges*

OVEN TEMPERATURE: 400°

1. Toast the bread, remove crusts, and spread with butter creamed with anchovy paste.
2. Remove the oysters from the shells, pat dry, and coarsely chop, reserving the liquor for another use.
3. Combine the cheese with 2 tablespoons of the bread crumbs and lemon zest, and mix with the oysters. Spread mixture on toast, and top with the remaining crumbs.
4. Place on a lightly buttered baking sheet, bake for 10 minutes, and place under the broiler to brown the crumbs. Serve with lemon wedges.

MAKE MINE DANISH
(*Serve with Fino Sherry*)

SERVES 4

2	*3 ³/₄-ounce tins smoked oysters*
4	*slices firm pumpernickel bread*
2	*Tablespoons butter*
1	*Tablespoon finely chopped chives*
3	*Tablespoons finely chopped parsley*
1	*large tomato*

A Book of Verses underneath the Bough,

A Jug of Wine, a Loaf of Bread—and Thou

Beside me singing in the Wilderness—

Oh, Wilderness were Paradise enow!

—RUBAIYAT OF OMAR KHAYYAM

$^1/_2$	green pepper
2	hard-boiled eggs
	Salt and freshly ground pepper

1. Drain and rinse the oysters; drain again, pat dry, and chill.
2. Remove the crusts and spread the bread with butter creamed with chives and 1 tablespoon of parsley.
3. Cut the tomato into 8 thin slices; slice the pepper lengthwise into thin strips. Halve the eggs, press the yolks through a sieve, and cut the whites into thin lengthwise strips.
4. Arrange 2 tomato slices on each piece of bread and sprinkle lightly with salt and pepper; place the oysters on the tomatoes, top with egg yolks, and cut each sandwich diagonally in half.
5. Garnish with the pepper and egg white strips, and sprinkle the remaining parsley over the top.

OYSTER CROQUE MONSIEUR

SERVES 2

A seaside version of this crispy French toasted sandwich can be achieved by using a toasting iron in the form of a scallop shell. Ideal for lunch on the patio or deck, the sandwich needs only a tossed lightly dressed green salad and a bottle of Alsace Riesling.

6	freshly shucked small oysters
	Seasoned flour
1	whisked egg
1	teaspoon water
$^1/_2$	cup cornflake crumbs
	Oil for frying
	Soft butter
4	thin slices white bread
2	slices ham
6	Tablespoons freshly grated Gruyère cheese
	Cornichons (optional)

1. Remove the oysters from the shells and pat dry; dredge in flour, dip in the egg mixed with water, and roll in crumbs. Refrigerate for 15 minutes.
2. Heat the oil to 375° and deep-fry the oysters; drain on absorbent paper.

3. Butter the bread on both sides, and line the iron with 2 pieces; place a slice of ham, 3 oysters, and a generous sprinkling of cheese on each piece. Cover with another slice of bread, close the iron, and heat on the top of the stove. Remove the sandwiches when they are golden brown.
4. Serve with cornichons, if desired.

OYSTERS DERRING-DO

SERVES 8

Although Welsh Rarebit can bring many contrasting sensations into play, it always looks *good*, smells *good*, tastes *good*, and is adaptable. In Gloucester, England, cooks add a little mustard and ale to the "baked" cheese and serve it over thick brown toast. In Portugal, a rarebit is made with a little tomato purée and topped with sardines. Indian recipes call for some mango chutney and curry powder. And, way down South, sautéed onions and tomatoes are added to the cheese before it is spooned over fried bread. So, for a little "derring-do," layer tomato slices, fried oysters, and crumbled bacon. And open a bottle of Nut Brown Ale.

16	*shucked large oysters*
1	*whisked egg*
1	*Tablespoon water*
	Cornflake crumbs
8	*slices bacon*
	Oil for frying
1	*teaspoon dry mustard*
1	*teaspoon Worcestershire sauce*
6	*ounces evaporated milk*
1/2	*pound grated sharp Cheddar cheese*
3	*Tablespoons grated Parmigiano-Reggiano*
2	*Tablespoons Kirsch*
8	*slices white toast*
8	*thin slices tomato*
	Chopped parsley

1. Remove the oysters from the shells, pat dry; dip in the egg mixed with water, roll in crumbs, and chill at least 15 minutes.
2. Cook the bacon until brown and crisp in a skillet or microwave oven, drain on absorbent paper, and crumble.

*If you think the oysters will
be too much done by baking
them in the crust you can
substitute for them pieces
of bread, to keep up the
lid of the pie.*

*Put the oysters with their
liquor and the seasoning,
chopped egg, grated bread,
etc. into a pan. Cover them
closely, and let them just
come to a boil, taking
them off the fire, and
stirring them frequently.*

*When the crust is baked,
take the lid neatly off
(loosening it round the
edge with a knife), take out
the pieces of bread, and
put in the oysters.
Lay the lid on again
very carefully.*

—75 RECEIPTS, BY A
LADY OF PHILADELPHIA,
1830

SERVES 4

3. Fry the oysters, a few at a time, in 375° oil until they are golden on both sides; set aside on absorbent paper, and keep warm.
4. Mix the mustard, Worcestershire, milk, cheeses, and Kirsch in the top of a double boiler; cook over boiling water, stirring constantly, until the mixture is hot, smooth, and thick. Add milk if a thinner consistency is desired.
5. Trim the crusts from the toast, place a tomato slice and 2 oysters on each piece, nap with the rarebit, and top with bacon and a bit of parsley.
6. Serve immediately.

BEGUILING BRIOCHE

Mushrooms and oysters are at the top of the list of *la cuisine amoureuse et magique*. And oysters accept a cream sauce beautifully, especially when prepared with fine mushrooms like morels. These piping hot brioches can be a captivating luncheon in seconds. Or, better yet, entertain a prince charming after the theater or concert. Serve with Meursault.

1	pint oysters and liquor
1/2	cup cream
4	ounces fresh morels
4	slices diced bacon
2	Tablespoons butter
2	Tablespoons chopped shallots
2	Tablespoons flour
1/4	cup dry Vermouth
	Pinch of nutmeg
	Salt and freshly ground white pepper
4	brioches

OVEN TEMPERATURE: 325°

1. Drain the oysters and set aside. Combine ½ cup of the oyster liquor with the cream and heat in a small saucepan.
2. Quarter the morels, soak in water, and rinse several times. Blanch in boiling water for a minute, and drain. Set aside.
3. Cook bacon in a skillet until crisp and drain on absorbent paper.
4. Melt the butter in a saucepan and sauté the shallots until translucent, stir in flour, and cook until pale yellow. Remove from the heat, and

whisk in the cream mixture. Return to heat and cook, stirring constantly, until the mixture thickens; simmer for at least 5 minutes.

5. Add the oysters, Vermouth, nutmeg, and morels. Season to taste.

6. Slice off the tops of the brioches, hollow out the centers, and arrange the tops and bottoms on a baking sheet. Spoon the sauced oysters and morels into the bottoms and top with bacon.

7. Place the baking sheet in the oven and heat until the brioches begin to brown. Remove from the oven and replace tops.

8. Serve immediately with a medley of spring vegetables.

FOGGY BOTTOM OYSTERS

SERVES 8 A first course of creamed smoked oysters on made-for-the-occasion corn sticks can certainly make Maryland a "merry land" during the holidays. Adding some scraped corn to the batter will ensure a moist center, and using the traditional cast-iron molds guarantees a crust that will stand up to the creamed oysters. All other matters pertaining to cheer depend on the customary comestibles and wines like a Chateauneuf-du-Pape Blanc or Palo Cortado.

| 2 | 3 ¾-ounce tins smoked oysters |

Corn Sticks (about 16):

1¼	cups all-purpose flour
¾	cup cornmeal
2½	teaspoons baking powder
1	Tablespoon salt
1	cup milk
2	Tablespoons melted butter
2	eggs
	Oil for molds

3	Tablespoons minced shallots
⅔	cup dry white wine
2	cups heavy cream
1	Tablespoon lemon juice
2	Tablespoons chopped parsley
	Salt and freshly ground white pepper
	Salad greens

1. Drain the oysters, rinse, and drain again. Set aside.

2. Make the corn sticks by sifting the dry ingredients together. Stir in the milk, melted butter, and lightly beaten eggs. The batter will not be completely smooth.

3. Oil the molds generously and place in the oven until hot. Remove and fill three fourths full of batter. Bake until golden brown, about 20 minutes. Remove from oven.

4. Simmer the shallots and wine in a heavy saucepan until the wine has almost evaporated. Stir in the cream and cook uncovered until reduced by one third.

5. Add the oysters, lemon juice, parsley, and season to taste. Cook until piping hot.

6. Slice the corn sticks in half lengthwise, and arrange 2 on each plate. Spoon the creamed oysters over the bottom halves, and cover with the top halves. Garnish with salad greens.

OYSTERS NARRAGANSETT BAY

SERVES 6

Rhode Islanders are particular about their corn bread and Jo(h)nny Cake. Rightly so, since "whitecap flint" corn is grown and milled exclusively in the Ocean State. For a total effect, spoon creamed oysters and chicken over this corn bread. You might hear the mermaids singing, or, maybe, it will only be the sound of all those water-powered buhrstones grinding away. Serve with an Oregon Pinot Blanc.

1	pint oysters and liquor
2¼	cups chicken stock (see p. 59)
½	cup heavy cream
4	Tablespoons butter
4	Tablespoons flour
2	Tablespoons lemon juice
	Pinch of nutmeg
2	cups diced cooked chicken
1	Tablespoon chopped fresh sage
	Salt and freshly ground pepper
	Tabasco
	Hot corn bread
	Herb sprigs

1. Drain the oysters and heat ¼ cup of the oyster liquor with the stock and cream in a small saucepan.
2. Melt the butter in another saucepan, stir in the flour, and cook until pale yellow. Remove from the heat and stir in the stock mixture. Return to heat, add the lemon juice, and boil, stirring constantly, until the sauce thickens. Simmer at least 8 to 10 minutes. Add the nutmeg, chicken, and sage, and cook until thoroughly heated.
3. Add the oysters, and cook until the oysters begin to curl. Season to taste.
4. Cut the corn bread into serving-sized pieces, split open, and spoon the oyster mixture over each bottom piece. Set the tops in place and cover/ with the remaining sauce.
5. Garnish with herb sprigs and serve with buttered blanched aparagus spears.

OYSTERS BENEDICT

SERVES 4

Certainly no traitor to the cause of regional cuisine, this adaptation of Eggs Benedict must be "found out" as soon as possible. The Hollandaise sauce complements the oysters admirably, and a glass of Champagne or high-quality sparkling wine from California would probably make the host punishable for the high crime of overindulging the guests.

16	*shucked medium oysters and liquor*
8	*slices Canadian bacon*
4	*English muffins*
2	*Tablespoons butter*
1	*Tablespoon dry Sherry*
2	*Tablespoons finely chopped shallots*
	Freshly ground white pepper
1½	*cups warm Hollandaise sauce*
4	*lemon wedges*

OVEN TEMPERATURE: HIGH BROIL

1. Remove the oysters from the shells, strain, and reserve ¼ cup of the liquor.
2. Lightly sauté the slices of Canadian bacon in butter.
3. Split the English muffins and toast them in the broiler.

4. Heat the butter, oyster liquor, and Sherry in a saucepan and simmer the shallots until tender; add the oysters, season with pepper, and cook until the oysters are hot and plump.

5. Place 2 muffin halves on each plate, top with a slice of bacon, 2 oysters, and some of the pan juices. Nap generously with Hollandaise. Serve immediately with lemon wedges.

OYSTERS NEWPORT NEWS

In the South these biscuits might be made with sour milk, but using buttermilk or yogurt will also guarantee a biscuit that is flaky and crisp on the outside and moist within. Perfect for a luncheon on the patio, simply split these little wonders in half, ladle creamy oysters over them, and serve with a glass of well-chilled Riesling from Oregon.

1	pint oysters and liquor
1¼	cups medium cream
5	Tablespoons butter
2	Tablespoons flour
	Pinch of mace
2	Tablespoons finely chopped scallions
2	egg yolks
2	Tablespoons dry Sherry
	Salt and freshly ground pepper
4	large baking powder biscuits
	Lemon wedges
½	cup sautéed oyster mushrooms

1. Drain the oysters and set aside. Add ¼ cup of liquor to ¾ cup cream and heat in a small saucepan.

2. Melt 3 tablespoons of the butter in another saucepan, stir in the flour, mace, and scallions, and cook until the scallions are soft. Remove from the heat and whisk in the cream. Return to heat and simmer, stirring constantly, until the mixture thickens. Simmer for 5 minutes.

3. Beat the egg yolks and the remaining ½ cup of cream in a bowl. Whisk in ½ cup of the hot mixture, a spoonful at a time. Slowly beat in the remaining hot mixture, then transfer the enriched sauce back to the saucepan and, stirring carefully, bring to a boil. Reduce heat.

SERVES 4

SHORTCAKE

Make a rich biscuit short-cake as for berries. Pick over the oysters carefully; strain the liquor, season and cook the oysters in this. Just as the shortcake comes from the oven split it and butter both inside crusts lavishly; lift the oysters with a fork and lay thick on the under buttered cake; season with pepper and salt and cover with the top crust. Thicken the gravy with flour rubbed smooth with butter; add cream and pour it hot over the shortcake the last moment before serving.

—MAY E. SOUTHWORTH,
One Hundred & One Ways of Serving Oysters,
1907

4. Add the oysters and Sherry, season to taste, and cook until the edges of the oysters start to curl.
5. Split and butter the warm biscuits. Put the bottoms on individual plates and ladle over a portion of the oyster sauce; replace the tops and cover with the remaining sauce.
6. Spoon sautéed mushrooms over the biscuits and garnish with lemon wedges.

MERRY OLDE OYSTER PYE

SERVES 4

Deep dish and "savoury" best describe the "main course" pies that England justifiably boasts. Topped with herbed biscuits or a flaky crust, this pie will surely prove that simple is best, as does a rich California or Oregon Chardonnay served with it.

1	pint oysters and liquor
1¹/₂	cups light cream
6	Tablespoons butter
6	Tablespoons flour
3	Tablespoons Madeira
	Salt and freshly ground pepper
6	partially baked 2-inch biscuits*
	Paprika

OVEN TEMPERATURE: 425°

1. Drain the oysters. Pour ¼ cup of strained liquor into a saucepan, add the cream, and heat.
2. Melt the butter in another saucepan, stir in the flour, and cook until golden. Remove from the heat and whisk in the hot liquids. Return to heat, add the Madeira, and cook, stirring constantly, until the mixture thickens. Simmer for at least 5 minutes.
3. Stir in the oysters, season to taste, and heat until the oysters plump.
4. Pour the hot oysters into a 1-quart buttered casserole, arrange the biscuits on top, and sprinkle with paprika.
5. Bake about 10 minutes until the biscuits are completely baked and golden brown. Serve immediately with a medley of cooked julienned root vegetables.

*Use a standard recipe for baking powder biscuits and mix ½ teaspoon sage or rosemary with the dry ingredients. Roll the dough ½ inch thick and bake the biscuits for 8 minutes.

Many of the old fashioned rusks were made with yeast dough. Rusks have come to have an entirely different meaning from what they had several generations ago. Today a rusk is looked upon as a dried sweetened bread, not unlike toast.

—IMOGENE WOLCOTT,
The New England Yankee Cook Book

PANCAKES, WAFFLES, CRÊPES

SERVES 4

OYSTER PIE

Line a deep dish that will hold rather more than a quart, with a good pie-crust nearly half an inch thick. Strain the liquor from a quart of oysters. Put in the bottom of the dish a layer of fine cracker or bread crumbs; then add the oysters, with bits of butter and mace, a little pepper and salt, and a part of the liquor. The liquor should fill the dish only about one-half. Over the oysters put another layer of fine crumbs, and cover with pie-crust. Cut an opening in the top of the crust, and ornament with leaves of pastry. Bake about an hour. Brown gradually. Serve the pie hot. A pie containing a pint, or a pint and a half of oysters, is large enough for a family of two or three.

—(MRS.) M. H. CORNELIUS, *The Young Housekeeper's Friend,* 1871

NIP AND TUCK GRIDDLE CAKES

With a little forethought and on-the-spot dexterity, these oyster griddle cakes can be made while the Sunday morning coffee is brewing. Tuck into place on a serving tray, and nip with a bit of sauce for a breakfast in bed that succeeds entirely. And as long as the Champagne bottle is open, a glass would be in order.

12	*shucked large oysters and liquor*
3/4	*cup Champagne*
1	*chopped small onion*
1/2	*cup bread crumbs*
2	*eggs*
3	*Tablespoons melted butter*
1/4	*cup milk*
3/4	*cup sifted flour*
1	*teaspoon baking powder*
	Salt
	Canola oil

Sauce:

1	*cup sour cream*
1/4	*cup mayonnaise*
1/4	*cup medium cream*
1	*Tablespoon prepared horseradish*
1	*Tablespoon chopped chives*

1. Make the sauce by combining the sour cream, mayonnaise, cream, horseradish, and chives in a mixing bowl and whisk until smooth. Refrigerate.
2. Remove the oysters from the shells; strain ¼ cup of the liquor.
3. Heat the oyster liquor and Champagne in a saucepan and lightly poach the oysters.
4. Pour the oysters and poaching liquid into the work bowl of a processor fitted with the steel blade. Add the onion, bread crumbs, eggs, butter, milk, flour, baking powder, and salt, and process until smooth. Add a little milk to the mixture if it is too thick to make thin pancakes.
5. Heat a griddle or skillet until a drop of water sizzles on the surface and brush with canola oil. Use 2 tablespoons of batter for each pancake, or

enough to make a 4-inch cake. When bubbles form on top, turn the pancakes, and brown the other side. Keep warm in the oven until all are fried.

6. Serve with butter and sauce.

WAFFLES HIGH HAMPTON

SERVES 4   A winter holiday breakfast with a festive glass of sparkling wine or a poolside brunch with Bellinis are engaging alternatives for these crowd pleasers. Either way, oysters and waffles are a feast for all seasons.

1	*pint oysters and liquor*
4	*Tablespoons butter*
¼	*pound button mushrooms*
1½	*cups cream*
¼	*cup dry Sherry*
2	*Tablespoons brandy*
6	*egg yolks*
	Salt and freshly ground pepper
	Paprika
4	*large hot waffles*

1. Drain the oysters, reserving ⅓ cup of the liquor.
2. Melt the butter in a 1½-quart saucepan, stir in the oysters and mushrooms, and cook until the oysters are plump; remove the oysters and mushrooms with a slotted spoon and set aside.
3. Add the oyster liquor, 1 cup cream, Sherry, and brandy to the saucepan and simmer, uncovered, for 3 minutes.
4. Whisk the egg yolks in a bowl with the remaining ½ cup of cream. Beat in ½ cup of the hot mixture, one spoonful at a time; then slowly whisk in the remaining hot mixture. Transfer the enriched sauce to the saucepan, and stir until bubbles form around the edge. Add the oysters and mushrooms, and season to taste. Keep hot.
5. Spoon over the waffles and add a dash of paprika. Serve with baked ham or fried Canadian bacon.

SERVES 6

Not a staple of Indian cuisine, oysters have, nevertheless, benefited from the range of spices and culinary styles exported from that country. The light curry flavor of these crêpes is a tempting "trade-off" for ordinary luncheon fare, especially if served with tall glasses of spiced ice tea.

$1^{1}/_{2}$ pints oysters and liquor
12   6-inch crêpes
2   finely chopped scallions
$^{1}/_{2}$ pound washed and stemmed spinach
1   cup dry white wine
1   cup medium cream
4   Tablespoons butter
2   Tablespoons flour
1   teaspoon curry powder
2   egg yolks
     Pinch of cayenne
     Salt and freshly ground pepper
     Chopped fresh coriander

1. Place pieces of foil between the crêpes and stack them on a heatproof plate; cover, and keep warm over boiling water or in the oven.
2. In a frying pan sweat the scallions in butter; add spinach and wilt. Drain and set aside.
3. Heat wine in a medium saucepan, add oysters and liquor, and poach until the edges begin to curl. Remove with a slotted spoon and, if they are large, cut in quarters, and set aside.
4. Reduce the poaching liquid to 1 cup; add ¾ cup of cream and reheat.
5. Melt the butter in another saucepan, stir in the flour and curry powder, and cook until dark yellow. Remove from the heat and whisk in the hot liquids. Return to heat and cook, stirring constantly, until the mixture thickens; simmer for at least 5 minutes.
6. Beat the egg yolks in a bowl with the remaining ¼ cup of cream. Whisk ½ cup of the hot mixture into the yolks, a spoonful at a time; slowly beat in the remaining hot mixture. Transfer the enriched sauce to the saucepan, and, stirring carefully, bring to a boil. Reduce heat, and season to taste with cayenne, salt, and pepper.

7. Combine oysters, scallions, and spinach in a bowl. Stir some of the sauce into the bowl to bind the oyster and spinach filling. Spoon about 2 tablespoons of the filling on each crêpe. Roll and arrange the crêpes, seam-side-down, on individual serving plates. Nap with the remaining hot sauce, garnish with fresh coriander, and serve immediately.

OYSTERS HAMILTON PLACE

SERVES 8

A century ago, this short avenue was where some of Boston's wealthiest families resided in "luxury and calm." Appropriately named, the following dish combines creamed oysters, paper-thin crêpes, and a whipped cream and caviar garnish to continue the tradition of elegance associated with the location, architecture, and distinguished past of Hamilton Place. Serve with Champagne.

1	*quart oysters and liquor*
1	*cup light cream*
3	*Tablespoons butter*
2	*Tablespoons flour*
4	*egg yolks*
	Pinch of nutmeg
1	*Tablespoon lemon juice*
	Salt and freshly ground pepper
16	*7-inch crêpes*
1	*cup whipped unsweetened cream*
	Caviar

1. Layer pieces of foil between the crêpes and stack them on an ovenproof plate; cover, and heat over boiling water or in a warm oven.
2. Drain the oysters, reserving ½ cup of the liquor. Heat the liquor and ¾ cup of the cream in a small saucepan.
3. Melt the butter in another saucepan, stir in the flour, and cook until straw yellow. Remove from the heat and whisk in the cream. Return to heat and cook, stirring constantly, until the mixture thickens; simmer for at least 5 minutes.
4. Beat the egg yolks and remaining ¼ cup of cream in a bowl. Whisk in ½ cup of the hot mixture, a spoonful at a time; then slowly beat in the remaining hot mixture. Transfer the enriched sauce to the saucepan, and bring to a boil. Reduce heat, and simmer.

5. Stir in the nutmeg, oysters, and lemon juice, and season to taste. Cook until the edges of the oysters begin to curl.
6. Place about 2 tablespoons of the filling on each crêpe. Roll the crêpes and arrange, seam-side-down, on a serving platter or on individual plates.
7. Garnish with whipped cream and a dab of caviar. Serve immediately.

CHARTWELL OYSTER CRÊPES

SERVES 12

These "do-ahead" crêpes are the passport to a perfect party. No need for the cook to do anything more than tossing a salad and opening a few bottles of Hermitage Blanc or dry Vouvray when guests arrive.

1	*quart oysters and liquor*
3	*cups chicken stock (see p. 59)*
3	*pounds broccoli*
1	*cup butter*
$^1/_2$	*cup flour*
1	*teaspoon nutmeg*
$^1/_3$	*cup dry Vermouth*
1	*pint crème fraîche*
$1^1/_2$	*cups freshly grated Fontina or Morbier cheese*
	Salt and freshly ground pepper
24	*7-inch crêpes*
1	*cup sliced almonds*

OVEN TEMPERATURE: 350°

1. Drain the oysters and place them in a large bowl, reserving ⅔ cup of the liquor. Heat the liquor and chicken stock in a saucepan.
2. Wash, peel stems, and blanch the broccoli in boiling salted water for 3 minutes; refresh in cold water, drain, finely chop stems, and separate florets.
3. Melt 4 tablespoons of butter in a large saucepan and toss the broccoli until it is well coated; remove and set aside with the oysters.
4. Melt the remaining butter, stir in the flour, and cook until straw yellow. Remove from the heat and whisk in the stock. Return to heat and cook, stirring constantly, for at least 10 minutes. Add nutmeg, Vermouth,

crème fraîche, and cheese. Cook on low to moderate heat until the cheese is melted into the sauce. Season to taste.

5. Stir enough of the sauce into the oysters and broccoli to bind.

6. Spoon some of the sauce on the bottom of a shallow buttered baking dish. Fill each crêpe with about 2 tablespoons of the oyster mixture; roll up the crêpes and arrange them in one layer, seam-side-down. Nap the crêpes with sauce, sprinkle sliced almonds on top, and bake until the sauce begins to brown at the edges of the dish, about 20 to 30 minutes. Serve immediately.

PASTRIES

OYSTERS LA NACELLE

SERVES 6

Up, up, and away in these puffy-pastry baskets. What oyster wouldn't feel on top of the world in this cream sauce brimming with mushrooms, peppers, and spirits? And for the ladies who lunch, a glass of California Sauvignon Blanc will add to the festive mood.

1	*pint oysters and liquor*
1	*cup light cream*
4	*Tablespoons butter*
3	*Tablespoons finely chopped celery*
2	*Tablespoons finely chopped green pepper*
2	*Tablespoons flour*
	Pinch of nutmeg
1	*Tablespoon dry Sherry*
$^1/_2$	*cup stemmed and quartered button mushrooms*
1	*Tablespoon chopped pimiento*
	Salt and freshly ground pepper
6	*large puff-pastry shells*
	Chopped chervil

1. Drain the oysters, pat dry, and cut in halves or quarters. Heat ¼ cup of the strained oyster liquor and the cream in a small saucepan.

2. Melt the butter in another saucepan and sauté the celery and pepper until soft; remove from pan and set aside. Stir the flour into the butter and cook until straw color. Remove from the heat and whisk in the cream. Return to heat and cook, stirring constantly, for 5 to 8 minutes.

...*secret and*
self-contained, and
solitary as an oyster.

—CHARLES DICKENS

Add the oysters, celery, green pepper, nutmeg, Sherry, mushrooms, and pimiento.
3. Heat until the edges of the oysters curl; season to taste.
4. Spoon the sauce into warm pastry shells, garnish with a bit of chervil, and serve immediately.

TWELFTH NIGHT OYSTER TARTS

SERVES 6   These Cognac-and-wine-laced tarts are exactly right for the wind-down of the Christmas holidays when a little heavy orchestration is needed for the last gathering of the season. Be traditional, serve with a glass of Macon and hide a pistachio nut in three of them in honor of the Three Kings. The festive topping hides all.

1	*pint oysters and liquor*
1¹/₂	*cups dry white wine*
¹/₂	*pound raw medium shrimp*
1	*cup medium cream*
7	*Tablespoons butter*
¹/₄	*cup minced shallots*
1	*pound sliced wild mushrooms (chanterelles, parasols, morels, meadows)*
4	*Tablespoons flour*
2	*egg yolks*
¹/₂	*teaspoon nutmeg*
2	*Tablespoons Cognac*
	Salt and freshly ground pepper
¹/₄	*cup fresh bread crumbs*
¹/₄	*cup grated Parmigiano-Reggiano*
¹/₄	*cup chopped almonds*
6	*4 ¹/₂-inch baked tart shells*

OVEN TEMPERATURE: 425°

1. Add 1 cup of wine to the oyster liquor and poach the oysters until plump; remove with a slotted spoon, pat dry, and set aside in a warm place.
2. Rinse the shrimp and poach for 2 minutes in the same liquid; refresh in cold water, shell, devein, and add to oysters. Reduce the liquid to 1 cup, strain, add 1 cup cream, and heat.

3. Melt 1 tablespoon of butter in a sauté pan, sauté the shallots until limp, add ½ cup of wine and mushrooms, and sauté until the liquid evaporates. Set aside.
4. Melt 6 tablespoons of butter in a saucepan. Spoon off 2 tablespoons into a bowl for the bread crumbs. Stir flour into the butter and cook until straw yellow. Remove from the heat and whisk in the hot poaching liquid and cream. Return to heat, and cook for 5 to 8 minutes, stirring constantly.
5. Beat the egg yolks in a bowl with the remaining ½ cup of cream. Whisk in ½ cup of the hot mixture, a spoonful at a time. Slowly beat in the remaining hot mixture and transfer the enriched sauce to the saucepan. Add nutmeg and Cognac and, stirring carefully, bring to a boil. Reduce heat.
6. Stir in the oysters, shrimp, and mushrooms, and season to taste.
7. Mix bread crumbs with the melted butter; add cheese and almonds.
8. Assemble the tarts on a baking sheet and spoon the shellfish and mushroom sauce into the shells. Top with the buttered crumb mixture.
9. Bake from 5 to 10 minutes or until hot and golden brown on top, remove from the oven, and serve.

GOVERNOR'S OYSTER PIE

SERVES 6

If this recipe brings Williamsburg to mind, then little will be lost in the translation of colonial Virginia's hospitality into a more contemporary idiom. Set an out-of-the-brick-oven pie on a King's Arms trivet, lay out the best "Queen's Ware," open a bottle of Macon, and light the tapers in the supper room—"That the Future May Learn From the Past." *Colonial Williamsburg Foundation*

1½   *pints oysters and liquor*
1   *cup cream*
4   *Tablespoons butter*
4   *Tablespoons flour*
      Pinch of nutmeg
¼   *cup dry Sherry*
1   *Tablespoon lemon juice*
1½   *cups sliced chestnut mushrooms*
      Salt and freshly ground pepper
      Cheddar cheese pastry dough for a 2-crust 9-inch pie*

*Substitute 1 cup freshly grated Cheddar cheese for 3 ounces of the regular shortening.

SOTTERLY OYSTER PYE

Take a quart of large oysters, parboil them in their liquor, a little bread grated, an onion and savoury spices. When the Pye is baked, take out the onion from the oysters, pour them in the Pye, lay on butter and close it with your Paste.

—MISS ANN CHASE'S BOOK, *Annapolis, 1811*

SERVES 6–8

OVEN TEMPERATURE: 400°

1. Drain the oysters, reserving ½ cup of liquor. Mix the liquor and cream, and heat in a small saucepan.
2. Melt the butter in another saucepan, stir in the flour, and cook until straw yellow. Remove from the heat and whisk in the cream mixture. Return to heat; add nutmeg, Sherry, and lemon juice; and cook, stirring constantly, for at least 5 minutes.
3. Add the oysters and mushrooms, and season to taste.
4. Roll the pastry ⅛ inch thick; line the bottom of the pie pan, fill with the oyster mixture, and cover with a top crust. Seal the edges and make a few 1½-inch slashes in the top crust.
5. Bake about 40 minutes until the crust is golden brown.

DOCKSIDE PIZZA

This adaptation of a Cote d'Azur recipe goes a long way toward transforming the plebeian image of pizza into a chic, dockside luncheon treat. Serve with a local wine like Tavel or any rosé from Provence.

1	pint oysters
2	Tablespoons olive oil
1	28-ounce can peeled chopped tomatoes
2	Tablespoons tomato paste
½	teaspoon chopped fresh thyme
½	teaspoon chopped fresh oregano
1	bay leaf
¼	teaspoon lemon juice
1	garlic clove
	Pinch of cayenne pepper
	Salt and freshly ground pepper
1	pound washed and stemmed spinach
½	cup thinly sliced onion rings
12	anchovy fillets
	Dough for 2 12-inch pizzas
2	cups shredded Mozzarella cheese

OVEN TEMPERATURE: 400°

1. Drain the oysters, pat dry, and set aside.
2. Heat 1 tablespoon of oil in a heavy 1½-quart saucepan. Add tomatoes, tomato paste, thyme, oregano, bay leaf, lemon juice, garlic, and cayenne. Cook, uncovered, over medium heat about 30 minutes until the sauce is thick. Discard the bay leaf and garlic. Season to taste.
3. Pour ½ tablespoon olive oil in a sauté pan, and sauté spinach until wilted. Drain well and season.
4. Add another ½ tablespoon olive oil to the pan, and cook onion slices until soft.
5. Rinse the anchovy fillets and drain.
6. Roll the dough into 2 12-inch circles and place on a greased baking sheet. Spoon tomato sauce over the dough, top with spinach, oysters, onion slices, anchovies, and cheese.
7. Bake in the center of the oven about 20 minutes until the crust is golden brown and the cheese is completely melted. Let stand a few minutes, cut, and serve.

Quiche

Recent popularity notwithstanding, quiche has long been a convenient and customary word in Continental cuisine. Spelled *kechel* in Old English, it meant a small cake. And when Chaucer, who was as interested in his characters' dining habits as he was in their tales, used it as a "Goddes Kechyl or trype of cheese," he probably had in mind a cake given as alms. While neither Escoffier nor Francatelli mention *quiche* in their cookery books, at some point in time the word quiche became useful to describe an egg-and-bacon flan popular in Lorraine and the three-cheese, open-face pie associated with Valenciennes.

Even today, quiche is thought of as regional—the English Cheddar flan, the New York smoked-salmon-and-dill quiche, and the ham and Swiss savory pie found in suburban shopping malls. As a rags-to-riches phenomenon any ingredient from the lowly onion to the opulent oyster will do, and is just right for a luncheon or supper entrée, especially when paired with a light Chardonnay.

The following recipes roam and range a bit, adding compatible spirits, herbs, vegetables, and cheese to the basic egg and cream mixture. The extravagance of using oysters has been its own reward.

YANKEE CLIPPER QUICHE

SERVES 6

1	pint oysters and liquor
1	teaspoon butter
1/2	pound washed, stemmed spinach
3	eggs
6	ounces cream cheese
1 1/2	cups half-and-half
2	Tablespoons flour
	Pinch of nutmeg
	Salt and freshly ground pepper
1	10-inch unbaked pie shell
1/4	cup chopped chives
1/4	cup chopped parsley
1/4	cup sautéed chopped scallions
1	cup grated Swiss-type cheese
3	Tablespoons grated Parmesan cheese

OVEN TEMPERATURE: 375°

1. Drain the oysters, pat dry, and cut in halves or quarters if large; strain and reserve ¼ cup of the oyster liquor.
2. Melt butter in a sauté pan, and wilt spinach. Squeeze moisture from spinach.
3. Put eggs, softened cream cheese, oyster liquor, half-and-half, flour, and nutmeg in a blender and mix. Season to taste.
4. Arrange the oysters in the chilled pastry shell; cover with chives, parsley, scallions, and grated cheese. Pour the egg mixture on top.
5. Bake about 45 minutes, until the custard is set and the top a golden brown; remove from oven and let stand for 5 minutes before serving.

KETTLE COVE QUICHE
(Serve with an Alsace Gewurztraminer)

SERVES 4

1	pint oysters
1	Tablespoon chopped fresh chives
1	Tablespoon chopped fresh tarragon
1	Tablespoon chopped fresh chervil

1	Tablespoon chopped fresh parsley
4	thin onion slices
1½	cups light cream
3	eggs
3	Tablespoons dry Sherry
	Salt and freshly ground pepper
3	Tablespoons diced smoked salmon
1	partially baked 9-inch pie shell
½	cup freshly grated Gruyère or Swiss-type cheese

OVEN TEMPERATURE: 375°

1. Drain oysters and pat dry.
2. Add the herbs and onion slices to the cream and scald in a saucepan. Remove the onions with a slotted spoon, and set aside. Strain the cream and cool.
3. Beat the eggs in a bowl, add the cream and Sherry, and season to taste.
4. Place the salmon in the pie shell; add the oysters, onion slices, and cheese. Pour the egg and cream mixture into the shell.
5. Bake in the upper third of the oven about 30 minutes until a knife, inserted near the edge, comes out clean.
6. Remove from oven and allow the quiche to stand for about 5 minutes before serving.

At an oyster supper, it is usual to have all the various preparations of oysters, fried, stewed, broiled, roasted, raw and in patties. Potatoes mashed, and browned, are generally added. The roasted oysters are served in the shell, on very large dishes, and brought in 'hot and hot,' all the time, as they are generally eaten much faster then they can be cooked. Small buckets (usually of maple or stained wood, with brass hoops) are placed on the floor, for the purpose of receiving the shells, beside the chairs of the gentlemen; as the business of opening the oysters mostly devolves on them. At the right hand of each plate is placed a thick folded towel and an oyster knife, which is used only to open the shell; at the other side of the napkin, fork, bread, tumbler, wine-glasses, etc. On the side-table let there be plenty of plates, knives and forks to change with; a basket of bread or light rolls; pitchers of water; bottles of port and cider; decanters of wine being on the table. Several butter plates, with a knife to each, should be set along the table. Sometimes the butter is made into the shape of a pineapple or basket of flowers.

—*Miss Leslie's House Book*, 1841

Oyster Entrées

Early accounts of "oyster suppers" at which bushels of "fried, steamed, boiled, roasted and [pattied]" oysters were consumed sound capricious today and thoroughly out of tune with contemporary culinary trends, lifestyles, and dining habits. Except for the regional once-a-year oyster festivals that are sponsored along the eastern seaboard and in the Pacific Northwest, all the tales of the surfeit of oysters enjoyed at Roman banquets, in Dickensian oyster bars, and at late evening suppers by the Diamond Jim Bradys of this world are simply reminders of a time long gone, the never-never wonderland of the Walrus and Carpenter and "oysters four," or four hundred.

No longer plentiful, threatened by complex coastal pollution problems, the oyster has literally become the "pearl of great price." And, like the pearl, it is valued, even treasured, and usually shown off to its greatest advantage. The celebrated celebrate with freshly shucked oysters on the half shell or with the legendary and luxurious Rockefellers. High life below the stairs at Grand Central Station means a bowl of creamy oyster stew. And *de rigueur* for the wee hours of Mardi Gras morning is a "po" boy loaf and a cup of *café brulot*.

Curiously, oysters as the main course in a well-orchestrated meal will not be found in the hallowed halls of haute cuisine, but seem to be the "regulars," the fried oyster entrée, featured in the fish-and-chip restaurants that line the harbors and piers of major ports.

It may be an image problem, and, perhaps, a culinary one as well. Seneca wrote that oysters "are not really food, but are relished to bully the sated stomach into further eating." Evidence of the absence of *cuisine minceur* in ancient Rome or at the court of Louis XIV are the bushels of oysters swallowed as a prelude to a meal, as appetite teasers but never as the main course.

Fortunately, a fresh new wind, gaining momentum on both the Atlantic and Pacific coasts, is blowing the briny scent of oysters across the land today. Lighter meals, low-sodium diets, simple sautéed and stir-fried methods of preparation, encourage greater use of the oyster as an elegant entrée.

The "secret and self-contained, and solitary oyster" like a demanding lover wants more than its share of time and attention in the kitchen. And its needs must be anticipated and respected. If neglected, an oyster will overcook in a split second or wallow in a soggy batter. Oysters resist steaming for so long that they are tough before their shells pop open. And, while stovetop, liquid cooking may be a brief and necessary first step in some recipes, poaching is not generally an effective way to prepare and serve oysters as a main course. Caution is "writ large" when planning an oyster entrée: careful timing and the fundamentals of each cooking technique should realistically be considered before selecting the mode of preparation.

French-frying virtually guarantees a succulent juicy oyster hidden within a firm tasty coating, providing the frying is done with the proper in gredients, utensils, and skill. The advantages of stir-frying, on the other hand, extend to the last-minute alliance of freshly shucked oysters and tender-crisp vegetables.

Sautéeing or pan-frying results in a crisper and tastier oyster dish than the "panned" or "mock-roasted" cooking method of yesterday, which often resulted in overcooked or "stewed"

oysters. And spooning a lightly thickened or reduced sauce over the oysters after frying instead of heating them in a sauce really enhances the flavor of all the ingredients used and keeps the oysters from sagging.

The benefits of baking oysters in a loaf or a simple crumb mixture effectively states the case that less is better than more when cooking this favorite mollusk of emperors and kings. "Scalloped oysters," served *en casserole* or in the traditional scallop shell, continues to be a classic way of preparing oysters, and a delicious one.

Whether the oysters are grilled on wood charcoal, or skewered and single-layered in a broiling pan, or kept on the half shell and laced with a bit of butter, the speed and intensity of broiling make this technique a "sorcerer's magic" way to transform raw oysters into an exciting entrée. Enhanced with a delicate, wine-scented, reduced sauce, they retain every ounce of flavor.

This chapter suggests that modern ovens, woks, deep-fryers, indoor and outdoor grills, and rotisseries are viable alternatives to the hot coals of colonial fireplaces and wood-burning stoves. And, while "Oyster Roasts" will never be elegant dining, a menu planned around an oyster entrée and an important bottle of Chablis can be a significant "visiting card" to a home where the old traditions have been transformed and yet respected.

Suggestions

- Bulk oysters may be considerably smaller than oysters purchased in the shell, which can be selected for size. An average-sized eastern oyster is 3 to 4 inches long; a large oyster is about 5 inches. Some Pacific oysters are larger, and "knife and fork" oysters are as large as a plate. In all cases the size of the oyster determines the appropriate number needed for a "main course" serving. Average-sized oysters are used in determining the number of servings suggested in the recipes unless large or small are specified.
- The amount of seasoning in a coating, batter, or "seasoned" crumb mixture depends on the saltiness of the oysters being prepared. Test the oyster liquor as a gauge of salinity.
- Oven temperature and thermostats vary considerably. The temperatures listed in the recipes may have to be regulated or adjusted to suit a specific unit.
- High-heat methods of cooking oysters result in a tastier dish if a marinade, basting sauce, simple coating, or batter is used in their preparation. The lighter the coating, the better.
- When frying oysters, use polyunsaturated oils that have a high "smoke point." They are more effective than olive oil, butter, lard, and other shortenings that have a low smoke point, or temperature at which the oil begins to break down. The ideal range for most recipes is 360° to 375°.
- The amount of oil depends on the fryer or pan. A commercial French-fryer is ideal but, lacking this, a saucepan can be used if filled at least half full of oil. Too much oil can make the oyster "greasy"; too little oil causes burning or rapid browning. Use enough oil to permit the oysters to "swim."
- Certain coatings need "basket" frying, and batter coatings require "dropping" into hot oil. The temperature of the oil will drop when the oysters are added. Care should be taken not to crowd the fryer. The second and third "batches" will have a tendency to brown faster if the temperature is not carefully regulated.
- Fried foods should be placed on absorbent paper to drain and be kept warm in a moderate oven until served. Do not stack or cover, and always serve on hot plates because cold plates cause condensation.
- Fritters are traditionally French-fried, but they can also be fried on a lightly coated griddle or in a skillet if a flat or "pancake" type of fritter is desired.
- French-fried oysters are usually served with sauces from the mayonnaise or Hollandaise family, or with one of the hot butter sauces.
- At a typical Chinese meal, at least four entrées are served. For ease in preparation, a soup and one or two steamed dishes will facilitate the preliminaries and last-minute cooking of the stir-fried dish.
- All the ingredients of a stir-fry dish should be similar in size and shape to accommodate the short cooking time.
- Stir-fry recipes cannot be doubled unless a second wok is used.
- When sautéing, it is important to use enough butter to prevent the coated oysters from sticking to the bottom of the skillet.
- Use clarified butter or butter fortified with a third the amount of vegetable oil.

- To keep the oysters crisp, sauce the dish just before serving. If a sauce has enough consistency, spoon it on the plate first and then place the oysters in the center of the sauce.
- A large grilling surface is essential to accommodate the number of oysters-in-the-shell needed for an entrée and for the heating pans required to keep them warm.

- Tongs and heavy gloves are helpful when taking the oysters from the grill and removing the top shell.
- Even when threaded through the adductor muscle, oysters resist skewering. It is advisable to wrap the oyster in bacon, leek leaves, or a layer of onion to keep it in place when grilling kebabs.

FRENCH-FRY

Oysters with Tartar Sauce
With Andalouse Sauce
Southwestern Style with Salsa Fresca
Tempura Style with Dipping Sauce
Crispy Sesame Style with
Ginger Sauce
In Beer Batter with
West Indies Hot Pepper Sauce
Oyster Croquettes with Saffron Sauce
Oyster and Corn Fritters with
Salsa Verde

STIR-FRY

Oysters and Vegetables in Oyster Sauce
Oysters in Black Bean and Oyster Sauce
Oysters and Chicken in Oyster Sauce
Oysters and Steak Oriental
Pork and Dried Oysters in Oyster Sauce
Oyster Egg Foo Yong

SAUTÉ

Oysters au Citron
Oysters Tarragon
Bard's Oysters
Oysters Parmigiana
Oysters Finocchio

BAKE

Scalloped Oysters
With Mushrooms
With Bacon
Baked Expectations

BROIL-GRILL

Charcoal-Grilled Oysters
Stageharbor Oysters
Mixed Grill en Brochette
Mustard-Glazed Oysters

FRENCH-FRY

Possibly no cooking technique has suffered more from abuse than French-frying or "deep-frying." Even the ingredients associated with it—oil, lard, fat, grease—make one shudder at the thought of calories, cholesterol, and corpulence. But nothing with "French" on the label can be all bad. Who hasn't savored a perfect potato puff teasingly placed next to a double-grilled lamb chop, or a heavenly hot plate of just-fried scallops rushed to the table with a wreath of parsley, or a perfectly French-fried oyster, thin-coated and crisp without, moist and delicious within? There is definitely something to be said about this import.

The current popularity of polyunsaturated oils and the convenience of commercial "deep-fryers," also, have gone a long way to dispel visions of sizzling grease, floating burnt particles, and heavy soggy food. Actually a "dry" method of cooking, French-frying is a plus in the preparation of many foods, especially the oyster. It seals in the natural flavor and juices, cooks the oysters quickly and uncompromisingly, and makes them the *pièce de résistance* of any supper or dinner menu.

The following recipes include simple coatings as well as batter coatings and a variety of cold and warm sauces. Many purists believe that a superlatively French-fried oyster needs little more than a wedge of lemon for its success, although tartar sauce is a classic accompaniment, and other sauces also can offer either a stingingly sharp piquancy or a delicate embellishment. Preference is the key to use. Planning and preparation is all.

OYSTERS WITH TARTAR SAUCE
(Serve with Pilsner)

SERVES 3

24   *shucked large oysters*
      Vegetable or peanut oil for frying
      Lemon wedges

Simple coating:
1½   *cups flour*
2   *whisked egg whites*
      Fine dry bread crumbs

Tartar sauce:
1   *cup mayonnaise*
½   *cup sour cream*
3   *Tablespoons minced cornichons*

1	minced shallot
2	Tablespoons chopped chives
2	Tablespoons minced parsley
1	Tablespoon minced fresh tarragon
1	Tablespoon capers
1	Tablespoon white wine vinegar
	Pinch of cayenne pepper

1. Make the sauce by combining all the ingredients and adding vinegar to taste. Refrigerate for at least 2 hours before serving.
2. Remove the oysters from the shells, drain, and pat dry, reserving the liquor for another use.
3. Dip the oysters in flour, egg whites, and roll in bread crumbs. Set aside.
4. Heat the oil to 375° in a deep-fryer or heavy-gauge saucepan.
5. Place a few of the oysters in the bottom of a fryer basket, taking care not to crowd it. Lower the basket into the hot fat and fry the oysters until they are golden brown. Remove, drain on a baking sheet lined with absorbent paper, and keep warm in a hot oven until all the oysters are fried.
6. Serve immediately with lemon wedges and tartar sauce.

OYSTERS WITH ANDALOUSE SAUCE
(Serve with Fino Sherry or light California Sauvignon Blanc)

SERVES 3

24	shucked large oysters
	Vegetable or peanut oil for frying
	Lemon wedges

Simple coating:

2	eggs
1/4	cup milk
1	Tablespoon vegetable oil
	Salt and freshly ground pepper
3/4	cup corn flour
	Fine dry bread crumbs

Andalouse sauce:

1/4	sweet red pepper
1/4	green pepper

1	Tablespoon extra virgin olive oil
2	Tablespoons tomato paste
1	cup mayonnaise
1/4	minced garlic clove
1/4	teaspoon sugar
	Pinch of salt

1. Char the skin of the peppers and peel when they have cooled; chop the peppers and sauté them in olive oil, drain, and cool. Add the peppers and tomato paste to the mayonnaise and season with garlic, sugar, and salt. Refrigerate until needed.
2. Remove the oysters from the shells, drain, and pat dry, reserving the oyster liquor for another use.
3. Combine the eggs, milk, oil, and seasonings, and mix well. Dip the oysters in the corn flour, then the egg mixture, and roll in crumbs.
4. Heat the oil to 375° in a deep-fryer or a deep, heavy saucepan.
5. Place a few oysters in a fryer basket, taking care not to crowd them. Lower the basket into the hot oil.
6. Fry the oysters until they are crisp golden brown. Remove and drain on a baking sheet lined with absorbent paper. Keep warm until all the oysters are fried.
7. Serve immediately with lemon wedges and Andalouse sauce.

OYSTERS SOUTHWEST STYLE WITH
SALSA FRESCA (*Serve with Iced Tequila*)

SERVES 3

24	shucked large oysters
	Vegetable or peanut oil for frying
	Lemon wedges

Simple coating:

1	cup finely ground yellow cornmeal
	Salt
1/2	teaspoon freshly ground pepper
	Cayenne pepper
1/2	cup light cream

Salsa Fresca:

1/2	cup finely chopped Spanish onion

2   *large, ripe, peeled, chopped tomatoes*
1¹/₂   *teaspoons chopped seeded jalapeño peppers*
¹/₄   *cup chopped cilantro*
      Pinch sugar
      Salt and pepper to taste

1. Make the salsa by combining all of the ingredients in a mixing bowl. Taste for seasoning and refrigerate until needed.
2. Remove the oysters from the shells, drain, and pat dry.
3. Mix the cornmeal and seasonings together on a large plate. Dip the oysters in the cream, drain, and coat with the seasoned cornmeal.
4. Heat the oil to 375° in a deep-fryer or a heavy-gauge, deep saucepan.
5. Shake off the surplus cornmeal before placing the oysters, a few at a time, in the bottom of a fryer basket. Lower the oysters into the hot oil and fry until they are golden brown.
6. Remove and drain on a baking sheet lined with absorbent paper. Keep warm until all the oysters are fried.
7. Serve immediately with lemon wedges and a bowl of salsa.

OYSTERS TEMPURA STYLE* WITH
DIPPING SAUCE (*Serve with sake*)

SERVES 3   24   *shucked large oysters*
               Vegetable or peanut oil for frying
               Lemon wedges

Batter coating:
¹/₂   *cup flour*
¹/₂   *cup cornstarch*
      Salt
1   *egg*
²/₃   *cup ice water*

Dipping sauce:
1   *teaspoon grated ginger*
1   *Tablespoon finely chopped scallion*

*Sixteenth-century Portuguese traders introduced the European notion of deep-frying to the Japanese. After four hundred years of refinement, Japanese tempura is probably the most delicate batter-fried food in the world.

$^1/_4$	teaspoon finely minced garlic
$^1/_2$	cup soy sauce
$^1/_4$	cup mirin
$^1/_2$	cup sake
1	Tablespoon sugar

1. Make the dipping sauce 1 or 2 hours in advance by combining the ingredients.
2. Drain the oysters and pat dry.
3. Heat the oil in a deep-fryer or heayy saucepan to 375°.
4. Sift the flour, cornstarch, and salt into a bowl, and whisk in the egg and water. Keep the batter chilled by placing the bowl on ice.
5. Dip an oyster in the batter and coat it well; remove with a spoon, and drop into the hot oil. Cook for about 2 minutes, moving the oyster around occasionally so that all surfaces become golden brown.
6. Remove and drain on a baking sheet lined with absorbent paper. Keep warm.
7. Fry the oysters in small batches until all are cooked.
8. Serve immediately with the dipping sauce.

CRISPY SESAME OYSTERS WITH GINGER SAUCE
(Serve with a dry California Gewurztraminer)

SERVES 3

24	shucked large oysters
	Vegetable or peanut oil for frying

Marinade:

2	teaspoons minced ginger root
$^1/_2$	cup rice wine
$^1/_2$	cup dry white wine
1	Tablespoon lemon juice
$^1/_2$	teaspoon sesame oil

Coating:

3	Tablespoons cornstarch
$^1/_4$	teaspoon sugar
	Salt
2	egg whites

| 1 | cup white sesame seeds |

Ginger dipping sauce:

1	cup rice vinegar
2	ounces sesame oil
1½	Tablespoons peeled minced ginger root
1	Tablespoon sugar
¼	cup chopped cilantro
	Salt and pepper

1. Make the marinade by combining the ingredients.
2. Drain the oysters, and marinate for about 15 minutes.
3. Combine ingredients for dipping sauce. Strain immediately before using.
4. Mix the cornstarch, sugar, and salt, and whip in the egg whites.
5. Drain the oysters, dip in the cornstarch mixture, roll in the sesame seeds, and allow to dry for 30 minutes.
6. Heat the oil to 300° in a deep-fryer or heavy saucepan. Fry the oysters, a few at a time, until golden brown. Remove and drain on a baking sheet lined with absorbent paper. Keep warm in the oven until all the oysters are fried.
7. Serve immediately with dipping sauce.

OYSTERS IN BEER BATTER WITH WEST INDIES HOT PEPPER SAUCE
(Serve with Nut Brown Ale)

SERVES 3

24	shucked large oysters
1	cup corn flour
	Oil for frying

Batter coating:

1	cup flour
	Salt and freshly ground pepper
3	Tablespoons melted butter
⅔	cup lukewarm water
½	cup beer
2	egg whites

Hot pepper sauce:

| 1 | minced seeded hot green chili pepper |

Parboil large fat oysters with a slice of onion, bit of mace and a sprig of parsley; drain, wipe dry, lay smooth on a buttered plate and put on the ice. When cold, roll each oyster in fine cracker-crumbs, then cover with thick mayonnaise dressing and roll in cracker-crumbs again. Allow them to dry for a couple of hours, and if necessary roll again in the crumbs, lay in a wire frying basket and plunge in smoking hot lard for one minute. Serve with the sandwiches made by buttering thin bread, freed from all crust, rolled around a crisp piece of celery, and tied with baby ribbon.

—MAY E. SOUTHWORTH,
One Hundred & One Ways of Serving Oysters, 1907

SERVES 4

2	Tablespoons minced sweet green pepper
1	minced garlic clove
1	minced small onion
2	Tablespoons fresh lime juice
1	teaspoon hot sauce (Barbadian style)
1	Tablespoon Cognac
$^2/_3$	cup extra virgin olive oil
	Salt and freshly ground pepper

1. Combine the ingredients for the sauce in a small saucepan. (If a smoother texture is desired, purée the minced vegetables and oil in a blender before heating.) Simmer over low heat, and correct the seasonings. Keep warm or reheat before serving.
2. Remove the oysters from shells, pat dry, roll in corn flour, and set aside.
3. Sift the flour, salt, and pepper into a 1½-quart bowl; whisk in the melted butter, water, and beer, just until blended. Set aside for 10 minutes.
4. When time to fry the oysters, add a pinch of salt to the egg whites, beat them until stiff, and stir 2 tablespoons into the beer batter, then fold in the remaining whites.
5. Heat the oil to 375° in a deep-fryer or heavy, deep saucepan.
6. Using a spoon, dip an oyster into the batter, lift out carefully, and drop it into the hot oil. Proceed to dip and drop several more oysters, but do not crowd the pan. Remove with a slotted spoon when the oysters are golden brown, and drain on a baking sheet lined with absorbent paper. Keep warm.
7. Serve the oysters with hot pepper sauce.

OYSTER CROQUETTES WITH SAFFRON SAUCE (*Serve with Pilsner*)

$1^1/_2$	pints oysters and liquor
$^1/_2$	cup cream
3	Tablespoons butter
3	Tablespoons flour
$^1/_4$	teaspoon nutmeg
3	egg yolks
2	Tablespoons dry Sherry
$^1/_4$	cup finely chopped parsley and chives

Salt and freshly ground pepper
Lemon juice
Vegetable or peanut oil for frying

Simple coating:

2   *cups flour*
2   *whisked eggs*
2   *cups seasoned fine bread crumbs*

Saffron sauce:

3   *large garlic cloves*
$^1/_2$ *teaspoon salt*
2   *egg yolks*
1   *cup extra virgin olive oil*
$^1/_4$ *teaspoon saffron*
$^1/_2$ *teaspoon cayenne pepper*
    Lemon juice

1. Drain the oysters and coarsely chop, measure ½ cup of the oyster liquor, and heat in a small saucepan with the cream.
2. Melt the butter in another saucepan, stir in the flour and nutmeg, and cook until straw yellow. Remove from the heat and whisk in the cream. Return to heat and boil, stirring constantly, until the mixture thickens; simmer for 5 minutes.
3. Whisk the egg yolks in a bowl. Add the Sherry. Beat ½ cup of the hot mixture into the egg yolks, a spoonful at a time. Then slowly whisk in the remaining hot mixture. Transfer the enriched sauce back to the saucepan and, stirring carefully, bring to a boil. Lower heat.
4. Stir in the oysters, salt, pepper, parsley, chives, and lemon juice, and heat thoroughly.
5. Spread the mixture on a large plate, cover it loosely with waxed paper, and set aside to cool.
6. Shape into 12 croquettes, roll in flour, dip in egg, and coat with bread crumbs. Dry for at least 2 hours.
7. Make the sauce by mincing the garlic with the salt until it becomes a paste. Place in a bowl, add the egg yolks, and whisk in the oil slowly, beginning with a few drops at a time. Add the saffron and cayenne pepper. Thin with a bit of lemon juice if too thick.

8. Heat the oil to 375° in a deep-fryer or deep, heavy-gauge saucepan.

9. Place the croquettes, a few at a time, in a fryer basket and lower into the hot oil. Fry until the croquettes are golden brown and remove to a baking sheet lined with absorbent paper. Keep warm in the oven until all are fried.

10. Serve the hot croquettes with a spoonful of sauce on the side.

OYSTER AND CORN FRITTERS WITH SALSA VERDE (*Serve with California Sauvignon Blanc*)

SERVES 4

24	shucked medium oysters
6	slices diced bacon
1	cup cornmeal
1	cup flour
3	teaspoons baking powder
$^1/_4$	teaspoon nutmeg
$^1/_2$	teaspoon salt
	Pinch of cayenne pepper
2	whisked eggs
$^1/_2$	cup milk
$^3/_4$	cup scraped corn
	Vegetable or peanut oil for frying

Salsa Verde:

1	10-ounce can tomatillos, drained
1	small finely chopped onion
$^1/_2$	chopped jalapeño pepper
1	Tablespoon fresh finely chopped cilantro
	Salt and freshly ground pepper
	Pinch of sugar

1. Remove the oysters from the shells and set aside; reserve the liquor for another use.

2. Make the sauce by combining the ingredients in a blender for a minute. Season to taste.

3. Cook the bacon in a skillet until it is brown and crisp; drain on absorbent paper.

4. Sift the dry ingredients into a bowl, add the eggs and milk, and mix well. Stir in the corn, bacon, and oysters, and adjust the seasoning.

OYSTER FRITTERS

Drain off the liquor, and to each pint of oysters take a pint of milk, a salt-spoonful of salt, half as much pepper, and flour enough for a thin batter. Chop the oysters and stir in, and then fry in hot lard, a little salted, or in butter. Drop in one spoonful at a time. Some make the batter thicker, so as to put in one oyster at a time surrounded by the batter.

—CATHERINE ESTHER BEECHER,
Mrs. Beecher's Housekeeper and Healthkeeper, 1876

5. Heat the oil in a deep-fryer or heavy saucepan to 350°. Drop a table-spoon of the batter, including 1 oyster, into the oil and fry from 2 to 3 minutes, moving the fritter around so the outside will be evenly browned.
6. Fry the fritters a few at a time, taking care not to overcrowd the pan. Drain on a baking sheet lined with layers of absorbent paper, and keep warm.
7. Serve immediately with a bowl of Salsa Verde.

STIR-FRY

When innovative cooks "jumped out of the frying pan" and into the wok in the early 1970s, a new trend in American cuisine began. Happily, it has survived the quick demise of less worthy culinary "fads," and for all the right reasons.

The wok is not only an age-old utensil, it is a symbol of a culinary style that has evolved for centuries. Behind all that steaming and stir-frying, all that slicing and shredding, is a cohesive philosophy of food that every Asian cook knows and respects.

The Taoist belief that food should be eaten as close to its natural state as possible literally mandates "quick" cooking, capturing the natural flavors and juices of foods by tossing and stir-frying in as little oil as possible over high heat. And the etiquette of Asian dining, which dictates that food should be bite sized and ceremoniously served, is reason enough for cutting all the ingredients into appetizing pieces.

It seemed inevitable. The widespread appreciation of Far Eastern cooking led to imitation and, ultimately, to creation. Vegetables appeared on American tables tender-crisp and glowing with color. And the "sampling" of dishes that makes Asian dining so distinctive has encouraged a movement away from the five-course meal to a freer pattern of serving several harmonious dishes together.

What an accommodating arrangement it all is for seafood cookery where light steaming or frying is so desirable, capturing the flavor of the sea so important, and variety so unexpected. If Oyster Egg Foo Yong and Oysters and Vegetables on a bed of rice in company with abalone, sea bass, and "ginger fish" (flounder) are considered simple meals, think of the feasts!

And, while oysters cannot compete with shrimp as the principal seafood ingredient of Asian dishes, they do add a special flavor and texture to some traditional recipes and some rather untraditional ones. Moreover, oysters play a substantial role in a special sauce that adapts to many basic foods. One way (stir-fry) or another (oyster sauce), Asian cooking and oysters are something to rhapsodize about.

OYSTERS AND VEGETABLES IN OYSTER SAUCE *
(Serve with California Sauvignon Blanc)

SERVES 6 †

24	shucked small oysters and liquor
1	small sweet red pepper
1	small green pepper
1/4	pound shitake mushrooms
2	ribs Chinese cabbage
1	small onion
1/2	cup water chestnuts
1/2	cup fresh bean sprouts
2	Tablespoons peanut oil
1/2	teaspoon sesame oil
3	cups cooked long-grain rice

Marinade:

1 1/2	Tablespoons oyster sauce
1	Tablespoon dry Sherry
1	minced scallion
1	teaspoon peeled, grated fresh ginger root

*Oyster sauce may be purchased or made with fresh oysters and light soy sauce: simmer a dozen chopped oysters and a cup of oyster liquor for about 20 minutes. Strain through a fine sieve and discard the oysters. Add 3 tablespoons of light soy sauce, pour into a sterilized bottle, and refrigerate.

†If this and the following stir-fry recipes are offered as part of a four-or-five-dish Chinese menu, it will be sufficient for 6 or 8 people. If a recipe is used as the main course, it will not serve more than 4.

Sauce:

2	teaspoons cornstarch
1	Tablespoon oyster liquor
1	Tablespoon oyster sauce
$1/_8$	teaspoon freshly ground pepper

Preparation:

1. Remove the oysters from the shells; strain and reserve 1 tablespoon of the liquor for the sauce.
2. Combine the oyster sauce, Sherry, scallion, and ginger root in a mixing bowl; add the oysters and marinate while the vegetables are being prepared.
3. Cut the peppers in ¾-inch squares; slice the mushrooms with the grain, and finely slice the Chinese cabbage and onion across the grain. Thin-slice the water chestnuts.
4. Mix the cornstarch sauce and set aside.

Stir-fry:

1. Heat the peanut oil in a wok until very hot.
2. Stir-fry the oysters in their marinade until they begin to curl at the edges. Remove and set aside in a warm heatproof dish.
3. Add more oil, if necessary, and stir-fry the peppers for about 2 minutes; add the mushrooms, cabbage, onion, water chestnuts, and bean sprouts, and toss for another 2 minutes.
4. Add the cornstarch sauce, stir until thickened, return the oysters, add sesame oil, and remove the wok from the heat after 1 minute.
5. Serve with hot rice.

OYSTERS IN BLACK BEAN AND
OYSTER SAUCE *(Serve with Nut Brown Ale)*

SERVES 4

24	shucked small oysters and liquor
1	small sweet red pepper
1	teaspoon grated lemon zest
2	teaspoons grated ginger root
2	finely chopped garlic cloves
$1/_4$	cup finely chopped scallions
$1/_2$	cup trimmed snow peas

2	Tablespoons peanut oil
2	cups cooked long-grain rice

Black bean sauce:

1¹/₂	Tablespoons fermented black beans
1	Tablespoon rice wine
¹/₂	teaspoon sugar
1	teaspoon light soy sauce
1	Tablespoon oyster sauce

Cornstarch mixture:

1	Tablespoon cornstarch
2	Tablespoons dry Sherry or water

Preparation:

1. Remove the oysters from the shells and set aside in a small bowl; strain and reserve 1 tablespoon of the liquor for the sauce.
2. Marinate the beans in rice wine for 15 minutes. Stir in the sugar, soy sauce, oyster sauce, and oyster liquor.
3. Cut the red pepper into fine julienne strips and set aside; combine the lemon zest, ginger root, and garlic in a small bowl.
4. Dissolve the cornstarch in Sherry and reserve.

Stir-fry:

1. Heat the oil in a wok until very hot and stir-fry the pepper, lemon zest, ginger, and garlic for 1 minute. Add scallions and snow peas.
2. Add the black bean sauce and bring to a boil.
3. Stir in the oysters and stir-fry until the edges begin to curl.
4. Stir the cornstarch mixture into the wok, and continue to stir until the mixture thickens.
5. Spoon over hot rice and serve immediately.

OYSTERS AND CHICKEN IN OYSTER SAUCE
(Serve with dry Alsace Gewurztraminer)

SERVES 4

24	shucked small oysters
1	large green pepper

1/4	cup bamboo shoots
1/2	cup drained canned whole straw mushrooms
1/2	peeled English cucumber
1	chicken breast
2	Tablespoons peanut oil
1/2	teaspoon sesame oil
2	cups cooked long-grain rice

Sauce:

1	sliced small onion
1	Tablespoon soy sauce
2	Tablespoons oyster sauce
3/4	cup chicken stock (see p. 59)
1	teaspoon brown sugar
1	teaspoon freshly grated ginger root
1	Tablespoon cornstarch
2	Tablespoons dry Sherry

Preparation:

1. Mix all the ingredients for the sauce together and simmer for about 10 minutes, stirring occasionally.
2. Remove the oysters from the shells, reserving the liquor for another use.
3. Cut the green pepper and bamboo shoots into fine julienne strips; slice the mushrooms, and dice the cucumber.
4. Skin, bone, and cut the chicken breast into ½-inch strips.

Stir-fry:

1. Heat the peanut oil in a wok until very hot.
2. Stir-fry the green pepper for 2 minutes. Add bamboo shoots and mushrooms and stir-fry 2 more minutes. Remove to a heated dish.
3. Add more oil if necessary and stir-fry the chicken for 3 or 4 minutes.
4. Pour the sauce into the wok, add the oysters, and stir-fry until they begin to curl at the edges. Add the cucumber and return the reserved vegetables to the wok. Toss until all the ingredients are coated with the sauce. Stir in the sesame oil and remove from the heat.
5. Serve over hot rice.

OYSTERS AND STEAK ORIENTAL
(Serve with Nut Brown Ale)

24	shucked small oysters and liquor
3/4	pound boneless sirloin steak
1	small sweet red pepper
1/4	pound cultivated cremini mushrooms
4	scallions
1/4	pound snow peas
2	Tablespoons peanut oil
1	teaspoon minced ginger root
1	cup chopped baby bok choy
4	cups cooked long-grain rice

Sauce:

1	Tablespoon cornstarch
1	Tablespoon oyster sauce

Marinade:

2	Tablespoons soy sauce
	Pinch of sugar
2	Tablespoons Sherry

Preparation:

1. Remove the oysters from shells and set aside. Strain and reserve ¼ cup of the liquor for the sauce.
2. Combine the oyster liquor, cornstarch, and oyster sauce.
3. Mix the marinade. Cut the steak into ¼-inch slices and marinate for at least 30 minutes.
4. Cut the pepper into thin julienne strips; slice the mushrooms; chop the scallions, including the stems. Trim and string the snow peas.

Stir-fry:

1. Heat the oil in the wok until very hot and stir-fry the pepper, scallions, and ginger for about a minute. Remove to a heated ovenproof dish.
2. Stir-fry the mushrooms, snow peas, and bok choy until tender. Remove and add the vegetables to the heated dish.

The great point to be borne in mind in frying, is that the liquid must be hot enough to act instantaneously, as all the merit of this culinary operation lies in the invasion of the boiling liquid, which carbonizes or burns, at the very instant of the immersion of the body placed in it.

MRS. BEETON'S BOOK OF HOUSEHOLD MANAGEMENT, 1861

3. Add more oil if necessary and stir-fry the steak until the slices are browned on the outside but rare inside.
4. Return the vegetables to the wok.
5. Add the sauce and stir in the oysters while the sauce is thickening. When the edges of the oysters begin to curl, remove from the heat.
6. Spoon the steak and oysters over hot rice and serve immediately.

PORK AND DRIED OYSTERS IN
OYSTER SAUCE (*Serve with Pinot Noir*)

SERVES 6

$^1/_2$	pound dried oysters or 2 3$^3/_4$-ounce tins smoked oysters
$^1/_2$	cup diced lean raw pork
10	dried Chinese straw mushrooms
1	cup bamboo shoots
1	cup water chestnuts
2	ribs Chinese cabbage
2	Tablespoons peanut oil
1	garlic clove
3	cups thin fresh Chinese egg noodles

Marinade:

2	Tablespoons sake or dry Sherry
1	Tablespoon soy sauce
1	teaspoon peeled and grated fresh ginger

Sauce:

1	Tablespoon cornstarch
$^1/_2$	teaspoon sugar
$^1/_4$	cup white wine
2	Tablespoons oyster sauce
1	teaspoon grated lemon zest

Preparation:

1. Soak the dried oysters for 5 hours, drain, and dice. If using smoked oysters, rinse, drain, dice, and set aside.
2. Mix the marinade and marinate the diced pork while the vegetables are being prepared.

3. Soak the mushrooms in warm water for about 15 minutes, drain, and dice.
4. Cut the bamboo shoots into fine julienne strips, slice the water chestnuts, and fine-slice the Chinese cabbage.
5. Fill a large pot three quarters full of salted water, and bring to a boil. Add noodles, stir to separate strands, and bring to a second boil. Cook for a minute, and drain. Before serving return to boiling water for a minute to reheat, and drain.
6. Mix the cornstarch, sugar, wine, oyster sauce, and lemon zest.

Stir-fry:

1. Heat the oil in a wok until very hot. Add the garlic clove and toss for 10 seconds. Remove and discard the garlic.
2. Add the pork and marinade, and stir-fry for about 3 minutes.
3. Add more oil if necessary and stir-fry the bamboo shoots, water chestnuts, cabbage, and mushrooms for about 1 minute.
4. Add the oysters and the sauce; stir until all the ingredients are evenly coated.
5. Serve over hot noodles.

OYSTER EGG FOO YONG *(Serve with Macon)*

SERVES 3

1	pint oysters and liquor
3	Tablespoons peanut oil
1/2	cup chopped brown mushrooms
3	eggs
1/2	cup bean sprouts
1/2	cup cooked green peas

Sauce:

1	Tablespoon cornstarch
1/2	teaspoon sugar
1/2	cup chicken stock (see p. 59)
1	Tablespoon oyster sauce
2	Tablespoons dry Sherry

1. Drain the oysters, reserve half of them and ⅓ cup of liquor for the sauce. Pat dry and chop the remaining oysters for the pancakes.

2. Heat 1 tablespoon of oil in a wok, stir-fry the mushrooms for about 30 seconds, and set aside to cool.

3. Add more oil if necessary and stir-fry the chopped oysters for about 30 seconds; remove and add to the mushrooms. Reduce the heat under the wok.

4. Combine the reserved oyster liquor with the cornstarch, sugar, stock, oyster sauce, and Sherry in a saucepan and cook, stirring constantly, until the mixture thickens; keep warm over low heat.

5. Break the eggs into a mixing bowl, beat well, and combine with the mushrooms and chopped oysters. Stir in the bean sprouts.

6. Add more oil to the wok and return to moderate heat.

7. Pour about ¼ cup of the egg mixture into the wok and fry without stirring for about a minute. Turn the pancake over and fry the other side to a light brown.

8. Transfer the pancake to a hot serving platter, add more oil if needed, and fry the other 5 pancakes.

9. While the pancakes are cooking, add the whole oysters and peas to the sauce, and cook until the oysters are plump.

10. Arrange 2 pancakes on each plate, and nap with the oyster sauce. Serve immediately.

SAUTÉ

Lightly sautéed–does it sound familiar? Perhaps one of the most frequently used techniques for tender, quick-cooked food, this simple "browning in butter" method of frying is right for everything from boned chicken breasts and veal scallops to fish fillets and oysters. And it gives a full range of possibilities to coat, dip, dredge, and roll in seasoned flour, fresh bread, cracker, or cornflake crumbs.

But, undoubtedly, the greatest advantage of serving a sautéed entrée is the lure of the saucière. From a simple butter, lemon juice, and wine sauce spooned over perfectly fried oysters to a full-bodied tomato sauce that will spark up an Oysters Parmigiana, a creative cook can transform ordinary fried oysters into a beautifully realized dish.

The following recipes, including a contemporary adaptation of an Elizabethan "stew," suggest what is possible for every "accomplisht cook." The first step is always the same—dredge, dip, roll, and lightly sauté; the last step is sheer alchemy.

HOW TO STEW OYSTERS

Straine the liquor from the Oysters, then wash them very clean, and put them into a pipkin with the liquor, a pinte of Wine to a quart of Oysters, two or three whole Onions, large Mace, Pepper, Ginger; let all the spices be whole, they will stew the whiter; put in salt, a little vinegar, a piece of butter and sweet Herbs; stew all these together till you think them enough, then take out some of that liquor and put to it a quarter of a pound of butter, a Lemmon minced, and beat it up thick, setting it on the fire, but let it not boyle; dreine the rest of the liquor from the Oysters thorow [through] a culender, and dish them; pour this sauce over them; garnish your dish with searced [sieved] Ginger, Lemmon, Orange, Barberries, or Grapes scalded; sippit it, and serve it up.

—JOSEPH COOPER,
The Art of Cookery Refin'd and Augumented, 1654

OYSTERS AU CITRON *(Serve with a Loire Muscadet)*

24	*shucked large oysters*
2	*eggs*
2	*Tablespoons milk*
$1/2$	*teaspoon salt*
$1/4$	*teaspoon pepper*
1	*cup all-purpose flour*
1	*cup fine bread crumbs*
	Clarified butter
	Lemon slices

Sauce:

1	*cup dry white wine*
1	*minced garlic clove*
1	*teaspoon Worcestershire sauce*
3	*Tablespoons unsalted butter (more for a thicker sauce)*
1	*Tablespoon lemon juice*
2	*Tablespoons chopped chives*

1. Remove the oysters from the shells and pat dry.
2. Beat the eggs in a bowl until frothy; whisk in the milk and seasonings. Combine the flour and bread crumbs in another bowl.
3. Roll the oysters, one by one, in the crumb mixture, dip in the egg, and roll again in crumbs. Set aside to dry for 30 minutes.
4. Melt enough clarified butter in a skillet to coat the bottom and prevent sticking. Sauté the oysters, a few at a time, adding more butter if necessary. Remove and drain the oysters on a baking sheet lined with absorbent paper. Keep warm until all the oysters are fried.
5. Add the wine, garlic, and Worcestershire to the pan juices, and boil until reduced by half. Swirl in the butter, a bit at a time. Remove from the heat and stir in the lemon juice and chives.
6. Place the oysters on individual plates, nap with sauce, and serve immediately, garnished with lemon slices.

OYSTERS TARRAGON (*Serve with Sancerre*)

SERVES 4

24   *shucked large oysters*
1   *cup flour*
2   *Tablespoons finely chopped fresh tarragon*
     Salt and freshly ground pepper
1   *cup fine cracker crumbs*
     Butter
     Vegetable oil
1   *cup crème fraîche*
2   *teaspoons lemon juice*

1. Remove the oysters from the shells, drain, and pat dry.
2. Combine the flour, 1 tablespoon of the tarragon, and seasonings. Dust the oysters in the flour, roll in crumbs, and set aside.
3. Heat enough butter and oil in a heavy skillet to prevent sticking. Sauté the oysters, about 6 at one time, turning so both sides are lightly browned, and add butter and oil to the pan as necessary. Keep the oysters warm until all are cooked.
4. Heat the *crème fraîche* and add lemon juice and the remaining tarragon.
5. Spoon *crème fraîche* on each plate and arrange 6 oysters on top.

BARD'S OYSTERS (*Serve with light Barbaresco*)

SERVES 2

12   *shucked large oysters and liquor*
1/4 *cup seasoned flour*
1/2 *cup fine bread crumbs*
2   *teaspoons grated orange zest*
    Clarified butter
4   *thin orange slices*

Sauce:
1   *Tablespoon butter*
1   *cup Cabernet Sauvignon*
1 1/2 *Tablespoons balsamic vinegar*
     Pinch of mace
1/2 *Tablespoon cornstarch*
2   *Tablespoons orange juice*

Take a pottle [two quarts] of large oysters, parboil them in their own liquor, then wash them in warm water, wipe them dry, and pull away the fins, flour them and fry them in clarified butter fine and white, then take them up and put them in a large dish with some white or claret wine, a little vinegar, a quarter of a pound of sweet butter, some grated nutmeg, large mace, salt and two or three slices of an orange, stew them two or three walms [moments], then serve them in a large scoured [clean] dish, pour the sauce on them, and run them over with beaten butter, slic't lemon or orange, and sippets around the dish.

—ROBERT MAY,
The Accomplisht Cook, or the Art and Mastery of Cooking, 1660

SERVES 4

1. Remove the oysters from the shells; strain and reserve the oyster liquor for the sauce.
2. Dust the oysters in flour, and roll in crumbs seasoned with the orange zest.
3. Simmer the oyster liquor, butter, wine, vinegar, and mace in an uncovered saucepan for 20 minutes or until reduced by half. Dissolve the cornstarch in orange juice, add to the wine, and cook, stirring constantly, until the sauce thickens.
4. Melt enough clarified butter in a skillet to coat the bottom and prevent sticking. Without crowding the skillet, sauté the oysters for about 2 minutes on each side. Remove, drain on absorbent paper, and keep warm until all are sautéed.
5. Arrange 6 oysters in the center of 2 individual serving plates, surround with hot sauce, and garnish with orange slices.

OYSTERS PARMIGIANA (*Serve with a Pinot Grigio*)

24	shucked large oysters
1	cup seasoned flour
2	whisked eggs
2	Tablespoons water
1	cup fine cornflake crumbs
	Butter
	Vegetable oil
1	cup fresh tomato sauce
¹/₂	cup freshly grated Parmigiano-Reggiano cheese

Fresh tomato sauce:

¹/₄	cup butter
³/₄	cup minced shallots
2	minced garlic cloves
2	cups peeled, seeded, diced plum tomatoes
	Pinch of sugar
	Salt and freshly ground pepper
¹/₄	cup chopped fresh basil

1. Remove the oysters from the shells and pat dry, reserving the liquor for another use. Dust the oysters in flour, dip them one by one in egg mixed with water, and roll in crumbs. Set aside to dry.
2. In a medium skillet melt butter, and sauté shallots and garlic until soft. Stir in tomatoes and sugar, and simmer for about 15 minutes. Put through a food mill or purée in a blender. Season to taste and keep warm. Add basil before serving.
3. Heat a little butter and oil in a large skillet, and sauté the oysters, turning them once to brown both sides evenly. Do not overcrowd the skillet and use more oil and butter as needed. Keep the oysters warm in the oven until all are cooked.
4. Arrange the oysters in individual serving dishes, nap hot sauce over the oysters, and top with a spoonful of cheese.

OYSTERS FINOCCHIO (*Serve with Pouilly-Fumé*)

SERVES 4

24	*shucked large oysters*
1	*cup flour*
	Salt and freshly ground pepper
1	*cup fine bread crumbs*
	Butter
	Olive oil
1	*cup cored thinly sliced fennel bulb; reserve green tops for garnish*
1/4	*cup chopped onion*
2	*Tablespoons chopped red pepper*
3	*Tablespoons white wine*

1. Remove the oysters from the shells, drain, and pat dry. Roll in flour seasoned with salt and pepper, and then in the bread crumbs.
2. Heat 1 tablespoon of butter and ½ tablespoon of oil in a saucepan and sauté the fennel and onion until tender. Add the pepper and cook 2 or 3 minutes more. Stir in the wine and season to taste. Keep warm.
3. Melt a tablespoon of butter and some oil in a large skillet and sauté the oysters, 6 at a time, for 2 minutes on each side, adding butter and oil if necessary. Remove with a slotted spoon and set aside in a warm oven until all are sautéed.
4. Spoon the fennel into the center of each plate, divide the oysters, and garnish with sprigs of green fennel.

BAKE

Whether as a hot appetizer on the half shell, in a vegetable casserole, or stuffed loaf, oysters are most frequently cooked in the oven. And there is no particular technique involved—only the reminder to set the timer or watch the clock to avoid overcooking. And then move on to other things.

There's something comforting about the ease and simplicity of preparing oysters this way, something equally pleasant about the distinctive aroma emanating from the oven when guests arrive or children come home from school in the already-dark, late fall afternoons. Perhaps that is why scalloped oyster recipes change so little and always seem to be what they were when made in Grandmother's kitchen or when one of the subjects most frequently discussed by the Ladies Guild was whether or not to add Sherry.

Scalloped Oysters, Oyster Loaf, and Crumbed Oysters are the "plain Janes" of oyster cookery. But don't underestimate the drama of these light dishes—there may be a surprise or two under that golden-brown topping. A dash of Sherry, pinch of nutmeg, some pungent fresh herbs, or a bit of this or that can, in almost no time at all, make one of these dishes the specialty of the house.

SCALLOPED OYSTERS (Serve with Graves Blanc)

SERVES 4

24	shucked medium oysters and liquor
8	Tablespoons melted butter
2	cups butter-cracker crumbs
	Salt and freshly ground pepper
1/4	cup heavy cream
3	Tablespoons dry Sherry (optional)

OVEN TEMPERATURE: 325°

1. Remove the oysters from the shells and pat dry; strain and reserve ¼ cup of the liquor.
2. Mix the butter and crumbs, and line the bottom of a shallow buttered casserole or 9-inch pie dish with a third of them. Arrange half the oysters on top, sprinkle with salt, pepper, 2 tablespoons of both oyster liquor and cream, and half the Sherry. Repeat the layers, covering with the remaining crumbs.
3. Bake for 30 minutes until the top is golden brown.

SCALLOPED OYSTERS WITH MUSHROOMS
(*Serve with aged Chardonnay*)

SERVES 4

1	pint oysters and liquor
1¼	cups light cream
6	Tablespoons butter
3	Tablespoons flour
1	teaspoon Worcestershire sauce
2	teaspoons lemon juice
1	cup sliced wild mushrooms (*porcinis, cepes, morels*)
	Salt and freshly ground pepper
½	cup fresh bread crumbs
	Herb sprigs

OVEN TEMPERATURE: 400°

1. Drain the oysters and set aside. Measure ¼ cup of the oyster liquor and heat it in a small saucepan with the cream.
2. Melt the butter in another saucepan; remove and reserve 2 tablespoons for the crumbs. Stir in the flour and cook 5 minutes. Remove from the heat and whisk in the cream. Return to heat, add the Worcestershire and lemon juice, and cook, stirring constantly, until the mixture thickens. Stir in the mushrooms and simmer for at least 5 minutes.
3. Stir in the oysters and adjust seasonings.
4. Spoon the oyster mixture into large buttered scallop shells or individual gratin dishes. Top with buttered crumbs.
5. Place shells or gratin dishes on a baking sheet and bake about 10 minutes until bubbling and golden brown. Garnish with herb sprigs.

SCALLOPED OYSTERS WITH BACON
(*Serve with Amontillado Sherry*)

SERVES 4

1	pint oysters
½	pound diced bacon
3	Tablespoons butter
½	cup finely chopped shallots
½	cup heavy cream
1	cup unsalted cracker crumbs

SCALLOPED OYSTERS

Scallop was the old-time term for mixtures baked in milk or in a cream sauce and served in a scallop shell. The term scallop has since been extended to a number of dishes baked in milk or in a cream sauce, but not served in a scallop shell—scalloped potatoes, for example. This recipe is simple, old-fashioned, and very good.

—*THE YANKEE MAGAZINE COOKBOOK*

Wash, drain and dry the oysters. Butter the bottom of a shallow baking-dish and spread thickly with the oysters; sprinkle with dried cépes powder and season with salt and cayenne. Have some very fine bread-crumbs that have been fried in olive-oil; mix with them double the quantity of grated cheese and cover the top of the oysters. Pour over a gill of champagne and brown in a quick oven.

—MAY E. SOUTHWORTH,
One Hundred & One Ways of Serving Oysters, 1907

SERVES 4

1/4   cup chopped parsley
2   teaspoons chopped fresh chives
       Salt and freshly ground pepper
2   Tablespoons lemon juice

OVEN TEMPERATURE: 350°

1. Drain the oysters and pat dry, reserving the liquor for another use.
2. Sauté the bacon in a skillet until almost crisp, remove with a slotted spoon, and set aside.
3. Pour off all but a tablespoon of fat from the skillet, melt the butter, and sauté the shallots until tender. Add one half of the bacon, the cream, crumbs, parsley, and chives.
4. Arrange the oysters in a buttered gratin dish or a 9- by 9-inch baking dish and season them with salt and pepper. Sprinkle with lemon juice and top with the crumb mixture and remaining bacon.
5. Bake for about 15 minutes or until the bacon is crisp and brown.

BAKED EXPECTATIONS
(*Serve with Alsace Riesling*)

1 1/2 pints oysters
1   minced garlic clove
1/2   cup olive oil
3/4   cup freshly grated Gruyère cheese
1/2   cup fresh bread crumbs
1/2   cup ground almonds
       Salt and freshly ground pepper

OVEN TEMPERATURE: 450°

1. Drain the oysters and pat dry; reserve the liquor for another use.
2. Mix the garlic and oil in a bowl. In another bowl, combine the cheese, bread crumbs, almonds, and seasonings.
3. Dip the oysters in the oil and roll in the crumb mixture. Arrange oysters in a single layer in a shallow buttered casserole, and top with the remaining crumb mixture.
4. Reduce the oven temperature to 375° and bake the oysters about 10 minutes until the top is golden brown.
5. Serve with a toss of salad greens.

BROIL-GRILL

To define broiling or grilling as "putting oiled foods into or onto a preheated broiler or white-hot wood charcoal grill" probably tells the story of one of the oldest and, ironically, one of today's trendiest forms of oyster cookery. In 1876, to "roast" oysters meant to "put oysters in the shell, after washing them, upon the coals so that the flat side is uppermost, to save the liquor; and take them up when they begin to gape a little." That's a far cry from Chez Panisse and the perfectly reduced creamy fumet sauce and teaspoon of caviar that distinguish the mesquitewood Charcoal-Grilled Oysters on the Café's *carte du jour*. But it surely proves the point that oysters are forever.

Beginning with grilled oysters and including various broiled and skewered recipes suitable for an indoor grill or oven broiler, the following recipes are presented with a bit of caution. Grilling is not an exact cooking technique. Wind, weather conditions, intensity of heat, and even the positioning of the oysters on the grill will vary the cooking time if an outdoor unit is used. And great care should be taken to remove the oyster from the grill at just the right moment. Yet, the pluses of preparing oysters this way definitely offset the minuses, because there is something so lighthearted about the informality of dining outdoors that the effort of planning a successful "Oyster Roast" is amply rewarded.

Like the other high-heat methods of cooking oysters, broiling them will result in a tastier dish if the oysters are lightly coated, rolled in crumbs or basted, and counterpoised with other compatible ingredients. Served *en brochette* with bacon, sausages, or vegetables, oysters can be as casual or as glamorous as desired. So . . . *en garde!* Skewer away.

CHARCOAL-GRILLED OYSTERS
(Serve with Muscadet)

SERVES 6

48	*unshucked oysters*
	Rock salt
	Lemon wedges

Sauce:

$1/4$	*cup white wine vinegar*
$1/4$	*cup dry Vermouth*
3	*Tablespoons chopped shallots*
$3/4$	*pound ice cold butter*
	Grated lemon zest
	Salt and freshly ground pepper

1. Scrub and rinse the oysters and set aside.
2. Light the charcoal grill and allow 30 to 45 minutes for it to reach the proper temperature.
3. Reduce the vinegar, Vermouth, and shallots in a saucepan over moderately high heat until only 2 tablespoons of liquid remain. Adjust to very low heat.
4. Cut the butter into ½-inch slices and whisk one piece at a time into the reduced liquid; whisk constantly with each addition until the sauce is creamy and thick. Add the lemon zest and season to taste. Keep the sauce warm over water that is the same temperature as the sauce.
5. Line two large shallow pans with rock salt and heat in the oven.
6. Put the oysters, flat-side-up, directly on the grill when the coals are white hot.
7. Remove with tongs when the shells begin to open. Wearing thick canvas gloves, shuck the oysters, discard the top shells, and place the oysters in their deep shells in the hot rock salt to keep warm.
8. Serve the oysters with the sauce and lemon wedges.

STAGEHARBOR OYSTERS (*Serve with Pilsner*)

SERVES 4

24	*shucked large oysters*
12	*slices bacon*
1	*cup fresh fine bread crumbs*
1	*teaspoon dry mustard*
¼	*teaspoon paprika*
	Salt
	Cayenne pepper
¼	*cup melted butter*
	Lemon slices
	Chopped cilantro

OVEN TEMPERATURE: HIGH BROIL

1. Cut the bacon in half and cook in a skillet or microwave oven until crisp and brown. Drain on absorbent paper. Set aside and keep warm.
2. Remove the oysters from the shells, drain, and pat dry, reserving the liquor for another use.
3. Combine crumbs, mustard, paprika, salt, and cayenne, and roll the oysters in the seasoned crumbs.

4. Arrange oysters on an oiled baking pan and spoon melted butter over them.
5. Broil 5 inches from the heat until golden. Turn, nap with the remaining butter, and broil until the other side is golden.
6. Serve oysters and bacon garnished with lemon slices and cilantro.

MIXED GRILL EN BROCHETTE
(Serve with light Chardonnay)

SERVES 4

24	*shucked medium oysters*
12	*slices thick bacon*
14	*breakfast sausages*
2	*large onions*
8	*Tablespoons butter*
$^1/_4$	*cup minced parsley*
1	*garlic clove*
	Salt and freshly ground pepper
	Cayenne pepper
	Corn flour
4	*12-inch skewers*
4	*thick slices toasted sourdough bread*

Sauce:

4	*Tablespoons butter*
$^3/_4$	*cup chili sauce*
2	*teaspoons Worcestershire sauce*
1	*teaspoon Tabasco*
1	*Tablespoon brown sugar*
1	*Tablespoon fresh lemon juice*

OVEN TEMPERATURE: HIGH BROIL

1. Remove the oysters from the shells, drain, and pat dry; reserve the liquor for another use.
2. Cut the bacon in half and place the bacon and sausages in a large saucepan of cold water. Bring to a boil and simmer for 5 minutes. Drain, rinse in cold water, and pat dry. Cut each of the sausages in half.
3. Peel the onions, cut into quarters, and use only the outer two layers of each quarter.

4. Melt the butter; add the parsley and garlic, and season with salt, pepper, and a pinch of cayenne. Lightly sauté the onion, remove with a slotted spoon, and set aside on absorbent paper.
5. Allow the butter to cool slightly, dip the oysters, and roll in corn flour.
6. Mix the ingredients for the sauce and simmer gently until the butter has melted. Remove the sauce from the heat and keep warm.
7. Wrap each oyster in a half slice of bacon. Skewer a piece of onion and sausage, then alternate the oysters and sausages, ending with sausage and onion. Place the skewers on an oiled broiler pan.
8. Broil about 5 inches from the heat for 3 or 4 minutes. Turn over when the bacon and sausage are golden brown and broil the other side until the bacon is crisp.
9. Place a slice of toasted bread on each plate and slip the oysters and sausages from the skewers onto the bread. Serve with warm chili sauce.

MUSTARD-GLAZED OYSTERS
(*Serve with India Pale Ale*)

SERVES 4

24	*shucked medium oysters*
12	*slices bacon*
4	*12-inch skewers*
24	*medium-sized lightly sautéed mushroom caps*
2¹/₂	*cups cooked long-grain rice*

Glaze:

¹/₃	*cup Dijon mustard*
¹/₂	*teaspoon dry mustard*
3	*Tablespoons white wine vinegar*
3	*Tablespoons brown sugar*
¹/₃	*cup honey*
2	*teaspoons peanut oil*
2	*teaspoons dark soy sauce*

OVEN TEMPERATURE: MEDIUM BROIL

1. Make the glaze by blending the mustards together in a saucepan and gradually mix in the remaining ingredients. Simmer for about 5 minutes over low heat. Cool to room temperature.

2. Remove the oysters from the shells, drain, and pat dry; reserve the liquor for another use.
3. Cut the bacon slices in half and wrap each oyster in one piece of bacon.
4. Thread the skewers with alternating oysters and mushroom caps.
5. Put the skewers on a platter and generously brush with the mustard glaze. Set aside for at least 15 minutes, turn the skewers, and repeat the process. Transfer to an oiled broiler pan.
6. Broil about 6 inches from the heat for 5 to 8 minutes, turning to brown all sides evenly. Brush with more glaze, if desired.
7. Serve on a bed of rice.

There are three kinds of oyster eaters:
those loose-minded sports who will eat
anything, hot, cold, thin, thick, dead or
alive, as long as it is oyster; those who will
eat them raw and only raw; and those who
with equal severity will eat them cooked
and no way other. The first group may
perhaps have the most fun, although there
is a white fire about the others' bigotry
that can never warm the broadminded.

—M. F. K. FISHER,
Consider the Oyster

Oysters & . . . Entrées

There is no better way to spend a rainy Saturday afternoon than to retreat to the attic or visit the browser's bookshop and pore over old cookbooks. They are the ones somebody's aunt added little marginal notes to before passing them along to a niece, the ones tucked away beneath the stairs of the local library to make way for the gloss and glamour of the new culinary tomes on display upstairs.

Explicit in instructions and no-nonsense in tone, the authors of those books were usually bent on more than a compilation of "receipts." They were concerned with the quality of culinary skill and never missed an opportunity to slip in a maxim here and a bit of homely wisdom there. The oft-repeated warning that "many waters cannot quench love, but an incompetent cook can turn the flame into a heap of smouldering ashes" must have sent many a novice cook to the stove with alacrity. And, of course, the observation that "there was never an angel who wouldn't take off her wings and cook for the man she loved" surely spurred her on as well.

To please, always to please, was the message, and not an altogether outdated one. It inspired those stalwart guild ladies to assemble an awesome number of recipes that still have charm and more than a little currency. Understanding the possibilities and limitations of the "food convenient to [them]" was perhaps their greatest contribution. And using whatever was seasonal was their triumph. It might have been "an old-fashioned rule" to pour oyster sauce over a plump fowl, but it also made good sense—the oysters were in the bay, the chicken in the barn. Why not "broil the steak, cover the top with raw oysters, and set it on the grate of the oven till the oysters curl," or take two dozen oysters chopped very fine for a "Delicious Stuffing for Fowl"? Call it thrift, call it a stroke of genius, the "huswive's affaires had never an end."

Yesterday's cooks were in many ways as cosmopolitan as they were committed to "What We Cook on Cape Cod" or elsewhere. The names of the recipes tell it all—Indian Pudding, German Apple Cake, Begorra, Portuguese Fish Stew, and Spaghetti: An Italian Receipt Brought from Palermo—complete with the instruction, "To have a perfect dish, buy your spaghetti from the Italian dealers. And do not use bottled cheese." They learned from the Indians and later from the waves of emigrés who brought recipes, utensils, and a distinctive cuisine to the melting pot or perhaps it was the "Kettle-Ho."

The recipes in this chapter capture something of the past and reaffirm the strong conviction that innovative cooking will continue to be found in every family kitchen where an open cookbook and the ingredients found in the refrigerator frequently determine the dinner to be served that evening. Meals come from the "food convenient to [one]"— the eggs in a basket on the kitchen counter, a pound of sirloin in the meat compartment, some freshly made pasta, or a package of rice.

And the instructions for every entrée begin with oysters.

Suggestions

- Some cooks prefer to add cooked pasta to the sauce to integrate the sauce more completely. On the other hand, some prefer to spoon the sauce over the pasta. Either method is a matter of choice.
- It is easier to cut pockets in steaks and chops if the meat has been placed in the freezer to firm up prior to cutting.
- Stuffing baked separately in a casserole dish is often recommended, but it is necessary to add more liquid if baked this way. Use chicken or vegetable stock rather than oyster liquor to prevent oversalting.
- The recipe for oyster sausage can be prepared as a terrine.
- Careful timing is essential in the preparation of fish and seafood. Overcooking reduces flavor and toughens.

PASTIFICIO

Oysters in Straw and Hay
Oyster Polenta Torta
Oysters Conchiglie
Genoan Tagliatelle
Oyster Tetrazzini

RICE BOWL

Colony House Oysters
Patchen Place Oysters
Jambalaya
Delight of Three
Crazy Oats

FROM THE EGG BASKET

Oysters Si Bon
Oyster Surprise
Oyster Aphrodisia
Incredible Omelet
Hangtown Fry
Pampered Oysters

CHICKEN, TURKEY, & A REPERTOIRE OF STUFFING

Carriage Trade Oysters
Traditional Turkey Croquettes
Rushy Marsh Bake
Eagle Pond Pie
Chanticleer Stifle
Herb and Oyster Bread Stuffing
for Poultry
Corn Bread, Apple, and
Oyster Stuffing for Turkey
Oyster and Bratwurst Stuffing for Goose
Wild Rice and Oyster Stuffing for Duck

BEEF, VEAL, LAMB, & PORK

Steak and Oyster Tartare
Oysters Casanova Grill
Oyster Sausages
Veal Roulades
Bayswater Pie
Buried Treasure
Drover's Inn Scallop

DOWN TO THE SEA

Lemon Tree Oyster Gratin
Oysters en Papillote
Port of Call Newburg
Sole Mates
Seafood Hot Pot
Top of the Cove Kebabs

PASTIFICIO

SERVES 6

The Italian legacy of a style of cooking totally allied with fresh, earthy, and wholesome flavors makes the venture into *ostrica cucina* as tempting today as exploring the Orient probably was for Marco Polo centuries ago. And the comparison may be less frivolous than it seems to be.

Allegedly the one who brought macaroni from China to his native land, the adventurous Venetian explorer may well have initiated the largesse of pasta available today. And he had more than a little to do with the succession of sauces that have been devised to accompany it.

In the beginning there was only an uncomplicated ginger-wine sauce and now there is an almost unbelievable range of full-bodied tomato, olive oil, basil, and garlic sauces that have come to be identified with the various regional cuisines of Italy. No ingredient, it seems, has been overlooked in the enduring partnership of pasta and vegetables, meats, and seafood.

For an excursion into this enticing world of pasta, follow the custom of generations of Italian fishermen who added clams to both white and red sauces. Substitute oysters for the clams, or serve oysters in a memorable pesto or "green" seafood sauce. The result can only be called *mescolando in gusto Italiano*, "getting it together, the Italian way."

OYSTERS IN STRAW AND HAY
A platter of egg and spinach pasta blanketed with a zesty white oyster sauce, a bottle of Tocai Friulano, and an *insalata russa* are all one needs for an evening of alfresco dining that may well bring back the lingering memory of a little trattoria just steps from the Rialto in Venice.

1	pint small oysters and liquor
1½	cups fish stock (see p. 58)
2	Tablespoons lemon juice
1	teaspoon grated lemon zest
5	Tablespoons butter
1	chopped medium onion
2	minced garlic cloves
3	Tablespoons flour
	Pinch of nutmeg
2	teaspoons chopped fresh basil
2	teaspoons chopped fresh oregano
½	cup minced parsley

O woeful, weeping Walrus,
your tears are all a sham!

You're greedier for Oysters
than children are for jam.

You like to have an Oyster to
give the meal a zest—

Excuse me, wicked Walrus,
for stamping on your chest!

—LEWIS CARROLL
FOR SAVILE CLARKE'S *Alice*

Salt and freshly ground white pepper
8   *ounces egg fettuccini*
8   *ounces spinach fettuccini*

1. Drain the oysters and set aside. In a small saucepan mix ½ cup of oyster liquor with stock, lemon juice, and zest, and bring to a simmer.
2. Melt 3 tablespoons of butter in another saucepan, and sauté the onion and garlic until soft. Stir in the flour, nutmeg, basil, oregano, and half the parsley, and cook for at least 5 minutes, stirring constantly. Whisk in the hot stock and stir until the mixture thickens, or at least 10 minutes. Keep warm.
3. Fill a large saucepan with 4 quarts of cold water, add 1 tablespoon of salt, and bring to a boil. Cook the fettuccini al dente. Drain and toss with the remaining butter.
4. Add oysters and remaining parsley to the sauce, and adjust seasonings. When the oysters plump, spoon the sauce over the fettuccini and serve.

OYSTER POLENTA TORTA

SERVES 6

One of the enduring qualities of Italian cuisine is its simplicity. What could be easier than to assemble this layered dish of spinach, leeks, pancetta, polenta, and oysters an hour or two before guests arrive? For a more interesting presentation use individual 8-ounce ramekins and follow the layering sequence. Bake and serve with a Piedmontese dry white wine.

1   *pint small oysters*
7   *cups water*
        Salt
7   *ounces coarse cornmeal*
1   *Tablespoon butter*
1   *washed, chopped leek, including green top*
1   *pound washed, stemmed spinach*
¹/₄   *pound pancetta*
2   *Tablespoons Parmigiano-Reggiano*
1   *cup tomato sauce (see p. 178)*

OVEN TEMPERATURE: 350°

1. Drain oysters and set aside.
2. Make the polenta by bringing the water to a boil, adding salt, and stirring in the cornmeal a little at a time. Continue stirring with a wooden spoon until the thickened polenta comes away from the sides of the saucepan, about 25 minutes.
3. Rinse a deep dish in cold water, pour the polenta into it, and cool.
4. Melt butter in a skillet and cook leeks until soft; remove and set aside. In the same skillet sauté the spinach, remove, and drain. Set aside. Add pancetta, lightly sauté, and dice.
5. Cut the polenta into ¼-inch slices. Butter an ovenproof pan and alternate a layer of polenta with a spinach-leek layer, and another polenta layer with spinach, oysters, and pancetta. Sprinkle cheese and dot butter over the last polenta layer and bake for about 30 minutes or until the top is golden brown.
6. Cut into diamonds or squares, and serve with a spoonful of tomato sauce.

OYSTERS CONCHIGLIE

SERVES 4 These shellfish- and spinach-stuffed pasta shells are so redolent of the seashore that one will be tempted to serve them on a bed of seaweed. But, perhaps, a nest of julienned zucchini could create the same effect and please the palate as well. A Chablis Premier Cru would be festive.

1	pint small oysters and liquor
½	cup milk
½	Tablespoon olive oil
	Salt
12	ounces large (2½-inch) pasta shells
4	Tablespoons unsalted butter
12	ounces bay scallops
1	Tablespoon minced shallot
½	minced garlic clove
2	Tablespoons flour
2	teaspoons lemon juice
½	teaspoon grated lemon zest
⅛	teaspoon freshly ground pepper
	Cayenne pepper
10	ounces stemmed fresh spinach
½	cup heavy cream

Lemon sauce:

2	*Tablespoons dry Vermouth*
1	*teaspoon lemon juice*
1	*teaspoon minced shallots*
1	*teaspoon chopped fresh sage*
1	*cup heavy cream*

OVEN TEMPERATURE: 350°

1. Drain the oysters and set aside. Mix ½ cup of the oyster liquor with the milk, and heat in a small saucepan.
2. Boil 3 quarts of water in a large saucepan; add the oil, 2 teaspoons of salt, and the shells. Cook the shells, stirring occasionally, until they are tender but firm. Drain in a colander and use only unbroken shells for the recipe.
3. Melt 2 tablespoons of the butter in a skillet over high heat. When the foam subsides, sauté the scallops and oysters for a minute or two; remove, quarter the oysters, and set aside.
4. Add 2 more tablespoons of butter to the skillet and lightly sauté the shallots and garlic. Stir in the flour and cook until bubbling. Remove from the heat and whisk in the hot milk. Return to heat and stir in the lemon juice, zest, pepper, cayenne, and salt to taste. Stir constantly and cook for 8 to 10 minutes.
5. Blanch the spinach, drain, and chop fine.
6. Add the spinach and seafood to the sauce, stirring lightly until mixed. Fill 20 of the pasta shells with the mixture.
7. Place the shells in a buttered shallow baking dish and pour the cream into the bottom of the dish.
8. Cover and bake about 20 minutes until the shells are thoroughly heated.
9. While the shells are baking, combine the Vermouth, lemon juice, shallots, and sage in a small saucepan. Cook, stirring frequently, until reduced to a tablespoon. Add the cream and cook until the sauce is reduced to ⅔ cup. Correct the seasoning.
10. Remove the shells from the oven and add the cream from the bottom of the dish to the sauce and additional cream if it is necessary to thin the sauce.
11. Arrange 5 shells on individual serving plates and pour some of the sauce over them. Serve immediately.

GENOAN TAGLIATELLE

SERVES 6

All the bounty of the sea spills over the pasta in this recipe that is definitely in the spirit of the Italian Riviera, although it was devised and served much closer to home and is delicious with a glass of Pinot Grigio.

1	pint oysters and liquor
¹/₂	cup olive oil
2	garlic cloves
2	minced shallots
1	Tablespoon chopped fresh oregano
1	cup dry white wine
	Salt and freshly ground pepper
1	pound tagliatelle
2	Tablespoons melted butter
¹/₄	cup brandy
¹/₄	pound cooked lobster
¹/₂	pound cooked, shelled, and deveined medium shrimp
2	peeled, seeded, and chopped medium tomatoes
1	Tablespoon chopped fresh basil

Ceres presents a plate of vermicelli,—

For love must be sustain'd like flesh and blood,

While Bacchus pours out wine, or hands a jelly:

Eggs, oysters, too, are amatory food.

—LORD BYRON, *Don Juan*

1. Heat the oil in a large saucepan and sauté the garlic and shallots until tender. Add the oregano, wine, and pepper to taste. Cook over moderately high heat until the liquid is reduced by half. Discard the garlic.
2. Bring 4 quarts of water to a boil in a large saucepan. Stir in 1 tablespoon of salt and drop in the pasta. Stir while the tagliatelle cooks and remove from the heat when tender but firm. Drain, toss with melted butter, and keep hot while finishing the sauce.
3. Add the oysters, oyster liquor, brandy, pieces of lobster, shrimp, tomatoes, and basil to the reduced wine, and adjust the seasoning. Cook until the mixture is thoroughly heated but do not boil.
4. Spoon the sauce over the tagliatelle and serve immediately.

OYSTER TETRAZZINI

SERVES 6

No telling what lengths a chef will go to in order to please a famous patron. This dish, named for Luisa Tetrazzini, an Italian coloratura soprano, was originally made with chicken. But think of the performance if it had been made with oysters. Toast with a high-quality dry Riesling.

1	pint oysters and liquor
2	cups chicken stock (see p. 59)
3/4	cup butter
1/2	pound sliced wild mushrooms
4	Tablespoons flour
2	egg yolks
3	Tablespoons cream
1/4	cup dry Sherry
	Salt and freshly ground pepper
	Tabasco
8	ounces spaghettini
1/2	cup toasted almonds

Patience is the joy of oysters.

—MARGE PIERCY

OVEN TEMPERATURE: 400°

1. Drain the oysters and set aside. Mix ½ cup of oyster liquor with the stock and heat in a small saucepan.
2. Melt the butter in another saucepan; spoon off and reserve ½ cup. Lightly sauté the mushrooms; remove with a slotted spoon and set aside.
3. Stir flour into the saucepan and cook until pale yellow. Remove from the heat and whisk in the stock. Return to heat and cook about 5 minutes, stirring constantly.
4. Beat the egg yolks and cream in a bowl. Whisk in ½ cup of the hot mixture, a spoonful at a time. Gradually beat in a cup of the hot mixture, then transfer the enriched sauce back to the saucepan. Season with Sherry, salt, pepper, and Tabasco and bring to a boil. Reduce heat.
5. Stir the oysters and mushrooms into the sauce and immediately remove from the heat.
6. Boil 3 quarts of water in a large saucepan, add 2 teaspoons of salt, and drop in the spaghettini. Stir, and remove from the stove as soon as it becomes limp. Drain the spaghettini and toss in a bowl with ¼ cup of the reserved melted butter.
7. Place half the pasta on the bottom of a buttered 2-quart baking dish. Cover with a layer of oyster sauce. Repeat the layers and drizzle with the remaining melted butter.
8. Cover the dish and bake for 20 minutes or until bubbling. Remove the cover and bake another 10 minutes.
9. Garnish with toasted almonds if desired.

RICE BOWL

From the ancient "paddy to pot" cuisines of China and India to the contemporary California-inspired style of cooking, rice dishes that have withstood the test of time are being re-created by cooks who have their own dining traditions and their own rules about how rice is cooked and served. Name a shallow pan of rice studded with seafood, paella, or jambalaya; refer to a plate of curry-spiced rice and fish as kedgeree or the Indian *kitcherie*; or describe a dish of mushrooms and rice as *ris al forno*, or *riz duxelles*, and the ethnic differences as well as the universality of rice are reaffirmed.

Most of the following recipes come from a country or region known for both its cultivation of rice and long tradition of seafood cuisine. They emphasize the proverb that cooking with ingredients "convenient" to one is frequently a necessity and always can be the art of the possible.

COLONY HOUSE OYSTERS

SERVES 6

Tradition holds sway over this curried rice entrée. Call it Indian; call it British. Either way, the combination of all those "curry" spices with rice and oysters is really a roaring success. Make the evening really cosmopolitan and serve with a Washington State Gewurztraminer.

1	pint oysters and liquor
2	Tablespoons butter
1	Tablespoon vegetable oil
2	finely chopped medium onions
1	teaspoon dry mustard
1	teaspoon turmeric
$^1/_2$	cup shredded unsweetened coconut
$1^3/_4$	cups chicken stock (see p. 59)
1	bay leaf
$^1/_4$	teaspoon red pepper flakes
$^1/_2$	teaspoon cinnamon
$^1/_4$	teaspoon ground cloves
$^1/_4$	teaspoon coriander
$^1/_4$	teaspoon cumin
$^1/_2$	cup cream
	Salt and freshly ground pepper
3	cups cooked long-grain rice

1. Drain the oysters and set aside, reserving ¼ cup of the liquor.
2. Heat the butter and oil in a skillet and sauté the onion until soft. Add the mustard, turmeric, and coconut; cook and stir over moderately high heat until the coconut turns golden brown.
3. Reduce the heat under the skillet and mix in the oyster liquor, stock, bay leaf, and spices. Simmer, uncovered, for 15 minutes. Remove bay leaf. Pour in the cream and simmer about 5 minutes.
4. Add the oysters and heat until the edges begin to curl. Season to taste with salt and pepper, and remove from the heat.
5. Spoon the hot rice into individual bowls and then add the oyster curry.

PATCHEN PLACE OYSTERS

SERVES 6

In this entrée both the rice and the seafood are prepared with the "trinity" of Creole cookery—green pepper, celery, and onions. The vegetables are as common to the garden patches that dot the Louisiana countryside as the rice fields are to the rich lowlands of the delta. And then there are all those oysters. Glory be. . . . Serve with Pilsner.

1	pint oysters and liquor
1½	cups long-grain rice
3½	cups chicken stock (see p. 59)
1½	Tablespoons corn oil
⅓	cup finely chopped celery
⅓	cup finely chopped green pepper
⅓	cup finely chopped onion
	Salt and freshly ground pepper
¼	teaspoon cayenne
2	Tablespoons butter
1	cup commercial clam juice
½	cup tomato purée
2	garlic cloves
	Pinch of thyme
½	cup cream
6	ounces lump crabmeat
1	pound shelled and deveined raw medium shrimp

OVEN TEMPERATURE: 350°

CURRIED OYSTERS

Put one tablespoonful of butter, one teaspoonful of grated onion, one-half teaspoonful of curry powder and one tablespoonful of flour in a hot chafing dish. When blended add the oyster liquor and cook a minute, stirring, add the oysters and when they curl serve on toast.

—WHAT WE COOK ON CAPE COD, *compiled by Amy L. Handy,* 1911

1. Combine the rice, chicken stock, corn oil, and 1 tablespoon each of celery, green pepper, and onion. Season with pepper, cayenne, and a pinch of salt. Bake in a tightly covered, buttered casserole for about 1 hour until the rice is tender.
2. Drain the oysters and set aside, reserving ⅓ cup of the liquor.
3. Melt the butter in a skillet; wilt the remaining celery, green pepper, and onion. Add the oyster liquor, clam juice, tomato purée, garlic, and thyme. Simmer uncovered for 15 minutes, stirring occasionally. Discard the garlic.
4. Stir in the cream and crabmeat and simmer about 5 minutes.
5. Add the oysters and shrimp and cook until the edges of the oysters begin to curl and the shrimp are pink. Adjust the seasonings.
6. Divide the rice into 6 shallow serving bowls and ladle the seafood over the rice.

JAMBALAYA

SERVES 6

Situated between New Orleans and Baton Rouge, Gonzales is one of the oldest Spanish settlements in Louisiana. Because the crown jewel of its local cuisine is a jambalaya that is heir apparent to Spain's own *paella*, it is well worth traveling to Gonzales to sample this one-dish meal in its authentic setting. Or try this recipe at home and serve with a light-bodied California Chardonnay if a visit to Gonzales is impossible.

1	*pint oysters and liquor*
12	*cherrystone clams in shells*
1	*pound lean pork*
1	*pound smoked mild sausage*
3	*Tablespoons butter*
¹/₂	*teaspoon chili powder*
¹/₄	*teaspoon thyme*
¹/₄	*teaspoon ground cloves*
1	*crumbled bay leaf*
¹/₄	*teaspoon freshly ground pepper*
	Pinch of cayenne pepper
4	*chopped medium onions*
3	*chopped scallions, including green parts*
2	*minced garlic cloves*

1 cup chopped tasso
1½ cups long-grain rice
3 cups chicken stock (see p. 59)
   Salt
2 Tablespoons chopped parsley

OVEN TEMPERATURE: 325°

1. Drain the oysters and set aside, reserving ⅓ cup of the liquor. Scrub the clams thoroughly.
2. Cut the pork into ½-inch cubes and the sausage into ⅛-inch slices.
3. Melt the butter in a large skillet over low heat and stir in the chili powder, thyme, cloves, bay leaf, and peppers. Sauté the onions, scallions, garlic, tasso, and pork about 15 minutes until they are brown, stirring frequently.
4. Stir in the sausage and cook for 20 minutes.
5. Transfer the contents of the skillet to a bowl, and keep warm.
6. Add more butter and the rice to the skillet; cook and stir over medium heat for 5 minutes until the rice is golden brown.
7. Pour in the oyster liquor and stock, and season to taste. When the stock comes to a boil, reduce the heat, cover and cook for 20 minutes or until the rice is almost tender and most of the liquid has been absorbed.
8. Spoon a third of the rice into a large buttered baking dish or paella pan. Place the meat in a single layer and spoon in more rice. Distribute the oysters, cover with the remaining rice, and add the clams to the top layer. Pour in more stock if the rice seems too dry.
9. Cover and bake about 15 minutes until the clams open.
10. Garnish with parsley and serve.

There's nothing in Christianity or Buddhism that quite matches the sympathetic unselfishness of an oyster.

—SAKI

DELIGHT OF THREE

The combination of ham, shrimp, and oysters in a dish of Oriental fried rice will certainly cause a division of loyalty between those epicures who prefer *chow fan* made with chicken rather than ham. But perhaps the "particularity" of oysters will bridge the gap. Serve with a dry Riesling.

1	pint oysters
	Vegetable or peanut oil
2	lightly whisked eggs
8	minced scallions, including green tops
1	minced slice fresh ginger root
1/2	pound shelled, deveined, raw medium shrimp
1/2	pound diced ham
1/2	cup shelled peas
3	cups cooked long-grain rice
2	Tablespoons soy sauce

1. Drain the oysters, pat dry, and set aside, reserving the liquor for another use.
2. Heat a wok to high heat, add 2 tablespoons of oil, and cover bottom and sides with a coat of oil. Lower the heat.
3. Pour in the eggs mixed with a few scallions. Cook until the eggs set. Transfer the eggs to a warm bowl and break the eggs into small pieces with a fork.
4. Add 1 tablespoon more oil to the wok and raise the temperature to medium high. Add the ginger and the remaining scallions and stir-fry for 1 minute.
5. Add the shrimp and stir-fry until pink. Add the ham and peas and stir-fry another minute. Remove all the ingredients from the wok to a warm bowl.
6. Add another tablespoon of oil to the wok and heat. Toss and stir-fry the cooked rice and oysters for 2 minutes; stir in the soy sauce.
7. Return all the ingredients to the wok; toss and mix together.
8. Remove from the heat and spoon the rice mixture onto a platter. Serve immediately as an entrée or as part of a Chinese dinner.

CRAZY OATS

What's in a name? Indians called it *manomin*, settlers called it water rice, French explorers called it "crazy oats," and now everyone calls it wild rice. For a truly "fare-thee-well," mix it with almonds, chicken livers, and oysters, and it will never be called anything less than provocative. Serve with an unabashedly rich and oaky California Chardonnay.

1	pint small oysters
1	cup wild rice
6	Tablespoons butter
$^1/_2$	cup chopped scallions, including green parts
1	cup blanched almonds
$2^3/_4$	cups chicken stock (see p. 59)
$^1/_4$	cup orange juice
1	Tablespoon grated orange zest
1	cup golden raisins
$^1/_2$	teaspoon salt
$^1/_8$	teaspoon freshly ground pepper
$^1/_2$	pound chicken livers

OVEN TEMPERATURE: 325°

1. Rinse the rice in several changes of water, and drain.
2. Melt 4 tablespoons of butter in a large skillet. Stir and sauté the rice, scallions, and almonds for 15 minutes.
3. Add the stock, orange juice, zest, raisins, and seasonings, and bring to a boil.
4. Transfer to a buttered 1½-quart casserole, cover, and bake 1 hour.
5. Drain the oysters and set aside, reserving the liquor for another use.
6. Cut the livers in 1-inch pieces and sauté quickly in a skillet in the remaining 2 tablespoons of butter. Remove with a slotted spoon when the livers begin to brown, and set aside.
7. After the casserole has been in the oven for 1 hour, stir in the oysters and livers, and fluff the rice with a fork. Cover and bake another 30 minutes.

FROM THE
EGG BASKET

Probably no other food has as much versatility as the dependable egg. It binds together, enriches, puffs up, thickens, fluffs, and enhances everything from sauces, custards, and pancakes to vegetables and cheese. And no other food is as comforting. An affirmative answer to the question: "Are there any eggs in the refrigerator?" virtually guarantees a meal that will stave off hunger any time of the day or night.

No longer regarded as the "autocrat of the breakfast table," the egg can perform dramatically at a festive brunch, lunch, dinner, or late supper, and it can be prepared in almost every imaginable way. As an added fillip, the absolute neutrality of its flavor makes an egg combined with fruit and sugar as delicious as it is zesty when mixed with spices and herbs.

Definitely a principal in a cast of two or more, an egg is at its best when partnered with other ingredients. So, from the inspired soufflé to a coddled egg on a breakfast tray, here are the "egg plus" recipes that work with oysters.

OYSTERS SI BON

SERVES 4

Anything as regal as Oysters Si Bon incurs a debt of gratitude. So, thank you, Catherine de Medici, for introducing the Florentine *sformata* to the royal court of France and making the soufflé a dish fit for a king. Perfect with a high-quality dry Alsace Riesling.

$^1/_2$	pint oysters
2	Tablespoons butter
3	Tablespoons flour
$^1/_4$	teaspoon nutmeg
$1^1/_2$	cups hot milk
3	slices smoked salmon
3	egg yolks
$^1/_4$	teaspoon salt
	Pinch of freshly ground pepper
2	teaspoons chopped fresh dill
4	egg whites

OVEN TEMPERATURE: 375°

1. Melt the butter in a 1½-quart saucepan; stir in the flour and nutmeg, and cook until straw yellow. Remove from the heat and whisk in the hot milk.

Return to heat and stir constantly for about 5 minutes, and then allow to cool.

2. Drain and coarsely chop the oysters, reserving the liquor for another use. Cut the salmon into ¼-inch strips, and set aside.

3. Beat the egg yolks lightly; add the salt, pepper, and dill. Whisk the yolks into the cooled sauce, one spoonful at a time.

4. Beat the egg whites until stiff in a large bowl. Stir a quarter of them into the yolk mixture. Fold the rest of the whites in quickly in order not to deflate or diminish their volume.

5. Spread an inch of the mixture on the bottom of a well-buttered and floured 1½-quart soufflé dish. Arrange the oysters and salmon on top of it and spoon in the rest of the mixture.

6. Bake in the center of the oven for 25 to 30 minutes, and serve immediately.

SERVES 4

OYSTER SURPRISE

Good things come in French brioches. Just open the lid and find the oysters and scrambled eggs inside. Marvelous with Cremant de Bourgogne, Kir Royales, or Bellinis on one of those revving-up-for-the-week-ahead Sunday brunches.

12	*shucked small oysters*
½	*cup corn flour*
	Salt and freshly ground pepper
	Cayenne pepper
6	*Tablespoons unsalted butter*
8	*eggs*
2	*Tablespoons cream*
	Tabasco
4	*3½-inch brioches*
	Herb sprigs

1. Remove the oysters from the shells and pat dry, reserving the liquor for another use. Dip the oysters in flour seasoned with salt, pepper, and cayenne.

2. Melt 2 tablespoons of the butter in a skillet and sauté the oysters over moderately high heat, browning both sides quickly. Set the oysters aside on absorbent paper.

Oysters are the usual opening to a winter breakfast. . . . Indeed, they are almost indispensable.

—ALMANACH DES
GOURMANDES, 1803

3. Beat the eggs and cream in a bowl, but do not homogenize. Season with pepper, Tabasco, and ¼ teaspoon salt.
4. Melt 4 tablespoons of butter in a large heavy-bottom skillet over low heat, add the eggs, and stir with a large fork until the eggs begin to thicken. Add the oysters and lightly stir until the eggs begin to solidify. Remove from heat.
5. Remove the lid from each brioche and hollow it out. Place the bottoms on heated plates and fill each with the scrambled eggs and oysters. Replace the lids and serve immediately with a garnish of herb sprigs.

OYSTER APHRODISIA

SERVES 4

Everyone dreams of that "betwixt the sheets" breakfast when *ambience* is the magic word, and Venus is in the kitchen preparing a feast of mangoes and melons, followed by scrambled eggs napped with an oyster and lobster sauce . . . and "love was the pearl of his oyster/ And Venus rose red out of wine."* Here is the recipe. And the wine is a Chablis Premier Cru.

½	pint oysters and liquor
¾	cup cream
5	Tablespoons butter
2	Tablespoons chopped shallots
1½	Tablespoons flour
2	teaspoons chopped fresh tarragon
2	Tablespoons dry Vermouth
1	teaspoon lemon juice
½	teaspoon tomato paste
½	cup coarsely chopped cooked lobster meat
	Salt and freshly ground pepper
8	eggs

1. Drain the oysters, reserving the liquor. If the oysters are large, cut in half or quarter, and set aside. Mix ¼ cup of the liquor with the cream, and heat in a saucepan.
2. Melt 2 tablespoons of butter in another saucepan and sauté the shallots until tender.

*Algernon Charles Swinburne, *Dolores*

OYSTER OMELET,
(Very Fine.)

*Take twelve large oysters
chopped fine. Mix the
beaten yolks of six eggs into
a tea-cupful of milk, and
add the oysters. Then put in
a spoonful of melted butter,
and lastly add the whites
of the eggs beated to a stiff
froth. Fry this in hot butter
or salted lard, and do not
stir it while cooking.
Slip a knife around the
edges while cooking, that
the centre may cook equally,
and turn it out so that the
brown side be uppermost.*

—CATHERINE ESTHER
BEECHER,
*Mrs. Beecher's Housekeeper
and Healthkeeper,* 1876

SERVES 1

3. Stir in the flour and cook until straw yellow. Remove from the heat and whisk in the cream. Return to heat; add the tarragon, Vermouth, lemon juice, and tomato paste. Cook, stirring constantly, for at least 5 minutes.
4. Stir the oysters and lobster into the sauce and adjust seasonings. Heat the sauce thoroughly and keep warm while scrambling the eggs.
5. Beat the eggs in a bowl and season with ¼ teaspoon of salt and pepper.
6. Melt the remaining butter in a heavy-bottom skillet over low heat, add the eggs, and stir with a whisk until they form a soft custard; continue breaking the curds until the eggs are almost solidified. Remove from heat, and let the heat from the pan finish cooking the eggs.
7. Serve immediately on hot plates, napping the eggs with the oyster and lobster sauce.

INCREDIBLE OMELET

Two eggs and 2 tablespoons of filling, and the Incredible Omelet becomes an edible masterpiece. Make and serve it individually like a precious *objet d'art*. It's the ultimate compliment to a guest. Serve with a high-quality California sparkling wine.

2	*fresh eggs*
	Salt
1	*teaspoon water*
	Freshly ground pepper
1	*Tablespoon unsalted butter*
¼	*cup of one of the following oyster fillings**

1. Crack the eggs into a small bowl; add a pinch of salt and water. Lightly beat the eggs with a fork, but do not homogenize the texture of the eggs. Crack in a bit of pepper and set aside.
2. Melt the butter in a 6-inch skillet over high heat. Pour in the eggs when the butter starts to foam.
3. Stir the eggs briefly with the flat of the fork; allow them to set, tipping the skillet to permit the uncooked egg to run to the bottom.
4. Spoon the filling across the center of the omelet while it is still moist. Fold the omelet over and tip it onto a warm plate. Garnish and serve.

* The amount of filling in each of the following recipes is sufficient for 4 individual omelets or an 8-egg omelet to serve 4 people.

CREAMED MUSHROOM FILLING

$^1/_2$	*pint oysters*
2	*Tablespoons unsalted butter*
	Pinch of nutmeg
$^1/_4$	*pound sliced button mushrooms*
$^1/_4$	*cup cream*
3	*Tablespoons dry Madeira*
2	*Tablespoons finely chopped parsley*
	Salt and freshly ground pepper

1. Drain and coarsely chop the oysters, reserving the liquor for another use.
2. Melt the butter in a skillet, stir in the nutmeg, and sauté the mushrooms over moderately high heat until the liquid has evaporated. Remove the mushrooms with a slotted spoon and set aside.
3. Lower the heat under the skillet, add the cream and Madeira, and simmer until reduced by half.
4. Before preparing the omelets, return the mushrooms to the skillet. Stir in the oysters, parsley, and seasoning, and heat thoroughly.

HAM AND CHEESE FILLING

$^1/_2$	*pint oysters*
2	*Tablespoons butter*
2	*chopped scallions*
2	*ounces julienned cured ham*
2	*Tablespoons shredded mild melting cheese, such as Fontina*

1. Drain and coarsely chop the oysters, reserving the liquor for another use.
2. Melt 2 tablespoons of butter in a skillet and sauté the scallions until wilted. Add ham and heat through. Add oysters and set aside. Allow to cool.
3. Before preparing the omelets, add cheese to the filling.

BACON AND POTATO FILLING

$^1/_2$	*pint oysters*
4	*slices diced bacon*
2	*Tablespoons butter*

1   *cup diced cooked potato*
¹/₂   *cup sliced onion*
      Salt and freshly ground pepper

1. Drain and coarsely chop the oysters, reserving the liquor for another use.
2. Fry the bacon in a skillet until brown and crisp. Remove with a slotted spoon and drain on absorbent paper. Pour off the drippings from the pan.
3. Add and melt the butter; sauté the potato and onion until well browned. Season to taste.
4. When preparing the omelets, return the bacon to the pan. Stir in the oysters and stir until thoroughly cooked.

HANGTOWN FRY

SERVES 4

Dry Diggings, Hangtown, and Placerville—all names for one small California town. And rumor has it that it wasn't gold, or desperadoes, or the Chamber of Commerce that put it on the map, but a certain cook at the Blue Bell restaurant who added a few oysters and bacon to a skillet of scrambled eggs. Another story of another golden egg! Serve with Cremant de Bourgogne.

24   *shucked medium oysters*
8   *slices bacon*
10   *eggs*
¹/₂   *cup flour*
      Salt and freshly ground pepper
1   *cup fine unsalted cracker crumbs*
4   *Tablespoons cream*
      Dash of Tabasco (optional)
6   *Tablespoons butter*

1. Cook the bacon in a skillet or microwave oven until brown and crisp. Drain on absorbent paper and set aside.
2. Beat 2 of the eggs in a bowl.
3. Remove the oysters from the shells, drain, pat dry, and coat with seasoned flour. Dip the oysters in the egg, and roll in cracker crumbs.
4. Beat the remaining eggs with the cream and seasonings.
5. Melt half the butter in a large skillet over moderately high heat and sauté the oysters quickly on both sides. Add the remaining butter, pour

the egg mixture over the oysters, reduce the heat to low, and cook until the eggs are set and the bottom of the omelet is lightly browned.

6. Fold the omelet and serve on a warm platter with the bacon slices.

PAMPERED OYSTERS

SERVES 6

Cosseted under this light crabmeat sauce, an oyster timbale will pamper even a reluctant diner and remind him of all those custards surrounded by cream sauce that were served in Auntie's kitchen. Serve with Puligny-Montrachet or a high-quality Graves Blanc.

Whoever eats oysters on
St. James Day will never
want money.

—PROVERB

1¹/₂	*pints oysters and liquor*
2	*cups milk*
4	*Tablespoons butter*
4	*Tablespoons flour*
2	*eggs*
2	*egg yolks*
¹/₄	*teaspoon salt*
¹/₈	*teaspoon freshly ground white pepper*
¹/₂	*cup heavy cream*
2	*Tablespoons Cognac*
6	*ounces lump crabmeat*
2	*teaspoons lemon juice*

OVEN TEMPERATURE: 350°

1. Drain the oysters and set aside. Measure ½ cup of the oyster liquor, mix with the milk, and heat in a saucepan.
2. Melt the butter in another saucepan, stir in the flour, and cook until straw yellow. Remove from the heat and whisk in the hot milk. Return to heat and cook, stirring constantly, for at least 5 minutes. Remove from the stove and allow the sauce to cool.
3. Place the eggs, yolks, salt, pepper, and oysters in a blender, and process at high speed for 1 minute. Add 1 cup of the sauce, 5 tablespoons of cream, and the Cognac, and process for 15 seconds.
4. Pour the mixture into 6 buttered ramekins. Place in a pan of boiling water and bake for about 30 minutes or until set.

5. While the timbales are baking, stir 3 tablespoons of cream, the crab-meat, and lemon juice into the remaining sauce. Adjust the seasonings and heat.
6. Unmold the timbales and nap with the crabmeat sauce.

CHICKEN, TURKEY, & A REPERTOIRE OF STUFFING

At our house there were always two turkeys roasted— one for dinner and the other to assure us of plenty of left-overs, for we were a family passionately devoted to cold turkey. To my mind, bits of cold turkey on toast for breakfast, and cold turkey served with salad, reheated stuffing and potato cakes are even more tasty than the roast turkey served at a formal dinner.

—JAMES BEARD, Delights and Prejudices

Looking over the "old" recipes for chicken stifle, deep-dish pie, and cream gravy is happily nostalgic, and there is a rightness about the honest, unclut-tered instructions to "add butter the size of an egg," and "pour over the fowl right away," that makes one wonder if these recipes can really be improved upon. There is also a certain reluctance to expose them to too much light, or too much scrutiny, for fear of losing something precious.

Undoubtedly, it is important to take what they have to offer, to join in the spirit of prodigality that existed at a time when it was commonplace and certainly nutritious to serve many chicken dishes with an oyster sauce or gravy and to stuff a brace of quail or a cavernous turkey with dozens of oys-ters. Important to remember, too, that it was considered a tad racy to add a pinch of thyme or a drop or two of Sherry.

The word *memories* best describes the repertoire of stuffings collected here. Thyme-sage-and-onion bread stuffing is such an "over the river and through the woods" kind of thing; it cannot be forgotten. And there are many who still believe that half the pleasure of a nicely roasted bird is the partnership that exists between the stuffing and the intrinsic flavor of the meat. So, here are a few not-so-familiar stuffing combinations for the cook who wants to preserve an old-fashioned, authentic recipe and still use the wondrous selection of ingredients available today.

Some of these are festive entrées for special holidays, some are Sunday fare, all of them are seasoned with oysters and . . .

CARRIAGE TRADE OYSTERS

SERVES 6 Anyone who keeps a dinner diary will record this one with four stars. The emphatic flavoring of the oysters, scallops, and shrimp adds a slight southern accent to a dish that needs only a potato puff, lemony artichoke, and a bottle of dry Vouvray for completion.

1	*pint small oysters and liquor*
4	*whole chicken breasts*
8	*Tablespoons butter*
2¹/₂	*cups chicken stock (see p. 59)*
¹/₄	*cup finely julienned leeks*
¹/₄	*cup chopped shallots*
2	*Tablespoons flour*
¹/₂	*cup heavy cream*
8	*ounces bay scallops*
8	*ounces peeled and deveined raw shrimp*
3	*Tablespoons brandy*
¹/₄	*cup chopped chives*
	Lemon wedges

Coating:

	Salt and freshly ground pepper
	Flour
2	*whisked eggs*
1	*teaspoon water*
2	*cups fine fresh bread crumbs*

1. Split the chicken breasts; remove the skin and bones. Flatten each piece with the broad side of a cleaver. Season with salt and pepper.
2. Dredge the chicken in flour, dip in eggs mixed with water, and roll in crumbs. Set aside to dry for 30 minutes.
3. Melt 5 tablespoons of butter in a large skillet and sauté the chicken on each side until golden. Remove to a platter, and keep warm.
4. Drain the oysters and set aside. Heat ½ cup of the liquor with the stock in a saucepan.
5. Melt the remaining butter in another saucepan, stir in the leeks, cover the pan, and cook over low heat for 5 minutes. Add the shallots and cook another minute. Stir in the flour and cook until straw yellow. Re-

move from the heat and whisk in the stock. Return to heat and cook, stirring constantly, until the mixture thickens.

6. Stir in the cream and simmer uncovered for 10 minutes, stirring occasionally.

7. Add the scallops, shrimp, and brandy, and simmer for a minute until the shrimp turn pink.

8. Add the oysters and heat until the oysters curl. Season to taste.

9. Nap some of the sauce over the chicken, garnish with chopped chives, and serve with lemon wedges.

TRADITIONAL TURKEY CROQUETTES

SERVES 4   Often referred to as Cutlets or Dodgers on turn-of-the-last-century oyster restaurant menus, these tasty croquettes can be Wedgwood and sterling fare with a bottle of Washington State Riesling and a tease of cranberry salsa.

1	pint oysters and liquor
²/₃	cup chicken stock (see p. 59)
3	Tablespoons butter
2	Tablespoons chopped shallots
3	Tablespoons flour
3	egg yolks
¹/₄	cup heavy cream
1	cup finely chopped cooked turkey
1	Tablespoon chopped fresh sage
	Salt and freshly ground pepper
	Cayenne pepper
	Peanut or vegetable oil for frying
	Cranberry salsa

Coating:

2	cups seasoned fine bread crumbs
1	egg
2	Tablespoons water

1. Drain the oysters, coarsely chop, and set aside. Measure ⅓ cup of the liquor and heat it with the stock in a small saucepan.

2. Melt the butter in another saucepan, and sauté the shallots until tender. Stir in the flour and cook until straw yellow. Remove from the heat and whisk in the stock. Return to heat and cook, stirring constantly, until the mixture thickens. Simmer for at least 5 minutes.
3. Beat the egg yolks and cream in a bowl. Whisk ½ cup of the hot mixture into the yolks, a spoonful at a time. Then slowly beat in the remaining hot mixture. Transfer the enriched sauce back to the saucepan and, stirring carefully, bring to a boil. Reduce heat, and add the oysters.
4. Remove from the stove and stir in the turkey and sage; adjust seasonings. Spread the mixture on a large plate, cover loosely with waxed paper, and set aside to cool.
5. Shape the mixture into 12 croquettes, roll in bread crumbs, then in the egg mixed with water, and again in the crumbs. Dry for at least 2 hours.
6. Heat the oil to 375° in a deep-fryer or heavy-gauge saucepan.
7. Place the croquettes in a fryer basket, a few at a time, and lower into the hot oil. Fry until the croquettes are golden brown and remove to a baking sheet lined with absorbent paper. Keep warm until all are cooked, or make ahead of time and reheat in a 400° oven.
8. Serve the croquettes with cranberry salsa.

RUSHY MARSH BAKE

SERVES 4

In New England, when the wind blows ripples across the marsh, the November clouds dull the sky, and the swans and ducks socialize in polite groups in the pond, then it's the time of year to build a fire in the fireplace, put the chicken in the oven, and open a bottle of Graves Blanc.

½	pint oysters and liquor
1	small chicken
⅓	cup dry pancake mix
½	Tablespoon chopped fresh rosemary
	Salt and freshly ground pepper
1	Tablespoon butter
2	cups chicken stock (see p. 59)
1	cup dry white wine
1½	Tablespoons flour
½	cup oyster mushrooms
½	cup blanched pearl onions

SMOTHERED FOWL AND OYSTERS

Dress a good, plump fowl as for roasting. Drain one pint of oysters and fill the fowl; sew up and set in a kettle to steam, put a rack under it to keep it out of the water. Put salt, pepper and some pieces of celery in the water. Boil hard until the fowl is tender but not broken. Serve with sauce made from the water in the kettle and one cup of cream thickened with flour. Add one pint of oysters and cook till they curl. Pour this over the fowl. An oldfashioned rule.

—*WHAT WE COOK ON CAPE COD, 1911*

SERVES 8

1. Cut the chicken into quarters and dip in dry pancake mix that has been seasoned with rosemary, salt, and pepper.
2. Place the chicken in a small roasting pan, dot with butter, and bake for about 1 hour until tender and browned.
3. While the chicken is baking, drain the oysters and set aside. Mix the oyster liquor, stock, and wine in a saucepan, and simmer uncovered until reduced by half.
4. Remove the chicken from the pan to a platter and keep warm while the pan gravy is being prepared.
5. Place the baking pan with chicken drippings over moderate heat, deglaze, and make a pan gravy by stirring in the flour. Simmer for at least 3 minutes. Whisk in the stock and cook, stirring constantly, until the gravy thickens.
6. Lower the heat, add the mushrooms (whole if small or cut in half), onions, and oysters. Simmer for 5 minutes and season to taste with salt and pepper.
7. Serve the chicken napped with the oyster gravy.

EAGLE POND PIE

After a skating party at one of the nearby ponds, a hot toddy or a glass of Riesling and an oyster and chicken pie crusted with fluffy biscuits is relaxation and reward all rolled into one.

1	pint small oysters and liquor
1	6-pound roasting chicken
1	bay leaf
1	garlic clove
	Salt
8	Tablespoons butter
1/2	teaspoon nutmeg
1	cup chopped leeks
1	cup chopped celery
6	Tablespoons flour
3	egg yolks
1/4	cup chopped parsley
	Biscuit dough for top crust

1. Cut the chicken into large pieces, place in a pot, cover with water, add the bay leaf, garlic, and 1½ teaspoons of salt, and simmer until tender, about 1½ hours.
2. Remove the chicken when cool; skin, bone, and cut it into 1½-inch pieces.
3. Degrease the broth; simmer in an uncovered saucepan until reduced to 4 cups. Keep warm until needed for the sauce.
4. Drain the oysters and set aside, reserving ½ cup of the liquor.
5. Melt the butter in a large saucepan, stir in the nutmeg, and sauté the leeks and celery for 5 minutes. Remove the vegetables with a slotted spoon and set aside.
6. Stir in the flour and cook until golden yellow. Remove from the heat and whisk in the hot broth. Return to heat and cook, stirring constantly, until the mixture thickens; simmer for 5 minutes.
7. Whisk the egg yolks and oyster liquor together in a large bowl. Beat in ½ cup of the hot mixture, a spoonful at a time. Gradually whisk in the remaining hot mixture and bring to a boil. Stir in the oysters, chicken, parsley, and vegetables; adjust seasonings.
8. Spoon into a buttered 2½-quart casserole. Cover with biscuit dough rolled ¼ inch thick and trimmed to fit the dish. Cut slits in dough to vent.
9. Bake about 25 minutes until the crust is golden.

CHANTICLEER STIFLE

SERVES 10

This saucy stifle really struts its stuff and has been doing so for a long time. Although it's in a class by itself, brussels sprouts and chestnuts or honey-glazed carrots do it proud, as does a glass of Macon.

1	quart small oysters and liquor
2¹/₂	cups half-and-half
5	whole chicken breasts
	Salt and freshly ground pepper
	Dry mustard
4	Tablespoons butter
1	Tablespoon oil
4	Tablespoons flour
¹/₂	cup dry Sherry
¹/₄	cup chopped parsley

OVEN TEMPERATURE: 325°

1. Drain the oysters and set aside. Mix ½ cup of the liquor with half-and-half and heat in a saucepan.
2. Split the chicken breasts and season with salt, pepper, and mustard.
3. Heat the butter and oil in a large skillet. When the foam subsides, cook the chicken, a few pieces at a time, until golden brown on all sides. Arrange the chicken in one layer in a buttered baking dish or roasting pan.
4. Stir the flour into the skillet and cook until golden. Slowly stir in the half-and-half, and cook, stirring constantly, until the mixture thickens. Add the Sherry, and pour the sauce over the chicken.
5. Cover the baking dish and bake for 1 hour. Baste at least twice during the baking time.
6. Remove the chicken to a hot platter and keep warm.
7. Pour the sauce from the pan into a blender and process to reblend the fat that has separated during the baking.
8. Transfer the sauce to a saucepan; stir in the oysters and parsley. Adjust the seasonings and heat until the oysters begin to curl.
9. To serve, nap the chicken breasts with the oyster sauce.

Stuffing

From the land of cotton plantations and bluegrass horse racing to the windswept bluffs and weathered captains' houses on Plymouth Bay, dressing a bird is part of a holiday ritual. Whether the stuffing base is bread, chestnuts, noodles, dried fruits, rice, or dozens of combinations of meat or seafood is often a matter of tradition, sometimes a matter of taste. But making it an integral part of the presentation of an entrée and not a taken-for-granted background is always a matter of care. Appropriate wines will depend on what is being stuffed—except in a few recipes, where the ingredients marry well with a certain wine choice.

HERB AND OYSTER BREAD STUFFING FOR POULTRY *

YIELD: 10 CUPS

1	pint oysters and liquor
1	cup unsalted butter
1	cup chopped onion
1	cup chopped celery
8	cups cubed day-old bread
2	well-beaten eggs
$^1/_2$	teaspoon ground sage
$^1/_2$	teaspoon dried thyme
$^1/_2$	teaspoon dried marjoram
$^1/_2$	teaspoon dried rosemary
$^1/_2$	cup chopped fresh parsley
	Salt and freshly ground pepper

1. Drain and coarsely chop the oysters, reserving ½ cup of the liquor.
2. Melt the butter in a skillet; pour off and reserve ½ cup.
3. Sauté the onion and celery in the skillet until tender. Stir in the oyster liquor and simmer for about 5 minutes.
4. Toss the bread cubes and vegetable mixture together in a large bowl, and allow the mixture to cool slightly.
5. Add the eggs and herbs, and mix until well blended. Gradually add the reserved butter to moisten the stuffing.
6. Add the oysters, and salt and pepper to taste.
7. Allow the stuffing to cool before using.

* This stuffing can also be used for fish, boned breast of veal, and boneless loin of pork.

CORN BREAD, APPLE, AND OYSTER STUFFING FOR TURKEY*

YIELD: 8 CUPS

1	pint small oysters and liquor
12	Tablespoons unsalted butter
1	coarsely chopped sweet onion
1	Tablespoon chopped fresh sage
6	cups crumbled corn bread
3	peeled, cored, and coarsely chopped tart apples
1/2	cup currants
	Salt and freshly ground pepper

Americans expect a stuffing with their roast turkey—but we think that the usual, heavy, wet, flavorless mass of bread is not worth the trouble just because it answers to the description of "stuffing." There are many marvelous flavors you can bring together in stuffings . . . and we have come to love lighter-textured stuffings in which the pieces of flavored bread barely hold together

—DAVID ROSENGARTEN

1. Melt the butter in a skillet; pour off and reserve ½ cup to moisten the stuffing. Sauté the onion until tender, and remove the skillet from the heat.
2. Add the sage and apples to the skillet and stir until well coated with butter.
3. Drain the oysters and reserve the liquor.
4. Toss the corn bread, oysters, onion, apples, and currants in a large bowl. Moisten with the reserved butter, add oyster liquor if needed, and mix well. Season with salt and pepper.
5. Allow the stuffing to cool before using.

OYSTER AND BRATWURST STUFFING FOR GOOSE† (*Serve with an Oregon Pinot Noir*)

YIELD: 8 CUPS

1	pint small oysters and liquor
5	cups dry bread crumbs
1	pound bratwurst
4	Tablespoons butter
1	chopped medium onion
1	minced garlic clove
1/4	cup dry white wine
1	Tablespoon chopped fresh sage
1	teaspoon chopped fresh rosemary
	Salt and freshly ground pepper

* This stuffing can be served with ham and medallions of pork or veal.
† This is an excellent stuffing for all poultry.

1. Drain the oysters and combine with bread crumbs in a large bowl. Reserve the liquor to moisten the stuffing.
2. Poach the bratwurst in water for 3 minutes. When cool, remove the casing and coarsely chop the sausage.
3. Melt the butter in a skillet and sauté the bratwurst, onion, and garlic for 5 minutes until lightly browned; remove from the stove. Mix the bratwurst and onion with the stuffing.
4. Return the skillet to the stove; stir in the wine, sage, and rosemary; scrape the pan to loosen bits of sausage, and cook until the liquid is reduced by half. Add this to the stuffing.
5. Use the reserved oyster liquor to moisten the stuffing to the desired consistency. Season with salt and pepper and cool completely before using.

WILD RICE AND OYSTER STUFFING FOR DUCK
(*Serve with an aged Oregon Pinot Noir*)

YIELD: 6 CUPS

1	pint oysters and liquor
1	cup wild rice
4	cups chicken stock (see p. 59)
3	Tablespoons butter
¹/₂	cup chopped onion
¹/₂	cup chopped celery
1	cup chopped shitake mushrooms
¹/₄	cup Madeira
	Dash of Tabasco
	Salt and freshly ground pepper

1. Drain and coarsely chop the oysters, reserving the liquor.
2. Rinse the rice in several changes of water, and drain. Simmer the rice in stock for 45 minutes or until tender. Uncover the pan, fluff the rice with a fork, and simmer to evaporate excess liquid. Set aside to cool.
3. Melt the butter in a saucepan and sauté the onion and celery until tender. Stir in the oyster liquor, mushrooms, Madeira, and Tabasco, and simmer uncovered until the liquid has evaporated.
4. Add the vegetable mixture to the rice, stir in the oysters, and adjust seasonings.
5. Cool the dressing before using.

BEEF, VEAL, LAMB, & PORK

What respectable member of the polo club would decline oysters and chopped sirloin on pumpernickel for a lunch that's as pukka as a chukka? And what finer way to give a real boost to a dinner for the Chairman of the Board than with beef fillets broiled to perfection and sauced with oysters in a glorious Béarnaise? There may be a better way to start the day than with a rasher of bacon and oyster sausages, but one wonders if anyone has discovered it.

The accommodation of oyster cookery to the meat-eating propensity of generations of Americans has been going on for years. And it's difficult, if not impossible, to ignore the appeal of a stuffed pork tenderloin, a tempting serving of Steak and Oyster Tartare, or a sizzling Oyster and Steak au Poivre. The votes are in—the togetherness of oysters and meat will always have an across-the-board appeal.

STEAK AND OYSTER TARTARE
(A Gentleman's Dish)

SERVES 4

This recipe, like "private stock," is only for the few. Decidedly decadent but not altogether disreputable, it's ideal for lunching in pub or club, especially with a tall cool glass of Pilsner at the ready.

12   *shucked oysters*
1   *pound hand-chopped beef fillet*
4   *finely sliced scallions or chopped shallots*
    Salt and freshly ground pepper
1   *Tablespoon capers*
1   *fresh egg (optional)*
2   *Tablespoons minced fresh parsley*
    Lime wedges
    Homemade rye bread

1. Drain, pat dry, and coarsely chop the oysters.
2. Combine the steak and scallions with a fork. Lightly mix in the capers and oysters, and season to taste. Handle gently and shape into 4 patties. Garnish with raw egg if desired.
3. Place a patty in the center of a serving plate. Sprinkle with parsley and surround with some lime wedges.
4. Serve with a basket of homemade rye bread cut into thin slices.

One cannot think well, love well, sleep well if one has not dined well.

—VIRGINIA WOOLF

OYSTERS CASANOVA GRILL

SERVES 4

"What becomes a legend most?" Steak and oysters, and, perhaps, the pleasure of his company. Serve with a Barbaresco.

8	shucked medium oysters and liquor
1/2	cup dry white wine
4	1-inch-thick strip steaks or fillets
	Salt and freshly ground pepper
3	Tablespoons butter
1/4	pound rinsed morels
1	Tablespoon lemon juice
1/2	cup Cognac
1	Tablespoon chopped chervil

A recipe left over from Gold Rush days Helen Brown calls "Carpetbagger's Steak," and the CALIFORNIA COOK BOOK (1925), an early regional book by Frances P. Belle, calls it "Spanish Steak with Oysters." This is a good mouthful for Bunyanesque appetites, consisting of a large thick sirloin, smothered in poached Pacific oysters and covered with hot chili sauce.

—BETTY FUSSELL, I Hear America Cooking

1. Lightly poach the oysters in the liquor and wine, drain, and pat dry.
2. Cut a deep pocket in the side of each steak with a sharp knife. Sprinkle the pocket with salt and pepper and insert 2 oysters. Rub the outside of the steaks with salt and pepper.
3. Melt the butter in a large skillet until it foams and begins to brown. Pan-fry the steaks to the desired degree of doneness. Remove the steaks to a heated platter and keep warm.
4. Sauté the mushrooms in the skillet. Stir in the lemon juice, Cognac, and chervil, and cook briefly over high heat.
5. Spoon the pan juices and mushrooms over the steaks and serve immediately.

OYSTER SAUSAGES

YIELD: 24

These sausages introduce oysters into contemporary charcuterie with uncompromising authority. As chic breakfast or brunch fare, they can be served with any number of egg recipes. And they can also be grilled over charcoal and enjoyed with a piquant sauce at lunch or supper. A match made in heaven with light Graves Blanc.

1	pint oysters and liquor
1 3/4	pounds marbled pork butt or shoulder
1 3/4	pounds veal
2	cups crème fraîche, milk, or water*

*If made with milk, the sausages should be eaten immediately or frozen for later use. If made with *crème fraîche* or water, they will keep about a week in the refrigerator.

OYSTER SAUSAGES

Beard, rinse well in their strained liquor, and mince, but not finely, three dozens and a half of plump oysters, and mix them with ten ounces of fine bread-crumbs, and ten of beef-suet chopped extremely small; add a saltspoonful of salt, and one of pepper, or less than half the quantity of cayenne, twice as much pounded mace, and the third of a small nutmeg grated; moisten the whole with two unbeaten eggs, or with the yolks only of three, and a dessert spoonful of the whites. When these ingredients have been well worked together, and are perfectly blended, set the mixture in a cool place for two or three hours before it is used; make it into the form of small sausages or sausage-cakes, flour and fry them in butter of a fine light brown; or throw them into boiling water for three minutes, drain, and let them become cold, dip them into egg and bread-crumbs, and broil them gently until they are lightly coloured.

—ELIZA ACTON,
*Modern Cookery in
All Its Branches,* 1858

2	*Tablespoons minced onion*
2	*Tablespoons minced parsley or chives*
	Salt[†]
$^1/_2$	*teaspoon white pepper*
1	*teaspoon brown sugar*
$^1/_2$	*teaspoon freshly grated nutmeg*
$^1/_4$	*teaspoon powdered ginger*
$^1/_4$	*teaspoon coriander seed*
1	*teaspoon lemon zest*
10	*feet good-quality sausage casing*

1. Drain the oysters and reserve 2 tablespoons of the liquor.
2. Cut the pork and veal into 1-inch cubes. Be sure the meat is below 40° in temperature before coarsely grinding in a food processor fitted with the steel blade.
3. Add the oyster liquor, *crème fraîche,* onion, and parsley, seasoning and mix thoroughly.
4. Coarsely chop the oysters by hand, and add to the sausage mixture.
5. Sauté a spoonful of the mixture, taste, and adjust seasonings.
6. Using a sausage stuffer, stuff into the casing, making each sausage about 4 inches long. Twist and tie.
7. Heat a large saucepan of water to 180° and cook the sausages for about 15 minutes or until the internal temperature registers 152°.
8. Remove from the water, and allow to come to room temperature.
9. Grill the sausages or sauté in unsalted butter until golden brown.

[†]Use ½ teaspoon of salt and adjust after tasting. The amount of salt depends upon the salinity of the oysters.

VEAL ROULADES

Especially attractive served on a bed of homemade parsleyed noodles, these stuffed veal scallops are parcels of pure flavor seasoned with oyster forcemeat and herbs. A light Beaujolais Villages seems just right for this veal entrée.

1½	pints oysters
3	slices diced bacon
12	veal scallops
	Pinch of mace
	Ground cloves
	Salt and freshly ground black pepper
	Flour
4	ounces ground veal
3	Tablespoons chopped parsley
1	teaspoon chopped fresh thyme
2	Tablespoons butter
2	Tablespoons olive oil
1	cup white wine
3	Tablespoons chopped shallots
½	cup heavy cream
8	Tablespoons unsalted butter
	Sprigs of fresh rosemary

1. Drain the oysters and set aside, reserving the liquor for another use.
2. Blanch the bacon in boiling water for 5 minutes, and drain on absorbent paper.
3. Season the veal scallops lightly with mace, cloves, salt, and pepper. Dip in flour, and pound flat between pieces of waxed paper.
4. Place the oysters, bacon, and ground veal (below 40°) in the work bowl of a food processor fitted with the steel blade and process for 1 minute. Add the parsley, thyme, and a pinch of salt and pepper, and process for 30 seconds more.
5. Spread some forcemeat on each veal scallop; fold up the ends and make a rolled package, securing with skewers or butcher's string.
6. Melt the butter and oil in a large skillet and sauté the veal quickly on all sides. Add the wine and shallots, cover, and simmer for 20 minutes or until tender.

7. Place the veal scallops on a heated platter, remove the skewers or string, and keep warm while the sauce is being prepared.
8. Boil down the pan juices until reduced to about 3 tablespoons. Stir in the cream and reduce again.
9. Strain the liquid into a saucepan. Place the pan over high heat and whisk in the butter, one spoonful at a time, until it is incorporated. Adjust seasoning.
10. Nap the veal scallops with the sauce, garnish with sprigs of rosemary, and serve immediately.

BAYSWATER PIE

This is a recipe that may well go back to the one found in *The Virginia House-Wife* written by Mary Randolph in 1824. Madeira seems to accent the flavors more subtly than Sherry; the shallots are more subtle than onions. But more than 150 years later, the recipe still pleases. Serve with Meursault.

1	*pint oysters and liquor*
	Salt
1	*teaspoon lemon juice*
1	*pair sweetbreads*
1	*cup heavy cream*
2	*Tablespoons butter*
2	*Tablespoons finely chopped shallots*
1	*Tablespoon flour*
2	*Tablespoons Madeira*
3	*egg yolks*
	Freshly ground white pepper
2	*unbaked piecrusts*

OVEN TEMPERATURE: 450°

1. Mix 1 teaspoon of salt and the lemon juice in water, add sweetbreads and bring to a simmer. Cook until tender. Drain, and plunge into a bowl of cold water. Remove the skin and membranes, and cut into bite-sized cubes.
2. Drain the oysters and set aside. Mix ⅓ cup of the liquor with ¾ cup of cream and heat in a small saucepan.

3. Melt the butter in another saucepan and sauté the shallots until tender. Stir in the flour and cook until straw yellow. Remove from the heat and whisk in the hot cream. Return to heat, add the Madeira, and cook, stirring constantly, until the mixture thickens. Simmer for 5 to 8 minutes.

4. In a bowl, beat the egg yolks with the remaining ¼ cup of cream. Beat in ½ cup of the hot mixture, one spoonful at a time. Gradually beat in the remaining hot mixture. Transfer the enriched sauce back to the saucepan and, stirring carefully, bring to a boil.

5. Remove from the stove and, when the sauce has cooled slightly, stir in the oysters and adjust seasonings.

6. Line a 1½-quart shallow casserole with a piecrust. Spoon a third of the oyster mixture into the casserole and cover with half the sweetbreads. Add more of the oyster sauce and another layer of sweetbreads, topping with the oyster mixture. Put the top crust in place; seal and crimp the edges. Cut a hole in the center to vent.

7. Bake in the upper third of the oven for 10 minutes. Reduce the oven temperature to 325° and continue baking for an additional 15 minutes until the crust is golden.

BURIED TREASURE

SERVES 4

It will take a little sleuthing to discover the oysters hidden inside the pork tenderloin in this recipe, but they're there. It's light, it's lean, it's the "other white meat" in a different setting. Serve with an Italian Dolcetto.

12	small freshly shucked oysters
2	Tablespoons butter
¼	cup finely chopped Spanish onion
½	cup sourdough bread crumbs
½	Tablespoon chopped fresh tarragon
½	Tablespoon chopped parsley
½	Tablespoon chopped chervil
½	Tablespoon chopped chives
	Salt and pepper
1	1½-pound pork tenderloin
6	thin slices pancetta
	Butcher's string
	Electric or charcoal grill

1. Remove the oysters from the shells, drain, and pat dry. Reserve the liquor for stuffing.
2. Melt butter in a sauté pan and wilt onions; add bread crumbs and herbs, salt and pepper, and enough of the oyster liquor to bind the stuffing.
3. Cut a deep pocket the length of the tenderloin and spread half of the stuffing along the pocket. Arrange the oysters over the stuffing, and cover the oysters with more of the stuffing. Close the pocket.
4. Wrap the pancetta around the tenderloin, and tie with presoaked butcher's string.
5. Place on an oiled rack and grill until the bacon begins to crisp and the inner temperature is 160°.
6. Remove the string, slice, and serve.

DROVER'S INN SCALLOP

SERVES 6

New England cooking at its tastiest. . . . After a day of cross-country skiing, scalloped oysters and ham are as inviting as a blazing hearth, the smell of baking bread, and a glass of dry Vouvray.

1	pint oysters
4	Tablespoons butter
2	Tablespoons flour
$1^{1}/_{2}$	cups scalded cream
$^{1}/_{4}$	cup dry Sherry
	Salt and freshly ground pepper
6	$^{3}/_{8}$-inch-thick slices baked ham
1	cup sliced cremini mushrooms
1	cup fresh bread crumbs
$^{1}/_{4}$	cup chopped chervil

OVEN TEMPERATURE: 350°

1. Drain the oysters, pat dry, and set aside. Reserve the liquor for another use.
2. Melt the butter in a saucepan; stir in the flour and cook until bubbling. Remove from the heat and gradually whisk in the cream. Return to heat, add the Sherry, season to taste, and stir vigorously while the mixture cooks and thickens. Simmer for 5 minutes.

3. Arrange the ham slices on the bottom of a 12- by 8-inch buttered baking dish. Distribute the oysters and mushrooms over the ham, and cover with the sauce. Sprinkle with crumbs.
4. Bake about 25 minutes until the crumbs are golden brown.
5. Garnish with chervil and serve immediately.

DOWN TO THE SEA

Along the Grand Banks of Newfoundland, up and down the Atlantic and Pacific coasts, in the Gulf of Mexico, Long Island Sound, and Chesapeake Bay, the sea talks to the fisherman in his trawler in a more intimate way than it talks to the people who walk along the shore, and it shares its bounty with him. From the lobster traps, clam baskets, and nets of the men who go down to the sea in ships come the ingredients for a score of seafood dishes.

The following recipes are specifically for the "catch of the day," for shellfish just out of the water and fillets of sole, haddock, and flounder so fresh that only the minimal embellishments of a brush of butter, a dash of wine, and a wedge of lemon are needed by way of preparation.

LEMON TREE OYSTER GRATIN

SERVES 4

Freshly shucked oysters and Maryland lump crabmeat are absolutely necessary in this recipe, which depends on the freshness of every ingredient, including the lemons, for its success. Nice with a California Chardonnay.

24	*shucked medium oysters and liquor*
4	*large portabella mushroom caps*
1	*Tablespoon olive oil*
	Salt and freshly ground pepper
1/2	*cup dry orzo pasta*
1 1/2	*quarts water*
1/2	*pound fresh spinach*
1/2	*cup oyster liquor*
1/2	*cup dry white wine*
1 1/2	*cups milk*
4	*Tablespoons butter*
1/2	*cup chopped scallions*
1/4	*cup chopped shallots*

4	Tablespoons flour
	Pinch of nutmeg
	Salt and white pepper
8	ounces cooked crabmeat
3/4	cup buttered bread crumbs
1	Tablespoon Parmesan (optional)
4	Meyer lemon wedges

OVEN TEMPERATURE: 325°

1. Remove the oysters from the shells; strain oyster liquor.
2. Remove stems from mushroom caps and place on a baking sheet; brush with olive oil, salt, and pepper, and roast in 325° oven for 10 to 15 minutes. Remove and set aside.
3. Cook orzo in lightly salted water until done, drain, add a trace of olive oil, cover, and set aside.
4. Rinse and stem spinach. With remaining olive oil, sauté spinach in a large shallow pan. When wilted, drain, season with salt and pepper, and set aside.
5. Heat oyster liquor and wine in a saucepan. Poach the oysters until the edges curl, remove with a slotted spoon, and set aside. Add milk to the poaching liquid and heat.
6. Melt the butter in another saucepan, add the scallions and shallots, and cook until they are tender. Stir in the flour and cook until the roux is a light straw color. Remove from heat and whisk in the hot liquid, add nutmeg, salt and pepper to taste, and cook until the mixture thickens, about 10 minutes. Add crabmeat and set aside.
7. Gently scrape out the darker part of the mushroom cap and discard. Assemble 4 caps on a baking sheet; place a fourth of the spinach on each cap. Spoon about 2 tablespoons of the orzo in the center and arrange 6 oysters around the orzo. Divide the crabmeat sauce among the 4 caps, and cover with bread crumbs mixed with Parmesan if desired.
8. Place under the broiler and remove when bubbling and golden. Arrange each cap on a plate, and serve garnished with a lemon wedge.

OYSTERS EN PAPILLOTE

SERVES 4

Up, up, and away with these brimming-with-flavor balloons. Place one on each of your guest's plates so they can cut it open and enjoy the aroma released. It's an elegant seafood entrée that can be prepared in less than 30 minutes. Serve with Graves Blanc.

16	*medium oysters*
16	*large raw shrimp*
$^1/_2$	*pound bay scallops*
1	*shrink-wrapped "gourmet" cucumber*
4	*sheets parchment paper*
5	*Tablespoons melted butter*
1	*Tablespoon chopped fresh tarragon*
1	*Tablespoon chopped parsley*
	Salt and white pepper
4	*Tablespoons dry Vermouth*

OVEN TEMPERATURE: 450°

1. Shuck oysters, drain, and reserve oyster liquor for another use.
2. Peel and devein shrimp, drain scallops, and set the seafood aside.
3. Peel and slice the cucumber.
4. Cut 4 heart-shaped pieces of parchment paper large enough to hold a quarter of the seafood and cucumber slices. Brush the side to be filled with melted butter.
5. Arrange a quarter of the cucumber slices on half of each heart.
6. Place the seafood over the cucumbers. Spoon approximately 1 tablespoon of butter over the seafood and sprinkle with tarragon and parsley. Season lightly with salt and white pepper.
7. Crimp the edges slightly on the half of the heart with the ingredients and add 1 tablespoon of Vermouth to each.
8. Fold over the other half of the heart and crimp the edges tightly together.
9. Place the parchment "balloons" on a baking sheet and bake in a 450° oven for about 10 minutes or until the paper puffs up and is brown. Serve immediately.

SERVES 6

Not one but six "gifts of the sea" add to the pleasure of this creamy New-burg. It can be served on waffles or in patty shells, but using deep-fried potato baskets adds a flavor and texture to the dish that is *non pareil*. It is es-pecially wonderful with a high-quality California sparkling wine.

1	pint oysters and liquor
1	cup dry white wine
4	ounces bay scallops
4	ounces haddock or flounder fillets
4	ounces raw medium shrimp
4	ounces cooked crabmeat
4	ounces coarsely chopped cooked lobster
2	cups light cream
5	Tablespoons butter
3	Tablespoons flour
2	egg yolks
$^1/_4$	cup Cognac
	Pinch of nutmeg
	Salt and freshly ground white pepper
6	French-fried shredded potato baskets
$^1/_2$	cup sautéed chanterelles

1. Drain the oysters and mix the liquor and wine in a 1½-quart saucepan. Bring to a boil and lightly poach the oysters. Remove when the edges be-gin to curl, drain, and set aside.
2. Use the same liquid to poach the scallops, fish, and shrimp. Set the scal-lops aside; coarsely flake the fish; shell and devein the shrimp. Add to the crabmeat and lobster and set aside. Strain and reserve the poaching liq-uid for another use.
3. Scald 1½ cups of the cream in a small saucepan.
4. Melt the butter in another saucepan, stir in the flour, and cook over moderate heat until straw yellow. Remove from the heat and whisk in the hot cream. Return to heat and cook, stirring constantly, until the mixture thickens. Simmer for 5 minutes.
5. Lightly beat the egg yolks and remaining ½ cup of cream in a bowl. Whisk in ½ cup of the hot mixture, one spoonful at a time. Gradually beat in the remaining hot mixture. Transfer the enriched sauce back to

the saucepan; add the Cognac and nutmeg. Continue stirring and cook until bubbles form on the edge of the pan.

6. Stir in the seafood, season to taste, and keep warm.

7. Spoon the creamed seafood into warm potato baskets and garnish with sautéed chanterelles.

SOLE MATES

SERVES 6

The catch of the day and the bounty of the garden pair up at the dinner table when these lettuce-wrapped fillets of sole are served. The lettuce cream sauce is very much in the French tradition, but if a zestier sauce is desired, substitute ¾ cup of sorrel for the lettuce, and *voilà*! Make the occasion special with a bottle of California Sauvignon Blanc.

½	pint oysters

Stuffing:

4	Tablespoons butter
1	Tablespoon fresh chopped chervil
1	minced garlic clove
3	Tablespoons chopped scallions
½	cup white wine
½	cup cooked rock or salad shrimp
	Fresh bread crumbs
	Salt and freshly ground pepper
6	large outer leaves iceberg lettuce
2½	pounds fillet of sole (6 ounces each)
	Chopped chives for garnish

Lettuce Cream Sauce:

1	Tablespoon butter
2	Tablespoons finely chopped shallots
2	cups lettuce chiffonade
1	cup crème fraîche
1	Tablespoon fresh chopped chervil
	Salt and white pepper

1. Drain the oysters, chop coarsely, and set aside.

2. Melt the butter in a saucepan, add chervil, garlic, and scallions, and sauté until soft.

3. Add the wine, oysters, and shrimp and cook briefly. Stir in enough bread crumbs to absorb most of the liquid. Season to taste. Set aside.

4. Blanch lettuce leaves in boiling water very quickly, remove, place in cold water, and drain on absorbent towels. Cut out hard core.

5. Wash and dry fillets, spread stuffing on half of a fillet, fold, and wrap in a lettuce leaf, forming a neat packet. Repeat until all 6 packets are complete.

6. Bring water to boil in the bottom of a steamer, and steam the packets flap-side-down for about 8 minutes per inch of thickness of a packet or until an internal temperature of 140° is reached.

7. While the fish is steaming, make the sauce. Melt butter in a sauté pan, and cook shallots until translucent. Add the lettuce and wilt. Transfer to a blender and purée. Heat *crème fraîche* in the same pan, add the puréed lettuce, shallots, and chervil, and stir into a smooth sauce. Season to taste.

8. Place a lettuce packet on each warmed plate, nap with the sauce, and garnish with chives.

SEAFOOD HOT POT

SERVES 4   This Asian-inspired seafood entrée is simplicity itself. It wants nothing but a chilled bottle of German Riesling Kabinett to accompany it.

12	*oysters and liquor*
2	*pounds flounder, sole, or sea bass fillets*
	Sesame oil

Marinade:

1/4	*cup aji-mirin (sweet cooking rice wine)*
1/4	*cup sake*
1/4	*cup soy sauce*

1/2	*pound soba noodles*
2	*quarts water*
	Freshly ground pepper
1	*Tablespoon oil*
1/3	*cup chopped scallions*
1/2	*pound fresh washed and stemmed spinach*
1	*Tablespoon cornstarch*
	Salt

1. Remove the oysters from the shells and set aside, reserving the liquor.
2. Rinse and dry the fillets, grease a shallow enamel cast-iron casserole with sesame oil, and arrange the fillets in the dish. Mix the marinade and pour over the fillets. Refrigerate for 15 minutes.
3. Bring the water to a boil, add soba noodles, and when water returns to a boil, cook for about 4 or 5 minutes until tender but firm. Drain in a colander. Season with sesame oil and pepper, and set aside.
4. Remove fillets from the refrigerator, and add enough water to come halfway up the side of casserole. Cover loosely, bring to a boil, reduce heat, and poach until the flesh is opaque but not flaky.
5. While fillets are poaching, heat oil in a sauté pan, sauté scallions, adding the spinach when the scallions are tender and cook spinach until wilted.
6. Remove the fillets and keep warm. Pour the poaching liquid and oyster liquor into the sauté pan with the scallions and spinach. Add the oysters and poach for a few minutes.
7. Mix cornstarch in a small amount of cold water and add to the sauté pan to thicken the broth slightly. Correct seasonings.
8. Place a mound of noodles in the center of each of the 4 warmed soup plates, place a fish fillet on top of the noodles, and ladle the thickened broth over the fish. Serve immediately.

TOP OF THE COVE KEBABS

SERVES 4

Oysters wrapped in leek leaves alternating with peppers, cherry tomatoes, and swordfish cubes, broiled, and served on a bed of rice—something for everyone, especially the swordfish devotee. Serve with a Nebbiolo d'Alba.

24	*shucked medium oysters*
2	*large leeks*
	Salt and freshly ground pepper
1	*pound swordfish*
3	*Tablespoons lime juice*
1	*cup butter*
1	*small quartered and seeded green pepper*
1	*small quartered and seeded red pepper*
3	*Tablespoons lemon juice*
8	*cherry tomatoes*
4	*12-inch skewers*

3   cups cooked long-grain rice
1½   Tablespoons minced parsley

OVEN TEMPERATURE: MEDIUM BROIL

1. Remove the oysters from the shells, pat dry, and set aside, reserving the liquor for another use.
2. Separate and rinse the leek leaves; blanch them in boiling salted water for 2 minutes; drain and chill in ice water. Drain again and pat dry.
3. Open the leaves and spread on a flat surface. Cut horizontally to accommodate the size of the oysters and wrap the oysters in the leaves before skewering.
4. Cut some of the remaining leeks into fine julienne strips to use in the sauce.
5. Cut the swordfish into 1-inch cubes, sprinkle with lime juice, salt, and pepper.
6. Melt 2 tablespoons of the butter in a skillet, lightly cook the peppers, remove, and set aside. Add the swordfish to the skillet and lightly brown on all sides. Set aside.
7. Heat the remaining butter and lemon juice in a saucepan.
8. Thread the oysters, fish, peppers, and tomatoes on 4 skewers, and brush with lemon butter.
9. Place the skewers on a hot, oiled broiling pan and broil for 2 minutes. Turn the skewers and broil on the other side for another 2 minutes.
10. Serve the kebabs on a bed of hot rice. Mix the parsley and reserved leeks with the melted butter, and spoon over the kebabs.

The oyster is the most disinherited of mollusks . . . Being acephalous—that is to say, having no head, it has no organ of sight, no organ of hearing, no organ of smell. Neither has it any organ of locomotion. Its only exercise is sleep; its only pleasure eating.

—ALEXANDER DUMAS

Oyster Glossary

ADDUCTOR: The single muscle, popularly called the "heart," that extends from the center of one valve, or shell, through the oyster to the other shell. When the adductor is relaxed, the shells open; under water, the shells remain partly open at all times unless counteracted.

AMERICAN: Often synonymous with *Crassostrea virginica*. Four other species are available in the United States: *Crassostrea gigas* (Pacific), *Crassostrea sikamea* (Kumamoto), *Ostrea lurida* (Olympia), and *Ostrea edulis* (farmed European *plates*). Within each species, oysters are named after the place the oyster came from, sometimes as specific as the actual tidal flat.

AQUACULTURE: Oyster farming; the oysterman considers himself a farmer of the sea rather than a fisherman. Oysters are seeded, cultivated, moved from bed to bed, and harvested by means of rakes, tongs, drags, dredges, and by divers. Oyster farming off the coast of Greece dates from the 4th century B.C., but there is evidence that it was practiced much earlier in China.

ATLANTIC: See *Crassostrea virginica*.

AMORICAINE: From the ancient name for Brittany (*ar-mor*: by the sea), the indigenous *Ostrea edulis* has become identified with the Gulf of Morbihan, which produces more than 80 percent of world production of the species. See *The Oysters of Loc-* *mariaquer* by Eleanor Clark for a detailed account of oystering in the area.

"BANANA": Name given by commercial oystermen to an elongated oyster; used only for stews and soups.

BANK: Oyster bed; oysters growing naturally, profusely, permanently.

BEAK: Hinged, narrow end of the oyster.

BEARD: Gills of the oyster, sometimes removed before cooking.

BELON: Commercial name for *Ostrea edulis* because through the years the shipment of local Gulf of Morbihan oysters was centered at Riec-sur-Belon. Generally, the place-name *Belon* refers to the maturing phase of the oyster, not the specific place of origin.

BILL: Thin end of the oyster shell.

BLUE POINT: Originally referred to oysters harvested from Great South Bay near the town of Blue Point, Long Island. Now a collective term for a medium-sized, mild East Coast oyster.

BROOD: Seed oyster; a 1- to 3-year-old adult that is ready to spawn.

BUYING: Raw shucked oysters constitute 80 percent of the oyster market; another 15 percent are sold in the shell, and the remaining 5 percent are frozen, canned, or processed for frozen or canned soups and stews. Of the shucked category, 90 percent are sold in fish markets and grocery stores, with the remainder going to restaurants. Bulk shucked oysters are graded as follows: Standards 30–40 to the pint; Selects 26–30 to the pint; Extra Selects 21–26 to the pint. Fresh shell oysters should be tightly closed when purchased.

CHAMBERING: Process by which a pocket inside the shell, started by water, or a worm, or grain of sand, is sealed off with a chalky substance manufactured by the oyster. Within the pocket, the foreign substance putrifies and gives off an odor if punctured. Does not affect the oyster as food.

COLCHESTER: Famous oyster from Colchester, England; also known as a Walflete oyster in Elizabethan times. Since 1318, the setting for an annual oyster festival held on October 8, St. Deny's Fair.

COLLECTOR: Culch, or the solid substance to which a free-swimming 2-week-old oyster may attach itself. The collectors may be tree roots, asbestos shingles, Styrofoam, or other man-made substances. They may be vertical rafts of shells or tiles strung on poles, or horizontal beds of rock or shells on the sea bottom.

COON: See *Crassostrea frons*.

COTUIT OYSTER COMPANY: Founded in 1837, the Cotuit Oyster Company is the oldest brand name of oysters in the United States. Seed oysters purchased from other eastern hatcheries are submerged in the bay waters to acquire the moderately saline flavor associated with these oysters.

Crassostrea angulata: The rough, cupped-shell oyster known as the Portuguese oyster. Of Asian origin, it is presumed to have been carried to Portugal on the hulls of explorers' ships, and was introduced to the coastal waters of southwestern France in the 1860s. Less difficult to cultivate than *les plates, portugaise* oysters now comprise most of the commercial production along the southwestern seaboard of France.

Crassostrea frons: A small oyster that attaches itself to tree roots and grows along the Carolina shores and southward. It is called the coon oyster because raccoons eat them when the oysters are exposed at low tides.

Crassostrea gigas: The rough-surfaced cupped Pacific oyster indigenous to Japan that was introduced to the northwest Pacific coast in 1905 to compensate for the depletion of the native Olympia oyster. Because it also is found in many of the British and European oyster beds, the species is commonly identified with oysters introduced to an area rather than native to it. Harvested mainly in northern California, Oregon, Washington State, and British Columbia, some of the easily recognized names are: Tomales Bay, Hog Island, Yaquina Bay, Willapa Bay, Wescott Bay, Golden Mantle, and Puget Sound.

Crassostrea sikamea: Known as the Kumamoto oyster, this small, deep, fluted-shelled oyster was first thought to be a subspecies of *C. gigas*. But its distinctive features have put it in a species of its own. It is cultivated in northern California and Washington State.

Crassostrea virginica, also C. virginiana: The cupped, common oyster indigenous to the Atlantic and Gulf coasts of North America, known as the American, Atlantic, and eastern oyster. Harvested from eastern Canada, New England, Long Island, mid-Atlantic states, and Chesapeake Bay to Florida and the Gulf of Mexico, some well-known names are: Bras d'Or, Malpeque, Bristol, Cuttyhunk, Wellfleet, Cotuit, Fisher's Island, Chincoteague, Apalachicola, Plaquemimes Parrish, and Galveston Bay.

CULCH: See Collector.

DÉGORGEOIR: A stone or cement basin used in Brittany in oyster cultivation. The oysters are placed in the basin for 3 or 4 days and water and food are withheld intermittently. The oysters respond to this treatment by keeping their shells closed during the intervals when they are exposed to air; they keep themselves alive by retaining their liquids. It is done to cleanse and to prepare immature oysters to keep their shells closed in order to retain water during shipment to distant markets.

EASTERN: See *Crassostrea virginica*.

EUROPEAN: See *Ostrea edulis*.

FREEZING: Shuck the oysters and pack in airtight containers. Allow ½ inch of head space. Storage life in a freezer at 0°F is about 6 months. Only useful in prepared cooked dishes.

FRILLED: Broad end of an oyster.

FRINGE: End of oyster opposite the hinge.

GALWAY: Famous oyster from the west coast of Ireland. International oyster festivals are held annually in Galway.

GENDER: Oysters are hermaphrodites, and some change sex at least once a year. Their sperm when developed go into the exhalant chamber and from there to the sea. In a female phase, the eggs are drawn by muscular machinery back through the gills against the normal current into a chamber for incoming food and waters. The *Ostrea* female takes in sperm with food and drink and 8 days later expels fertilized larvae. The *Crassostrea* female expels eggs directly into the water where they come in contact with sperm and fertilize. Temperature is the most important factor in sex change.

GILL: Organ for obtaining oxygen from water. Also called the beard, it lies along the broad end of the shells where they open. The gill filters from 10 to 12 gallons of water each hour, retaining microscopic plankton for food.

GREENING: Process by which the oyster's gills become colored when the oyster is placed in water with minute marine algae. The treatment lasts from 3 weeks to 1 year, and is considered by oyster epicures especially delicious.

HALF-WARE: Name for the 2- to 3-year-old oyster.

HO TSEE: Chinese dried oyster.

MANTLE: Membrane embracing the oyster and lining the shell, it secretes shell-building material.

Meleagrina margaritifera: Pearl oyster. It is not a true oyster; it is more closely related to the mussel; widely distributed in the Indian Ocean, Red Sea, Pacific, Gulf of California, Caribbean; the oldest fisheries are in Ceylon. The pearl substance is aragonite.

MSX: *Minchinia nelsoni*; microorganism fatal to mollusks; destroyed large portions of the Virginia, Maryland, and New Jersey oyster populations in the 1960s and 1970s, and periodically contaminates other eastern beds.

NUTRITION: Six oysters contain: 59 calories, 1.6 grams fat, 66 mgs. sodium, 45 mgs. cholesterol. Oysters have significant quantities of A, B complex, and C vitamins, and are valuable for minerals: iron, copper, iodine, some calcium, phosphorus, and zinc. The eastern oyster measures 74.7 mgs. zinc per 100 grams of weight; the Pacific oyster measures 9.0 mgs.

OLYMPIA: See *Ostrea lurida*.

OSTENDS: Belgium oyster of the *O. edulis* species.

Ostiones: An oyster found in the Caribbean, a small 2-inch narrow oyster that grows on tree roots.

Ostrea edulis: Known as the European oyster. It has a flat, smooth shell and mild sweet flavor. Historically, natural banks of *O. edulis* were found from Sebastopol on the Black Sea to latitude 65 on the shores of Norway. Romans discovered them in England and the mouth of the Gironde. But because of man's intervention and climate changes, the natural banks of these oysters were eventually destroyed, with the result that many places that might still be suitable for adults of the breed became impossible for *captage du naissain*. Today a very small area of inlets and islands along the Gulf of Morbihan are the breeding ground and nursery for much of the world's supply of *les plates*. From this area the bulk of the crop will go to other places like Britain and Belgium for *elevage* (raising until 2 or 3 years old). At that stage they will become Whitstable, Colchester, Zeeland, Pied de Cheval, and Belon oysters. Initially, New Hampshire, Maine, and the Pacific Northwest imported larvae from the Gulf of Morbihan for the farming of *O. edulis*. Now both nurseries and raising areas are established in the United States. And places like Wescott Bay produce hybrids of "Belons" and other species.

Ostrea lurida: The Olympia oyster is indigenous to North America's Pacific coast. It is being cultivated again after near extinction due to pollution. Olympias are tiny in size: over 200 are required to make 1 pint.

OYSTER: Classified in the phylum Mollusca, class Pelecypoda, order Filebranchia, family Ostreidae; an edible bivalve mollusk. The shell is made up of two valves, the upper one flat and the lower convex. Said to be the most prolific of all living creatures, there are 70 different species of oysters around the world and over 300 different varieties.

OYSTER CATCHER: Any of certain wading birds of the widely distributed genus *Haematopus*; 16 to 20 inches in length; stout legs and heavy wedge-shaped bill are usually pinkish or bright red. Its bill is used to open bivalves; usual habitat is mudflats, sandy beaches, and rocky shores.

OYSTER CRAB: *Pinnotherer ostreum*; a crab that lives as a commensal in the gill cavity of the oyster; approximately ⅜-inch shell diameter.

OYSTERLEAF: Sea mertensia (*Mertensia maritima*); a seaside plant of the Forget-me-not family; the fleshy, glaucous leaves taste of oysters.

OYSTER MUSEUM OF CHINCOTEAGUE: Opened to the public in 1972, this museum, dedicated to preserving the heritage of oystering on the island, is the only one of its kind in the United States. Among many other exhibits, the one that features the farming of oysters with many of the turn-of-the-century methods is one of the most valuable in the permanent collection.

OYSTER MUSHROOM: An edible agaricaceous fungus or mushroom (*Pleurotus ostreatus*) growing in clusters of overlapping tiers on deadwood. As the name suggests, the cap is shell shaped and in noncultivated varieties measures 2½ to 5 inches across.

OYSTER PLANT: Salsify; a fusiform root. In late 19th-century cookbooks, this root vegetable was used in vegetarian recipes for oyster stews and chowders. It has a mild flavor of the sea when cooked.

PACIFIC: See *Crassostrea gigas*.

PARK: Pond for farming oysters, as opposed to a natural bed; tidal waters may be controlled by sluices and floodgates.

PEARL: See *Meleagrina margaritifera*.

PETTICOATS: Shoots, rings, or layers of the oyster shell that help establish its age.

Pinctada margaritifera: A pearl oyster; a nonconformist genus of *Ostrea*.

PLUMPING: Moving oysters just before harvesting to a lower-density water for a few days; they fatten, but lose flavor.

PORTUGUESE: See *Crassostrea angulata*. Name of an oyster from Vancouver, B.C., not *C. angulata* but *C. gigas*.

PRAIRIE OYSTER: In some western states, a local cure for a hangover made with 1 raw egg, measure of Sherry, dash of Worcestershire sauce, salt, and pepper.

PREDATORS: Starfish, oyster drills, whelk tingles, certain species of crab, shrimp, fish, and worms, oyster catchers, and herons.

RED COLORATION: May appear in the liquor of shucked oysters within 48 hours after shucking or after freezing.

ROCKY MOUNTAIN OYSTERS: Cooked lamb's testicles, which, allegedly, resemble fried oysters.

ST. MARY'S COUNTY OYSTER FESTIVAL: Since 1967, this annual affair held in Maryland has been distinguished by oyster-shucking and original oyster-recipe contests.

SALSIFY: See oyster plant.

SEATTLE OYSTER OLYMPICS: For the past 10 years, the city of Seattle has hosted this 1-day event on the last Tuesday of March. Wine and oyster identification, shucking, and competing restaurant teams as well as various awards distinguish this celebration.

SEED: Brood oyster; name for the 1- to 2-year-old oyster that is approximately 1 inch in size; used for transplanting purposes.

SET: A newly settled oyster; spat.

SHELL: Substance of the oyster shell is calcium carbonate. The shell-building material is secreted by the oyster's mantle and extruded in rings which help define the oyster's age. Historically, oyster shells have been used for road surfacing, to make a type of cement, and for chicken feed.

SHUCK: To remove the shell. Traditionally there are four methods: Stabbing or Sticking, Cracking or Billing, Side Knife, and Hinge. To open an oyster by the Hinge method, scrub under cold running water to remove silt; wear a glove on the hand holding the oyster or protect the hand with a heavy towel. Hold the oyster flat-side-up, grip the broad edge with the fingers, and insert the tip of a shucking knife directly into the hinge, twist, and pry the shells apart. Run the knife under the top shell and sever the muscle that attaches the oyster to the shell. For serving purposes, sever the muscle attached to the bottom shell, and turn the oyster over. Save as much of the oyster liquor as possible. Shucking can be facilitated by relaxing the muscle of the oyster by heat or by extreme cold. Neither method is advisable when serving fresh oysters raw.

SHUCKING KNIFE: A sharp pointed knife with a strong blade that may be straight, slightly curved, or protected by a flange. It is designed specifically for this purpose. The most common are: Chesapeake Stabber, Crack Knife, New Haven, Southern, and Galveston.

SPAT: Young oyster under the age of 1 year.

SPATTING: Ejecting of spat by the parent oyster.

TROCHOSPHERE: Larva of a fertilized egg. In the oyster it swims freely by means of a rudder and ciliated velum, or foot. After a week, the young oyster secretes a limey deposit through its foot, positions itself on its left side, and attaches itself to a smooth surface, to which it clings until disturbed.

UNION OYSTER HOUSE: Restaurant in Boston that is considered to be the country's oldest restaurant still in operation today. When it started serving oys-

ters in 1826, its semicircular oyster bar was fre-
quented by Daniel Webster.

Vase: Dark sea mud of an oyster bed made
"gluish" from the mucus excreted by the oysters.

WARE: An oyster that is more than 3 years old.

WHEATON SHUCKING MACHINE: Infrared light machine used to open oysters at the rate of 60 per
minute, designed by F. W. Wheaton at the University of Maryland, 1968.

Index